Administration
of
Construction Contracts

ADMINISTRATION

OF

CONSTRUCTION CONTRACTS

Santosh Srivastava

Notion Press

Old No. 38, New No. 6

McNichols Road, Chetpet

Chennai - 600 031

First Published by Notion Press 2016

Copyright © Santosh Srivastava 2016

All Rights Reserved.

ISBN 978-93-5206-756-5

Contents

This book includes eleven (11) chapters and each chapter is briefly described below:

Chapter 1: Introduction

Introduces contract administration to the reader and provides details of actual spending on this industry by the top spenders (countries). It also lays down the broad expectations from a contract administrator.

This chapter also touches on current development that is likely to have an impact on a contract administrator's job in future.

Chapter 2: Contract Overview

This chapter explains a Contract and thereafter touches upon the types of procurement that a contract administrator is likely to come across while performing his duty.

This chapter moves on to explain the different parties to an agreement and explains different types of contract.

Chapter 3: Contract Administration

This chapter is dedicated to the actual function of a contract administrator. We try to understand the role and responsibilities of a contract administrator. This chapter explains latent/patent defects, under-runs and over-runs before taking us explain on defects or impropriety in contractor's invoicing. We understand variations, Extension of Time (EOT) and Acceleration clauses and the reason to have them in the agreement.

This chapter moves-on to explain cost of delay and about delay events, importance of notices and assessment of claims. We further move on to read about methods of delay analysis & their strengths and weaknesses besides reading about acceleration and assessment thereof.

We also touch upon breach of contract and conclude by a topic on interpretation of contract.

Chapter 4: Contract: Pre-Award stage

This chapter highlights the importance of maintaining strict confidentiality of correspondence during the tendering process. It highlights the requirements of archiving and retention of documents. Thereafter, we proceed to know more about the Tendering Activities and Process, Types of tendering and then take us through a tender process.

We also learn about the available Standard tender documents. Explains how communication with bidders needs to be done and the information management. We also learn about the actual evaluation process of a tender, before learning about the Contractors appointment and finally conclude by understanding the Tendering stages.

Chapter 5: Contract: Post-Award stage

In this chapter we try to understand Contract Administration Activities. Learn about Advance Payment, Interim Payments and the Final Payment.

We also learn about Variations under contract and Valuation thereof. We try and understand how and why Variations may be a source of conflict.

We then proceed on to understand what a Claim is in construction industry. We talk about Guarantees, Insurances, Collateral warranties, Retention, try to understand Liquidated Damages.

We go through the topic of Communication with Contractors and the maintenance of relationship with the appointed contractor, before reading about Contract termination process and the Contract close out.

Chapter 6: Valuations

This chapter highlights the requirements and provisions concerning valuations and payments. Requirement and the process of advance, interim and final payment to a contractor.

We also see when and how to make payment of retention monies before proceeding to the topic of Correction of statement, final statement, discharge of obligations, time for payment, Defects Liability Certificate and recourse available in case of unfulfilled obligations.

This chapter also contains templates/forms of Payment Certificate (including its Appendices) and the Final Statement.

Chapter 7: Variations

This chapter begins with defining a variation before moving on to explain Valuation of Variations. We also see how a variation may be a source of conflict within a contract. Thereafter, we learn about the limits on variations set by standard conditions.

We also go through a process of variation after a potential contract variation has been identified and initiated and the responsibility of parties to carry out the required functions.

Suggested formats and Forms have also been provided to convey the requirements of variation documentation.

Chapter 8: Contract Claims

This chapter explains the concept of Claims within the construction industry. We see who and how one party may affect a claim under contract. We learn about the cause and effect issues, before proceeding to learn about Notices and importance thereof. We also go through the requirements of Particulars that needs to be provided by a contractor.

Thereafter, we learn about Concurrent Delays. We will also learn how we need to quantify a Claim and learn about Claims Management.

We would proceed on to learn about the preparation of a Claim report and eventually the Claim finalization, before moving on to learn about Alternate Dispute Resolution (ADR) that is getting all the more important within this industry due to obvious reasons.

Chapter 9: Risk: within the Construction Industry

This chapter commences with the definition of hazard, uncertainty and common risks associated with a construction project. Thereafter, we read about the basic risks of a construction project and learn about risk mitigation & its control with an ultimate aim of cost and time optimization for any given project.

Chapter 10: Contract Close-out

This chapter explains a contract close out process. We learn about contract completion, and about activities involved in closing out a Contract. We also would learn what it means by physical completion of a contract and contract close-out.

We would also learn about questioned costs and what does administrative completion of a project mean. Towards the close of this chapter we will see why a lesson learned report is important and know about the post project review of construction projects.

Also enclosed are some relevant Forms (i.e.; PTOC, TOC, DLC and Final Statement)

Chapter 11: Construction Disputes

This chapter begins with an understanding of the reason(s) of occurrence of Construction Disputes and how different factors have an effect on the dispute within the industry.

We will learn briefly about the Alternate Dispute Resolution (ADR) available within the industry and the reason why it needs to be encouraged on all construction projects.

Construction industry has a great amount of impact on both, the micro and macro economy of a country and hence it can be a major contributor of the well-being of its population. Therefore, and in order to do justice to his works, a contract administrator is highly expected to be aware of the ramifications of his actions.

Preface

The construction industry around the world and in particular within Asia and the Middle East region, has been observed to have remarkably grown over the past decade and is expected to keep up with the accelerated growth rate at least for a few decades necessitating requirement of new projects and completion of the on-going projects on priority. The author is an experienced contracts and commercial professional in the field of buildings and infrastructure development with over 20 years of sound contract administration experience on major projects within India and United Arab Emirates.

This book is intended to serve a stakeholder in the administration of a contract with an aim to make the most of the available (read as "expressed" conditions within the contract) contents within the contract in order to fulfill the basic need thereof i.e.; the completion and hand-over of the project to the user in the manner that it was envisaged at the first instance.

The intention behind publishing this book is to serve a stakeholder in the administration of a contract for a proposed or an on-going project. Since we are in a dynamic environment, it is envisaged that the book will have to be fine-tuned with time. With this intention, I request the readers to complement the reading by posting suggestions and recommendations to the author for the improvement of this book.

Best Regards,
Santosh Srivastava,
BE (Civil Engineering), MBA (Finance), MRICS, ACIArb

Foreword

This book is probably unique in having its focus on the administration of construction contracts which holds un-parallel importance within the construction industry. Role of a Contract Administrator (CA) has increased over the years and is almost certain to further increase in the coming years.

With the introduction of new approaches to construction procurement, a Contract Administrator is required to manage his duties and responsibilities in the most efficient way that may be possible. Numerous software(s) are available in the market to facilitate an Administrator's job. However, a Contract very rarely closes (completes) without issues, claims and counter-claims. It is very common to hear within the industry that a particular dispute could have been prevented, had the Stakeholders took extra care of a (or a few) specific issue.

A well-managed contract is the outcome of detailed planning and an efficient administration of all intended actions envisaged within the contract and use of the best industry practices.

While a Contract document lays down the intricacies of the overall requirements and lays down a path to achieve the end result, it is the administration thereof that holds the key to its success.

The publication of this book is timely to advice on contract administration to both construction professionals and students in a comprehensive manner. The text is presented as a practical manual, providing forms that may be used with as-needed amendments by the users.

It is highlighted that the standard reference used within this book is from FIDIC contract conditions. However, cross-references to other forms of contract have also been explained where applicable.

Acknowledgment

I would like to acknowledge and thank the following persons who have directly or indirectly made this book possible:

Special and heartfelt thanks to Mr. Saeed Al Zaabi for his continued guidance, motivation and extraordinary support, without which this book would not have been possible.

To Andy Hewitt for his review and expert advise, Graham Bland and Reuban Devadass for being there when needed and for sharing their knowledge and professional experience.

To my parents, my wife & her parents, and my two lovely daughters for their understanding, love and support.

I would also like to thank my past and present colleagues who directly or indirectly have been instrumental in the completion of this book.

Chapter 1

Introduction

Construction industry mirrors the general economy of the land at any given time and therefore, has its own highs and lows. However, there would seldom be a time when construction industry would seem to have stopped.

In the more recent times, the construction industry, fuelled by the increasing spending power of the population around the world, has been showing an increased activity. Construction industry has shown robust growth and a sustained development in the North America and Europe since the last century. Thereafter, and during the last few decades, growth has been remarkable, particularly in the Middle East and Asia. Within Asia, the leaders in this growth were China and India and within the Middle East, this has been more visible in the United Arab Emirates (UAE) & Qatar, and the trend is expected to continue in the future. The coming years is expected to witness major boost to government spending on infrastructure, driven by the ever fluctuating oil and gas prices, the award of Expo 2020 to Dubai (UAE) and the FIFA World Cup 2022 to Qatar.

A general study of the headlines from any business news of the region in particular (or the world in general) shall advise the significance of contract administration. It is very easy to come across stories of multi-million losses to business houses due to poor contract administration (and may not always be due to contract practices or the contract set-up).

Modern day contracts are in many ways more complex than those of the past. Factors such as globalization, increased regulations, changing technologies and the pace of change have all contributed to an environment in which it is difficult to manage the dynamics involved in the successful administration of a contract. This has led many organizations to view a contract as a tool to control by imposing rigid standards and conditions and allow for negotiations only to the specific areas such as the pricing schedules or the deliverables.

Unfortunately, this thinking has led to many organizations stepping away from their role in the contract process, viewing the contract requirement purely as a procedural or legal requirement. The consequences are the business news carrying the tough messages.

It would not be incorrect to state that contract administration is one of the most important jobs related to construction projects and it involves numerous tasks occurring before and after contract execution and work order issuance. All work must be administered in accordance with the contract specifications, terms and conditions, common laws and regulations, and company policy.

Proper contract administration includes:

➢ Developing proper and accurate bid and contract documents
➢ Complying with contract documents and specifications
➢ Enforcing state and federal regulations
➢ Ensuring quality control by overseeing, inspecting and reviewing sampling and testing of all materials and work
➢ Keeping and maintaining accurate project records
➢ Recording, verifying and preparing monthly pay estimates
➢ Negotiating and processing of change orders, supplemental agreements and other contract modifications in a timely manner
➢ Promoting good public relations and
➢ Setting-up and maintenance of a high professional standard.
➢ Contract administration also provides for the following related activities:
➢ Pre-qualification of construction contractors
➢ Pre-qualification of construction contractors
➢ Claims analysis and processing
➢ Provision of materials and testing specifications
➢ Business Opportunity Programs (BOP) administration
➢ Subcontractor policy development and program administration
➢ Contractor/consultant workforce issues.

This book seeks to provide insight to the good contract administration practices that will attempt to contribute to the success of a contract. Making (contract execution) and managing (contract administration) Contracts can be easy or tough. This book will try to combine commercial process knowledge with an understanding of the role of a Contract Administrator in making contracting an easy, effective and efficient task.

This book also contains a few relevant case studies to provide an insight into the reasons for having a good contract administration in place for the proper management of a construction contract. Also, provided are a few important and commonly used forms within the construction industry that if used, with proper details therein shall result in capturing pertinent details of the progress of a contract resulting in overall sound administration of the contract.

Before we get into the details of contract administration within the construction industry, let us have a look at the importance of this industry to the general economy of countries around the world.

Below is a list of countries that has the largest output within construction industry:

Position	Country	Construction Output (in billions USD)
1	United States of America	599
2	China	562
3	Japan	333
4	France	147
5	India	144
6	Germany	143
7	United Kingdom	131
8	Canada	131
9	Australia	115
10	Russia	111
11	Brazil	109
12	Italy	107
13	Spain	104
14	Indonesia	93
15	Mexico	92
16	South Korea	59
17	Turkey	35
18	United Arab Emirates	34
19	Venezuela	34
20	Netherlands	34
21	Poland	34

(Contd.,)

22	Switzerland	33
23	Kingdom of Saudi Arabia	32
24	Iran	29
25	Colombia	29

Figures from data published in UN National Accounts database for the year 2012.

Below is a list of how the global construction market would look like in the year 2020:

Position	Country	Global Market Share in Percentage
1	China	21%
2	United States of America	15%
3	India	7%
4	Japan	3%
5	Canada	3%
6	Indonesia	3%
7	France	3%
8	Germany	3%
9	Australia	3%
10	Spain	2%
11	Italy	2%
12	United Kingdom	2%
13	Brazil	2%
14	Russia	2%
15	Mexico	2%
16	Others	24%

(Figures from data published by Global Construction Perspectives and Oxford Economics).

Some of the recent developments within the construction industry that are already impacting, however would have greater impact to the contract administration function of future are discussed below:

Building Information Modeling (BIM)

BIM is an intelligent model-based process that provides insight to help the planning, design, construction and management of buildings and infrastructure. BIM gets the right information to the right people at the right time, helping firms innovate and compete.

A true BIM model consists of the virtual equivalents of the actual building parts and pieces used to build a building. These elements have all the characteristics, both physical and logical, of their real counterparts. These intelligent elements are the digital prototype of the physical building elements such as walls, columns, windows, doors, stairs etc. that allow us to simulate the building and understand its behavior in a computer environment way before the commencement of the actual construction.

With the advent of mobile technologies such as smartphones/iPhones/iPads and the likes, utilization of BIM has stepped out from the close circle of professionals. Employers, building owners and operators are getting more and more access to BIM models through their mobile devices even without the need to installing a BIM application at the first instance. This shift would definitely require the adoption of BIM onto the next level so that a contract administrator, as a construction professional really cannot afford ignoring BIM. Fortunately there is ample availability of software and training facilities to learn about BIM and be prepared for the upcoming latest major paradigm shift in the construction industry.

3 Dimensional (3D) Visualization:

While there can be several different goals to fulfill by the creation of a purpose built BIM model that may differ both in their focus, scope, complexity, level of details and the depth of information added to the 3D model, the most trivial use of a BIM model is for making better visualizations of the buildings and infrastructure to be build. This is good for both helping the design decision by comparing different design alternatives and for finalizing the design at an early stage of the project life cycle.

Change Management:

Since data is stored within a central place in a BIM model, any modification to the building design will automatically replicate in each views such as floor plans, sections and elevation. This would not only help in the creation of faster documentation, but would also provide stringent quality assurance by automatic coordination to the different views, thereby aiding the management of change in a structured manner.

Comparing CAD and BIM:

BIM and CAD (Computer Aided Design) represent two fundamentally different approaches to building design and documentation. While CAD applications imitate the traditional paper & pencil process in so far as two-dimensional electronic drawings are created from 2D graphic elements such as lines, hatches and text, etc. CAD drawings, similarly to traditional paper drawings, are created independently from each other so design changes need to be followed up and implemented manually on each CAD drawing. However, BIM applications imitate the real building process. Instead of creating drawings from 2D line-work, buildings are virtually modeled from real construction elements such as walls, windows, slabs and roofs, etc. This allows the architects to design buildings and infrastructure in a similar way as they are actually built. Also, since all data is stored in the central virtual building model, design changes are automatically followed-up on individual drawings generated from the model. With this integrated model approach, BIM not only offers significant increase in productivity but also serves as the basis for better-coordinated designs and a computer model based building process.

Therefore, while switching from CAD to BIM is already justified by the benefits achieved during the design phase, it is noted that BIM offers further benefits during the construction phase and the actual use of the buildings and the related infrastructure.

Building information modeling is a process involving the generation and management of digital representations of physical and functional characteristics of places. Building information models (BIMs) are files which can be exchanged or networked to support decision-making about a place. Current BIM software is used by individuals, businesses and government agencies who plan, design, construct, operate and maintain diverse physical infrastructures such as water, wastewater, electricity, gas, refuse, communication utilities, roads, bridges, airports and seaports, houses, apartments, schools, colleges, shops, offices, factories, warehouses, prisons, etc.

Origins of BIM:

Although the concept of BIM has existed since the early 1970s, the term Building Information Model first appeared in the 1990s. However, the terms Building Information Model and Building Information Modeling (including the acronym "BIM") had not been popularly used until 10 years later when Autodesk released the white paper entitled "Building Information Modeling".

The US National Building Information Model Standard Project Committee has the following definition of BIM:

Building Information Modeling (BIM) is a digital representation of physical and functional characteristics of a facility. A BIM is a shared knowledge resource for information about a facility forming a reliable basis for decisions during its life-cycle; defined as existing from earliest conception to demolition.

Traditional building design was largely reliant upon two-dimensional drawings (plans, elevations, sections, etc.). Building information modeling extends this beyond 3D, augmenting the three primary spatial dimensions (width, height and depth) with time as the fourth dimension and cost as the fifth dimension. BIM therefore covers more than just geometry. It also covers spatial relationships, light analysis, geographic information, and quantities and properties of building components (for example, manufacturers' details).

BIM involves representing a design as combinations of "objects":vague and undefined, generic or product-specific, solid shapes or void-space oriented (like the shape of a room), that carry their geometry, relations and attributes. BIM design tools allow extraction of different views from a building model for drawing production and other uses. These different views are automatically consistent, being based on a single definition of each object instance. BIM software also defines objects parametrically; that is, the objects are defined as parameters and relations to other objects, so that if a related object is amended, dependent ones will automatically also change. Each model element can carry attributes for selecting and ordering them automatically, providing cost estimates as well as material tracking and ordering.

For the professionals involved in a project, BIM enables a virtual information model to be handed from the design team (architects, contract administrators, surveyors, civil, structural and building services engineers, etc.) to the main contractor and subcontractors and then on to the owner/ employer, who eventually manages the facility through a dedicated Facility Management team. Each professional adds discipline-specific data to the single shared model. This reduces information losses that traditionally occurred when a new team took ownership of the project, and provides more extensive information to owners of complex structures.

BIM throughout the Project Life-Cycle:

Use of BIM goes beyond the planning and design phase of the project, extending throughout the building life cycle, supporting processes including cost management, construction management, project management and finally the facility management.

Management of Building Information Models:

Building information models span the whole concept-to-occupation time-span. To ensure efficient management of information processes throughout this span, a BIM manager may need to be appointed. The BIM manager is retained by a design build team on the employer's/client's behalf from the pre-design phase onwards to develop and to track the object-oriented BIM against predicted and measured performance objectives, supporting multi-disciplinary building information models that drive analysis, schedules, take-off and logistics. Companies are also now considering developing BIMs in various levels of detail, since depending on the application of BIM, more or less detail is needed, and there is varying modeling effort associated with generating building information models at different levels of detail.

BIM in Construction Management:

Participants in the building process are constantly challenged to deliver successful projects despite tight budgets, limited manpower, accelerated schedules, and limited or conflicting information. The significant disciplines such as architectural, structural and MEP designs should be well coordinated, as two things can't take place at the same place and time. Building Information Modeling aids in collision detection at the initial stage, identifying the exact location of discrepancies.

The BIM concept envisages virtual construction of a facility prior to its actual physical construction, in order to reduce uncertainty, improve safety, work out problems, and simulate and analyze potential impacts. Sub-contractors from every trade can input critical information into the model before the beginning of construction, with opportunities to pre-fabricate or pre-assemble some systems off-site. Waste can be minimized on-site and products delivered on a just-in-time basis rather than being stock-piled on-site.

Quantities and shared properties of materials can be extracted easily. Scopes of work can be isolated and defined. Systems, assemblies and sequences can be shown in a relative scale with the entire facility or group of facilities. BIM also prevents errors by enabling conflict or clash detection whereby the computer model visually highlights to the team where parts of the building (e.g.: structural frame and building services pipes or ducts) may incorrectly intersect. Thereby, providing the project team an opportunity to correct the upcoming error much before the actual planned physical event on the field.

BIM in Facility Management:

BIM can bridge the information loss associated with handing a project from design team, to construction team and to building owner/operator (who may or may not be the Employer), by allowing each group to add to and reference back to all information they acquire during their period of contribution to the BIM model. This can yield immense benefits to the facility owner or operator.

For example, a building owner may find evidence of a leak in his building. Rather than exploring the physical building, he may turn to the model and see that a water valve is located in the suspect location. He could also have in the model the specific valve size, manufacturer, part number, and any other information ever researched in the past, pending adequate computing power.

Dynamic information about the building, such as sensor measurements and control signals from the building systems, can also be incorporated within BIM to support analysis of building operation and maintenance.

BIM in India:

In India, BIM is also known as VDC (Virtual Design and Construction). India, as an emerging market has an ever increasing/expanding construction industry and has huge potential for large scale residential and commercial development (because of the population and economic growth). It has many qualified, trained and experienced BIM professionals who are implementing this technology in Indian construction projects and also assisting teams in other countries such as USA, Australia, UK, Middle East, Singapore and North Africa to design and deliver construction projects using BIM

Soft Landings:

The term Soft Landings refers to a strategy adopted by project professionals to ensure that the transition from construction phase to occupation is bump-free or smooth and that the operational performance is optimized.

There is a broad consensus that buildings in operation do not perform as well as they could, or as well as it was initially envisaged to perform. There is often a significant gap between predicted and achieved performance that results in part from short-comings in briefing, design and construction and in part from poor operation. This problem gets compounded by the almost complete separation of construction and operation.

This transition needs to be considered throughout the development of a project, not just at the point of handover. Ideally the client should commit to adopting a soft landings strategy in the very early stages so that an appropriate budget can be allocated and appointment agreements and briefing documents can include relevant requirements. This should include agreement to provide the information required for commissioning, training, facilities management, etc. and increasingly will include requirements for Building Information Modeling (BIM).

To ensure that a soft landings strategy is implemented properly from the outset, it may be appropriate to appoint a Soft Landings leader to oversee the strategy. Facilities managers should also be involved from the early stages. It is worth highlighting here that the contracts administrator can either be an advisor to the Soft landings leader or in smaller projects, may work as one.

In order that a project gains from the concept of soft landing, it is recommended that a Soft Landings Framework is prepared under the Soft landings leader that enables designers and contractors to improve the performance of buildings and generate feedback for the project teams. This would require involvement in the project for the first two:three years of occupation and so will have budgetary implications.

Recommended Soft Landings Framework may include the following five stages:

1. Ensuring that the Employer's/client's needs and required outcomes are clearly defined.

2. Reviewing comparable projects and assessing proposals in relation to facilities management and building users.

3. Ensuring operators properly understand systems before occupation.

4. Establishment of a Soft Landings team on site to receive feedback, fine tune systems and ensure proper operation.

5. Outstanding issues are resolved and post occupancy evaluations are fed-back for future projects.

Soft Landings leader would be required to propose an appropriate guidance and process map to adopt a plan of work that may need to have the following plan of action in order to achieve the desired result:

> Strategy

> Brief

> Concept

> Definition

> Design

> Build and Commission

> Handover and close-out

> Operation and end-of-life

Therefore, Soft Landings may be described as the process of alignment of interests of the designers and construction team with the interests of the users and the managers of the facility. It aims to improve employer's and the user experiences, with reduced re-visits, and to provide a product that meets and performs to the client expectations in a manner that the facility was envisaged at the first place (and at a reasonable cost). It suggests that the reason for the creation of an asset and its intended business purpose, that could often be lost in the construction process, is maintained in order to ensure its continuation into the building's productive use stage.

Soft Landing therefore goes together with the Building Information Modeling (BIM), as BIM feeds into Computer Aided Facility Management (CAFM) systems, and helps enable proper operations and future alterations to the completed buildings and/or infrastructure.

Below listed are some important functions of a contracts administrator at pre-award and post-award stage.

Contract Pre-Award Stage Functions:

1. Scope building

2. Budget information and its allocation

3. Drawings/sketches preparation for bidding information

4. Specification building

5. Finalization of Contract Conditions

6. Preparation of Instruction to Tenderers document

7. Technical and commercial submission forms

8. Preparation of Bill of Quantities (BOQ)

9. Compilation of Request for Proposal (RFP) Document

10. Prequalification and preparation of a compatible Bidders list

11. Tender Bulletins/RFP Addendums

12. Site Visit

13. Pre-Tender meetings

14. Mid-Tender meetings

15. Review of Bids submissions and Bid Bonds

16. Post tender clarifications

17. Negotiation meetings

18. Contract finalization and award

19. Correspondence with regards to sending out of regret letters to all participating (but the winner) bidders

20. Maintenance of impartiality throughout the tendering process

Contract Post-Award Stage Functions:

1. Kick-off meeting

2. Contract Commencement

3. Submission of Performance Bond and return of Bid Bond

4. Advance Payment

5. Submission of insurances

6. Submission of Programme of works

7. Mobilization

8. Execution of Works/Services

9. Monthly Interim Payments

10. Substantial Completion

11. Issuance of Taking Over Certificate

12. Release of 50% of retention money

13. Defects Liability Period

14. Issuance of Defects Liability Certificate

15. Release of 100% of retention money

16. Issuance of Final Statement

17. Issuance of Certificate of Discharge

18. Final Payment

19. Return of Performance Bond

20. Contract Close-out

Chapter 2

Contract Overview

Contract:

A Contract is a legally enforceable agreement between two or more competent parties in which an offer is made and accepted, and lawful consideration is exchanged or agreed to be exchanged.

Essentials of a Contract

Any contract needs to have certain essential elements that would make it legally enforceable and be of value and use to the parties in contract. Therefore, a contract may also be called a practical document that intends to provide a clear understanding of the intentions of the contracting parties. However, what distinguish a construction contract from other types of contracts is their factual complexity and the widespread use of standard forms of contracts. However these characteristics merely increase the burden of forensic analysis rather than changing the rules of such analysis.

There are primarily four essentials of a Contract:

➤ It is between two (2) or more parties

➤ There needs to be an intention to create legal relations

➤ An agreement is in-place or is agreed to be executed within a reasonable time

➤ A consideration for the Works to be performed

Essentials of a Contract: Two or More Parties

There must be two or more parties present to create a contractual obligation. This statement may seem self-evident; however the law defines party by reference to legal capacity as well as physical existence. For example, if there is a parent company with subsidiary companies then contracts can be made between the parent and the subsidiary and between the various subsidiaries provided of course they are all registered companies. However, if a company operates by way of a divisional structure then the various divisions do not have a legal capacity to enter into contracts. Therefore, selling to one own-self cannot be allowed as there could not be a contract with oneself.

However, a drunk, insane, bankrupt, an enemy alien or a minor would have an impaired legal capacity to get into an agreement, although all of these will have to provide for a legal back-up through a guarantor.

Essentials of a Contract: Intention to Create Legal Relations

It is presumed that domestic or social arrangements are not intended to be legally binding. For example, if A agrees to take B, his wife to a cinema provided that B gets his car serviced, there is a promisor A and consideration moving from the promisee B.

However, in commercial transactions there is no such presumption although there may be particular circumstances where the parties are not animo contrahendi (an intention to form a contract).

Essentials of a Contract: Agreement

The presence or otherwise of an agreement is determined by an objective test and not a subjective test. Objectivity is based upon a reasonable man's understanding of a particular set of circumstances or facts. In its purest form the test needs to exclude what was actually in the minds of the parties.

However, a basic rule that an agreement exists is evidenced by offer and acceptance.

Essentials of a Contract: Agreement (offer)

An offer is a written or oral statement by a person of his willingness to enter into a contract upon terms that are certain or are capable of being made certain. It needs to be noted that an offeror's intention to enter into a contract may be actual or apparent. An apparent intention is determined by the objective test (as discussed earlier).

An offer must be distinguished from what is merely a request for information or an invitation to offer. An invitation to offer is a request for an offer. Neither a request for information nor an invitation to offer be converted into a binding Contract by its acceptance. Competitive bidding is a common method of procurement in the construction industry. In the absence of special circumstances the invitation to tender sent out to bidders by the employer is an invitation to offer, and not an offer. It is the bidder's submission of tender which constitutes the offer and which in turn must be accepted by the employer to give rise to a formally binding contract. Therefore, the employer is not bound by the lowest tender or is responsible for the contractor's costs of preparing and submitting the proposal.

An offer can be withdrawn at any time prior to it being accepted. This is so, even is the offeror stipulates that the offer shall be kept open for a particular period of time.

An important aspect to bear in mind is that the withdrawal of an offer is not effective until the withdrawal has been communicated to the offeree, and that this communication may be written or oral.

Essentials of a Contract: Agreement (Acceptance)

An acceptance is a written or verbal expression of acceptance of the terms and conditions of the offer. It must be unequivocal and unconditional. For example, acknowledgement of the receipt of an offer is not an unequivocal acceptance nor is an acceptance that fails to distinguish between alternative offers.

A conditional acceptance is not a real acceptance. In fact, a conditional acceptance maybe treated as a counter offer terminating the original offer so that it is no longer capable of being accepted even though an unconditional acceptance is subsequently sent to the offeror.

As a general rule an acceptance must be communicated by the offeree to the offeror to create a binding contract. In the absence of any particular requirements set out in the offer, communication of an acceptance may be oral or in writing.

Silence cannot be taken as an acceptance of an offer even if the offer stipulates the same. This is to be contrasted with conduct that may constitute a binding acceptance. Consider for example the situation where a sub-contractor for the supply of ready mix concrete has forwarded an offer in response to a main contractor's enquiry. The main contractor responds with a purchase order that sets out the main contractor's standard terms of contract, some of which are at variance with the terms of the sub-contractor's offer. The sub-contractor intends to negotiate these matters with the main contractor, however the first deliveries of concrete have already been sent from the batching plant. Subsequently if the sub-contractor communicates to the main contractor that its terms and conditions of contract are not acceptable, it can be held that the delivery of the concrete by the sub-contractor to the main contractor constitutes an acceptance through his conduct that is based upon the terms of the main contractor's purchase order.

Essentials of a Contract: Agreement (The 'Last shot' Doctrine)

In construction industry, commercial negotiations can be both lengthy and tortuous. Offers being superseded with counter-offers and counter-offers with counter-counter offers, each party intending to impose a standard form contract or their own terms and conditions of trade to the other party.

However, the law of contract requires the offer and the acceptance to be in the same terms, and in case of a dispute the difficulty that one faces is decide whether what contract came into existence. The 'last shot' doctrine provides that where there is a series of conflicting documents they shall all be treated as counter offers and the contract, if indeed one comes into existence is to be based upon the last document in time.

It cannot be over-emphasized that the modern commercial practice of making quotations and placing orders with attached conditions generally produces a battle of forms between parties, and hence needs to be minimized to the maximum.

Let us try and understand this by an example:

Company A sends details (offer) of his project to company B for pricing and in turn B proposes to complete the project at a value say X. However, B's offer has a condition that A changes the payment terms contained within the offer. Now, if A accepts to get into an Agreement with B, the contract shall be on the payment term proposed by B.

Essentials of a Contract: Agreement (Incomplete agreements)

To create a legally binding contract the process of offer and acceptance must result in the parties being in agreement on all the terms which are essential to their bargain; there must be consensus ad idem (meeting of minds).

As a general rule the essential terms of a construction contract are parties, description of the works/services, specifications, price, payment terms and the period of construction. A failure to agree on price or time for performance is not necessarily fatal, in certain circumstances a dispute resolution authority may apply terms that is a reasonable industry practice.

However, particular difficulties may arise in respect of collateral warranties/third party liabilities in so far as the ultimate beneficiary of the warranty may not be known at the time the parties enter into an agreement

In order to have a good contract there must be a concluded bargain and a concluded contract is one which settles everything that is necessary to be settled and leaves nothing to be settled by agreement between the parties. "An Agreement to agree" does not constitute a binding contract. Statements such as parties must continue to negotiate in good faith continues to adversely affect a binding contract.

Essentials of a Contract: Consideration

There must be a valuable consideration to a contract. Valuable consideration is 'something of value in the eye of the law'. Clearly the payment of money or a promise to pay money is valuable consideration. It is noted that in the eyes of the law any insignificant consideration may also provide valuable consideration. For example a promise to pay AED 1.00 "if you come to my house" is also a valuable consideration.

"A Contract is about reinforcement of trust by bringing together the parties on a level playing field that tends to create something of value through mutual understanding and cooperation."

Contract/Agreement that tends to damage trust:

Contract exists to foster trust, but they can actually do the opposite. Overly detailed contracts leave no room for spontaneous acts of kindness to create goodwill between parties; too-rigid contracts leave parties unable to respond to the unanticipated; and, strangely enough, incentives can end up being just plain insulting.

Contract or an Agreement is primarily prepared to reinforce trust between the contracting parties and reduce or clearly assign the associated risks. Unfortunately, when they're too detailed or do not clarify the issue, they can accelerate the very problems they are supposed to circumvent. It cannot be over-emphasized that loosing trust is any manager's biggest nightmare and needs to be curtailed at all costs.

Trust requires that parties see each other as ethical and with good intentions.

A contract needs to be reasonable and just in terms of being not too rigid and at the same time, not too lenient to amendments.

Contracts that are too rigid can be problematic if it tends to lock parties into arrangements that may look like a good idea at a point of time but won't allow for necessary circumstances when circumstances warrant. For example, a group of three technocrats started a online travel company, and at the time of drafting the contract had the provision of equally dividing the equity from all three. However, a person A was allocated a higher share of profit as the start-up was his original idea. However, problems started to surface, when this person A began feeling that he was doing more work than his other two partners and requested for a renegotiation of the terms. The other two partners did not agree and there was no mechanism in the Contract to allow for this in-equation resulting in a conflict.

A question that comes to our mind of course is; was this conflict avoidable? Perhaps yes, if the contract had enough flexibility to accommodate these conflict arising out of ones' feelings of doing more than the others.

Contracts that are too flexible can also be contentious. If the parties to a contract get a feeling that the contract that binds them is too flexible and can be swayed in any direction that a party wants, the reasonableness to be bound by that agreement is depleted. For example, if a contract mentions the duration for approval of submitted drawings by an Employer between 7 to 28 days, the Contractor may tend to believe that he wants the employer to approve a submitted drawing in 7 days, while the Employer may see up to 28 days taken by him as no delay to the approval. Again we ask the same question; is this confusion of understanding conflict avoidable? Definitely yes, if the contract had been rigid enough to provide a clear and expressed provision on the time for the Employer to approve, there would not have been an ambiguity. If the intention of the contract had been that a drawing of a certain phase was required to be approved within 7 days and other phases within 28 days, the contract needs to have said this clearly.

It is not uncommon to see that parties to a contract often overestimate the level of certainty in the environment and underestimate the likelihood of a future divergence in perspectives. As a result, they tend to include fewer contingencies than they should have and are generally too eager to finalize the terms of the contract.

Letter of intent

A Letter of Intent (LOI) is a document expressing an intention to enter into a contract at a future date but creating no contractual relationship until that future contract has been entered into. A Letter of Intent is not an 'agreement to agree'. However, in construction industry, it's not very uncommon to see that a contractor is requested to mobilize and commence Works on the basis of a Letter of Intent while the Agreement is still being drafted.

It is important to bear in mind that 'Letter of Intent' is a term of commercial convenience and not a term having a substantive legal meaning, as for example 'subject to contract'. Therefore, each and every Letter of Intent needs to be construed on its own particular meaning. It is suggested that the legal effect of a Letter of Intent may fall into one or more of the following categories:

> The expression of an intention to enter into a contract at a future date which does not give rise to any legal obligation, whether in contract or quasi ex-contractu (as if from a contract) on a quantum meruit (a reasonable amount for labour and materials, payable even in the absence of an enforceable agreement); or

> The expression of an intention to enter into a contract at a future date which does not give rise to any liability in contract but does not exclude or negate a right to recover reasonable expenditure on a quantum meruit; or

> The creation of a conditional or ancillary contractual obligation which may, but not necessarily will, be subsumed by a wider contractual obligation upon formal contracts being exchanged; or

> A legally binding executable contract in that the Letter of Intent is an offer capable of being accepted or is the acceptance of an offer.

Letters of intent are most commonly sent at a time when it is anticipated that the recipient will be incurring costs and overheads. They can be used as an interim arrangement to mobilize construction prior to a formal contract being engrossed, but they should never be seen as an alternative to a full contract and should place a limit on expenditure and the client's liability prior to the contract being put in place.

A comprehensive Letter of Intent should address the following:

- Client authorization to the contract administrator to represent them.
- Acceptance of the contractor's offer and definition of the project.
- The agreed contract sum.
- Reference to the tender documents and subsequent amendments (with dates).
- Instruction to proceed on a certain date.
- Site possession date.
- Contract completion date (including details of any phases).
- A full description of the proposed form of contract, including warrantees and performance bonds.
- A fall-back date for signing the contract (this is important, as beyond a certain time in the progress of the works it may no longer be in the interests of the contractor to sign the contract).
- Direction as to whether the contract will be executed by Deed, under seal or under-hand.
- Restriction of the work authorized by the Letter of Intent, by proceeding with which the contractor has fully accepted the terms of the Letter of Intent.
- Terms and provisions for cancelling the letter and determining the works at any time prior to signing the full contract:specifically, the terms will limit the client's liability for costs and exclude claims for loss of profit, opportunity, good will, indirect or consequential losses.
- Provision for the contractor to have access to the site under license only, with no (tenancy) rights to possession and limited rights described in a separate license that sets out conditions and the license period.
- Client and agents access provisions during the license.
- Insurance provisions and indemnification.

- ➢ Agreement that there are no rights to assign the works.
- ➢ Disputes resolution procedures.
- ➢ Agreement that there are no rights to assign the works.
- ➢ Liquidated and ascertained damages may be applied to late commencement or completion of projects.

It is contracts administrator's/project manager's duty to ensure that a contract is entered into rather than relying on a letter of intent (LOI) to commence works while still finalizing the Agreement.

Letter of Intent: Legal and negotiating position (1)

In a legal judgment relating to letters of intent that was made in a case, company B (Consultant) was appointed as a project manager for a number of projects at the premises of Company A (Employer). On the advise of company B, a contractor (company C) was appointed on the basis of a Letter of Intent (LOI) to allow an early start on site. In the event, eight (8) letters of intent were written and the contract itself, despite being substantially agreed, was never signed. The contractor was four months late in completing the works, but as there was no contract in place, the settlement that was reached was not as favourable for the Employer (company A) as it was expected. Therefore, company A began proceedings for professional negligence against his consultant (company B). The judgment awarded damages to company A on a *loss of chance* basis because the Letter of Intent failed to make provision for liquidated and ascertained damages, although such a provision was set out in the proposed contract that was yet to be signed.

In essence, the advice for employers/clients is to avoid letters of intent because they do not cover all the eventualities set out in a standard contract. They also reduce the pressure for a contractor to sign a more comprehensive set of obligations and allow the contractor an opportunity for back-negotiation from a position of strength.

Herein, it is highlighted that as a good practice the Tender documentation needs to set out the proposed contact documentation and the terms & conditions, so that there is no reason for agreement of the contract to be delayed.

Letter of Intent: Legal and negotiating position (2)

A Letter of Intent is different from a provisional contract. A Letter of Intent is usually a unilateral assurance intended to have contractual effect if acted upon, whereby reasonable expenditure incurred in reliance upon such a letter of Intent will only be reimbursed. Such a letter places no obligation upon the recipient to act upon it and there is usually no obligation to continue with the work or to undertake any defined parcel of work, the recipient being free to stop work at any time. The effect of a LOI is to promise reasonable reimbursement if the recipient does act upon it.

Contents of a contract document:

Any kind of business arrangement requires specific understanding of the roles, responsibilities and the expectations from each party. In a fast moving business environment, it becomes all the more important that "all that matter" is captured in the most concise manner in a document. Contracts are fundamental to any construction project, and it lays down the depth and breadth of requirements from the parties to the Contract. It will at the minimum include the following:

- Contract Agreement
- General terms and conditions
- Particular terms and conditions
- Scope of work
- Specifications
- Bill of Quantities
- Notes, if any

Procurement:

Procurement describes the merging of activities undertaken by the employer to obtain a project (product or service). There are many different methods of construction procurement; however the three most common types of procurement are:

- Traditional (design-bid-build)
- Design and build
- Construction Management
- Management contracting
- Turnkey form of procurement

There is also a growing number of new forms of procurement that involve relationship contracting where the emphasis is on a co-operative relationship between the principal and contractor and other stakeholders within a construction project. New forms include partnering such as Public-Private Partnering (PPPs), Private Finance Initiatives (PFIs) and alliances such as "project" alliances or "strategic" alliances. The focus on co-operation is to diminish the many problems that arise from the often highly competitive and adversarial practices within the construction industry.

Types of procurement:

New acquisitions or ordering of properties in construction industry is defined as "procurement". It refers to a wide array of strategies, rules, forms of procurement and responsibilities arising from material, services and construction equipment. It also includes design, construction and rectification works during the defects liability period.

There are several forms or methods of procurement and each one of those involves a different type of contract, contractual relationships, information flow, roles and responsibilities within a planning team.

Common available forms of procurement are the following:

Traditional (lump sum or re-measured):

Traditional form, used very extensively within the construction industry. This method of procurement is the most popular among small and middle sized construction projects. Those rules have been formed in the beginning of 20th century (hence the name, 'traditional'). The constructor works according to a detailed plan provided by the employer (or owner).

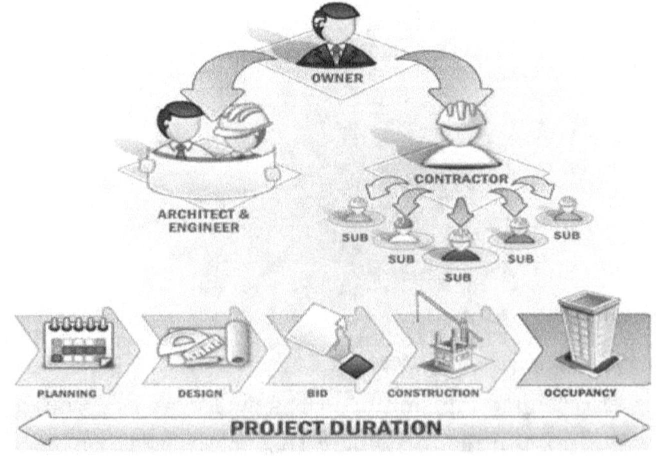

This is the most common method of construction procurement and is well established and recognized. In this arrangement, the architect (or engineer) acts as the project coordinator. His or her role is to design the works, prepare the specifications and produce construction drawings, administer the contract, tender the works, and manage the works from inception to completion. There are direct contractual links between the architect's client and the main contractor. Any subcontractor will have a direct contractual relationship with the main contractor.

Design & Build (D&B):

This form of procurement is becoming more and more popular in middle sized and larger projects. It was first introduced in the 1980s and is now used extensively on projects that intend to commence works before the completion of drawings. It obliges the contractor to undertake a large part of project works (preparation of a detailed project), while the employer only provides an outline of a project requirements. This method of procurement is not very common in smaller projects.

This approach has become more common in recent years, and involves the client contracting a single entity to both provide a design and to build that design. In some cases, the Design and Build (D & B) package can also include finding the site, arranging funding and applying for all necessary statutory consents.

The owner produces a list of requirements for a project, giving an overall view of the project's goals. Several D&B contractors present different ideas about how to accomplish these goals. The owner selects the ideas he or she likes best and hires the appropriate contractor. Often, it is not just one contractor, but a consortium of several contractors working together. Once a contractor (or a consortium/consortia) has been hired, they commence the Works in phases, starting with the first phase of the project. Generally, as they build phase 1, they design phase 2. This is in contrast to a design-bid-build contract, where the project is completely designed by the employer (or owner), then bid on to award the Work to a contractor who is thereafter, tasked to complete the Works.

It is highlighted that employers usually use design build contracts as a way of getting projects done when they don't have the resources.

Construction Management (Management procurement system):

In this arrangement the employer plays an active role in the procurement system by entering into separate contracts with the designer (architect or engineer), the construction manager, and individual trade contractors. Employer takes on the contractual role, while the construction or project manager provides the active role of managing the separate trade contracts, and ensuring that they complete all work smoothly and effectively together.

Management procurement systems are often used to speed up the procurement processes, allow the client greater flexibility in design variation throughout the contract, give the ability to appoint individual work contractors, separate contractual responsibility on each individual throughout the contract, and to provide greater client control.

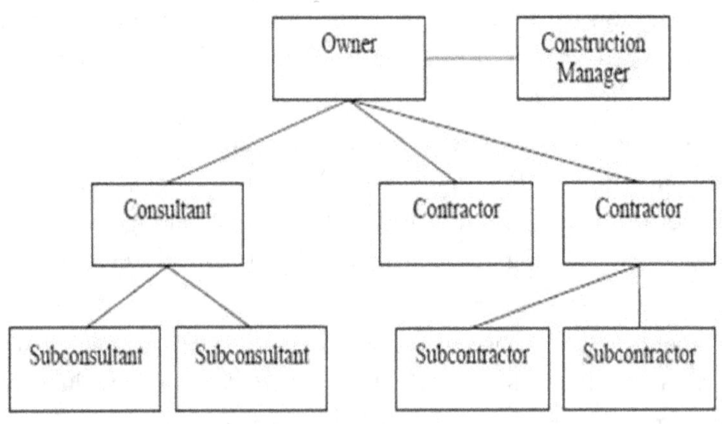

Note: Owner may also be referred to as an Employer.

This method of procurement has been developed in the United States of America (USA), where it initially gained popularity in the 1930s. It is still commonly applied, especially in technologically complex projects, where speed of completion is crucial. In construction management form of procurement, the contractor acts as a consultant, and even though they manage the construction works undertaken by subcontractors, they are not directly responsible for subcontractors. Therefore, Construction Manager manages the project on behalf of the employer. The employer enters into separate direct contracts for the works either using the Construction Management Trade Contract (CM/TC) or a special Trade Contract. It is suitable where separate responsibility for management, design and construction is required. Provisions are included for collaborative working, sustainability, third party rights and collateral warranties.

Management Contracting:

This is a hybrid form of procurement as it basically is a fusion between traditional method and construction management. Management Contractor undertakes to manage the carrying out of the work through work contractors, and those work contractors are contractually accountable to the Management Contractor. The client normally engages the Management Contractor to take an active role in the project at an early stage, and because of this the Management Contractor is normally an experienced contractor.

Management Contractor is responsible for the administration operation of the Works Contractors. However, the Management Contractor is not liable for the consequences of any default by a Works Contractor so long as the Management Contractor has complied with the particular requirements of the management contract.

An alternative view of management contracting is that it is an effective method for the client to retain control of the design whilst drawing on the experience of a construction specialist as part of the professional team. Management contracting is popular in some areas and is becoming increasingly popular when constructing major projects.

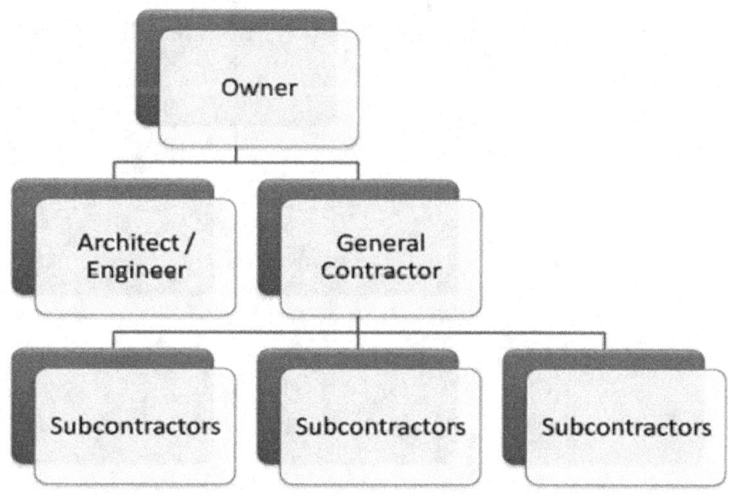

Note: Owner may also be referred to as an Employer/Client.

Turnkey Form of Contract:

This form of procurement is preferred mostly by the process industry clients, who wish to award the contract on a turnkey basis and is willing to wait for the approved concept design from an appointed Consultant.

This approach has becoming popular within oil and gas industry wherein the Employer first appoints a FEED (Front End Engineering Design) Consultant to prepare the concept design that forms the basis of the lump sum turnkey contract appointment.

Following are some of the procurement methodologies in use that would eventually be formed out of the above mentioned procurement types:

Private Finance Initiative (PFI):

Design & Build form used at large projects, where the contractor provides an investment in return for license to charge fare for using it in a designated period of time. It has a very complex settlement structure, suitable only to multimillion public use projects.

PFI devises a method of providing funds for major capital investments where private firms are contracted to complete and manage public projects. Under a private finance initiative, the private company, instead of the government, handles the up-front costs. The project is then leased to the public, and the government authority makes annual payments to the private company. These contracts are typically given to construction firms and can last 25 years or longer. In the United States, PFIs are called public-private partnerships.

Private finance initiatives were originally started as part of Great Britain's strategy for providing high quality services. PFIs were first implemented in the nineties and become popular within a few years. They are used to fund major public works projects such as schools, prisons, hospitals and infrastructure. Instead of funding these projects up front from tax receipts, private firms construct them and then make their money back through long-term (25+ years) repayments, plus interest, from the government. Thus, the government does not have to outlay a large sum of money at once to fund a large project. PFIs are also supposed to improve on-time project completion and transfer some of the risks associated with constructing and maintaining these projects from the public sector to the private sector. Financial advisers such as investment banks help manage the bidding, negotiating and financing process.

A key drawback is the interest and payments associated with PFIs burden future taxpayers. In addition, the arrangements sometimes include not only construction, but also ongoing maintenance once the projects are complete, which further increases these projects' future cost and tax burden.

In the United Kingdom in the 2000s, a scandal surrounding PFIs revealed that the government was spending significantly more on these projects than they were worth, to the benefit of the private firms running them and to the taxpayer's detriment. The same scenario is not uncommon in other countries encouraging PFIs for building infrastructure. PFIs have also been criticized as an accounting adjustment to reduce the appearance of public-sector borrowing.

Public-Private Partnership (PPP):

This is a form of procurement that envisages a long-term cooperation between government and private organizations.

A business relationship entered between a private-sector company and a government agency for the purpose of completing a mega project that will serve the public. Public-private partnerships can be used to finance, build and operate projects such as public transportation networks, parks and convention centers. Financing a project through a public-private partnership can allow a project to be completed sooner or make it a possibility in the first place.

Public-private partnerships often use private-sector investments to finance a public project when sufficient public funding is not available. For example, a city government might be heavily indebted, but a private enterprise might be interested in funding the project's construction in exchange for receiving the operating profits once the project is complete.

Framework Contracting:

This method is mostly is use at large projects, where the contractors are chosen following selective criteria and not only the prices. It is usually connected with long-term cooperation contracts including many different projects.

A framework agreement will generally allow a purchaser more flexibility around the goods or services contracted for under the framework, both in terms of volume and also the detail of the relevant goods and services. A multi-supplier framework allows a contracting authority to select from a number of suppliers for its requirements, helping to ensure that each purchase represents best value.

Prime Contracting:

This form is an expanded traditional form including long-term partnership. The contractor is usually obliged to undertake construction works and further building maintenance. It is commonly used by governmental institutions.

The prime contractor is responsible to the employer for all of the goods and services in the contract. A sub-contractor may be employed by the prime contractor to complete a portion of work that that prime contractor wishes him to do. Employer may also provide restrictive covenants wherein he may state that certain companies may not be eligible to be hired as sub-contractor for certain portions of the works (use of local companies or suppliers only, etc.).

Lump Sum contract basics

Most of small projects are carried out under traditional form of procurement (Lump Sum contract). Most importantly, such approach divides the design and construction functions. A detailed plan should be provided by the employer or its planning team and supplied to the contractor prior to cost estimate preparation.

However, in practice it happens rarely. Very often, some elements of the project are not finalized and the details are provided to the contractor at latter date. It is important that all doubts and errors in documentation are identified by the contractor at the time of preparing the tender.

In this procurement form, employer is fully responsible for all planning matters. The contractor should not make any decisions regarding the project, since it puts him at risk of having to redo the works if the employer does not approve their decision. On the other hand, all additional works arising from changes of faults on behalf of the employer have to be paid for by the employer.

There is a possibility to partially transfer the design duties to the contractor. It can be done by using adequate contract form. It often happens in case of technologically advanced elements, e.g. air conditioning/district cooling installation etc. It is associated with additional responsibility and costs, to the contactor.

Procurement routes and the information flow:

In the traditional contract form, relationship is separate to the information flow.

All members of design team have direct contract with the employer even though they are supervised by the architect (employer's representative). This offers them a lot of independence and limited contractual responsibility. On the other hand, in the construction team all members are contracted to main contractor, who in turn has access to the employer. Such structure makes main contractor liable for performance of all subcontractors and suppliers.

Every exchange of information between construction and design teams should take place via main contractor-architect. This means, that legally, requests made by employer should not be implemented until they are confirmed in adequate form (in writing) by the contract administrator.

Theory versus Practice:

The above mentioned information refers of course to contractual theories. However, reality can often be very different. One has to bear in mind that in case of disputes it is the fundamentals and contract terms that will be taken into consideration: not common sense or good will of the parties. Following and complying with the contractual procedures it to contractor's best interest, especially if the form of contract (which is common) is generally in favor of the employer, not contractor. It is not very uncommon to come across contractors who have not been paid at the completion of the contract because they had failed to follow the procedures set out within the contract.

For instance, if the employer requested a partition to be moved, that was not approved by the employer's representative (engineer/architect). It may turn out (at a later point of time) that this may cause the previously ordered wardrobe not to fit. Now if the employer denies ever giving the instruction and employer's representative, according to contact, deduced and amount from the final payment to cover the additional cost of moving the partition back.

Therefore, following the contractual procedures and detailed organization of contract documentation protects the contractor against wrongfully imposed penalties and problems with payment. An adequate contract strategy allows maximizing profits and minimizing the risk of construction works.

Contract Conditions typically deals with:

- ➢ General obligations to perform the Work
- ➢ Provisions of instructions, including variations
- ➢ Valuation and payments
  - • Liabilities and insurances
  - • Provisions of quality and inspections

- Completion, delay and Extension of Time (EOT)
- Role or power of Engineer or PM
- Disputes

"One of the main objectives of the conditions of contract is to facilitate an efficient control and administration of works, while at the same time providing certainty that the project duration is maintained and payments are done on time".

Parties to a Contract:

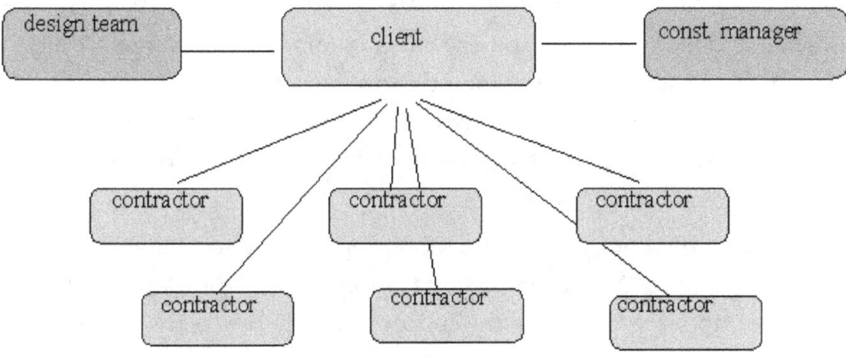

Employer (or client)

The most essential person within a contract is a client, who requests and commissions the work. He may be referred to as building owner, promoter or by a term that we will mostly use in this book as "Employer". An employer may have practically any status. He may be an individual, a company or government. Two or more entities may also come together in a joint venture and form an employer.

Contractors and sub-contractors

A large proportion of construction works is performed by a main contractor or general contractor. Professional services including design and/or small portions of the works may be done by specialist contractors who do not have a direct contract (agreement) with the employer but have their agreement with the main contractor. These entities are generally referred to as sub-contractors, and are indirect parties to the contract as they team-up with the main contractor to complete the works for the employer.

Main contract may provide for certain specialist sub-contracts to be provided for by sub-contractors chosen by the employer, usually identified as prime cost (PC) work. The sub-contractors appointed such are usually called nominated sub-contractors.

Virtually all standard forms of contract permit the main contractor to sublet (subcontract) main portions of the work to firms of its own choosing (provided that certain conditions are met), it is the main contractor who is responsible towards his contractual commitment towards the client (though some of it is passed on to the sub-contractor via the sub contract agreement). The subcontractor chosen such are termed 'Domestic' subcontractors.

The restrictions imposed on the main contractor (for hiring a domestic subcontractor) vary from one standard form to the other; generally a form of contract may state that "the contractor shall not subcontract the works of any part thereof without the written consent of the Architect whose consent shall not be unreasonably withheld."

Similar (sometimes simpler or more complex or restrictive) provisions may be included in a form of contract, supplemented by various additional stipulations, about the terms of the subcontract. These essentially ensure that, if the main contract is determined, then the subcontracts are also determined, and that title to any unfixed goods and materials on the site passes to the employer as soon as the main contractor has been paid for them.

A general form of contract may state that, although the Employer's (or Engineer/Architect) permission to sublet is required, this shall not be unreasonably withheld. Domestic subcontractors are commonly divided into the following three basic types:

- ➢ Subcontractors carrying out complete parcels of work, including providing all necessary labor, plant and materials. Examples are piling, plumbing, installations, and the fabrication and erection of structural steelwork.

- ➢ Labor only subcontractors, where all necessary materials and plant are provided by the main contractor. Examples are bricklaying gangs and concreting gangs.

- ➢ Labor and plant subcontractors, where materials are provided by the main contractor. This arrangement may have some advantages in cases where the work requires specialized plant but the main contractor wishes to exercise tight control of materials purchasing and supply.

Authority having Jurisdiction:

In construction, the authority having jurisdiction (AHJ) is the governmental agency or sub-agency which regulates the construction process in a particular geographic region. In most cases, it is the municipality in which the project is located. However, construction performed for supra-municipal authorities are usually regulated directly by the owning authority, which becomes the AHJ i.e.; Airport Authorities, Nuclear Agencies, etc.

Before the foundation can be dug, contractors are typically required to verify and have existing utility lines marked, either by the utilities themselves or through a company specializing in such services. This lessens the likelihood of damage to the existing electrical, water, sewage, phone, and cable facilities, which could cause outages and potentially hazardous situations. During the construction of a building, the municipal building inspector inspects the building periodically to ensure that the construction adheres to the approved plans and the local building code. Once construction is complete and a final inspection has been passed, an occupancy permit/building completion certificate may be issued.

A modern operating building must always remain in compliance with the fire code. The fire code is enforced by the local fire department or the civil defense.

Changes made to a building that affect safety, including its use, expansion, structural integrity and fire protection items, usually require approval of the AHJ for review concerning the building code.

Professionals within the construction industry:

Quantity Surveyor (QS): Typically holds a bachelor's/master's degree in quantity surveying. Chartered status is gained from the Royal Institution of Chartered Surveyors (RICS).

Architect: Typically holds undergraduate degree in architecture, post-graduate degree (Dip. Arch or B. Arch) in architecture, plus a minimum of 2-3 years of experience within the construction industry. To use the title "architect" the individual must be registered on the Architects Registration Board register of Architects of the land.

Civil Engineer: Typically holds a degree in a related subject. The Chartered Engineer qualification is controlled by the Engineering Council, and is often achieved through membership of the Institution of Civil Engineers. A new university graduate must hold a master's degree to become chartered. A person with bachelor's degree may become an Incorporated Engineer.

Building Services Engineer: Often referred to as an "M&E Engineer" typically holds a degree in mechanical or electrical engineering. Chartered Engineer status is governed by the Engineering Council, mainly through the Chartered Institution of Building Services Engineers.

Project Manager: Typically holds a 4-year or higher education qualification and may also be qualified in another field such as quantity surveying or civil engineering.

Structural Engineer: Typically holds a bachelor's or master's degree in structural engineering. New university graduates must hold a master's degree to gain chartered status from the Engineering Council, mainly through the Institution of Structural Engineers.

Civil Estimators are professionals who typically have a background in civil engineering, construction project management, or construction supervision.

Safety:

Construction is one of the most risky occupations in the world, incurring more occupational fatalities than any other sector anywhere in the world. Published data around the world confirms that the fatal occupational injury rate among construction workers in the United States was nearly three times that for all workers (similar data is reported from other countries as well). Trips, slips and falls are the most common causes of fatal and non-fatal injuries among construction workers. Proper safety equipment such as harnesses and guardrails and procedures such as securing ladders and inspecting scaffolding can curtail the risk of occupational injuries in the construction industry. Other major causes of fatalities in the construction industry include electrocution, transportation accidents, and trench cave-ins.

Roles in traditional procurement

Individuals or organizations involved in supplying the project in traditional system can be divided into the following groups:

Client

➢ The Client

➢ Their employees and representatives

Design Team

- Architect:team leader
- Structural Engineer
- Mechanical Engineer
- Quantity Surveyor
- Other designers

Construction team

- Main contractor
- Subcontractors
- Suppliers
- Their employees and representatives

There is also a role of contract administrator, that is usually carried out by the architect and it involves dispute resolution, certifying payments and managing changes to the project/contract. This role should be performed separately from design functions and the decisions made by contract administrators should be objective.

In the modern industrialized world, construction usually involves the translation of designs into reality. A formal design team may be assembled to plan the physical proceedings, and to integrate those proceedings with the other parts. The design usually consists of drawings and specifications, usually prepared by a design team including surveyors, civil engineers, cost engineers (or quantity surveyors), mechanical engineers, electrical engineers, structural engineers, fire protection engineers, planning consultants, architectural consultants, and archaeological consultants. The design team is most commonly employed by (i.e. in contract with) the property owner or the employer. Under this system, once the design is completed by the design team, a number of construction companies or construction management companies may then be asked to make a bid for the work, either based directly on the design, or on the basis of drawings and a bill of quantities (BOQ) provided by a quantity surveyor. Following evaluation of bids, the owner will typically award a contract to the most cost efficient bidder or the best techno-commercial bidder (the best offer).

The modern trend in design is toward integration of previously separated specialties, especially among large firms. In the past, architects, interior designers, engineers, developers, construction managers, and general contractors were more likely to be entirely separate companies, even in the larger firms. Presently, a firm that is normally an "architectural firm" or "construction management" firm may have experts from all related fields as employees, or to have an associated company that provides each necessary skill. Thus, each such firm may offer itself as "one-stop shop" for a construction project, from beginning to end. This is designated as a "design build" contract where the contractor is given a performance specification and must undertake the project from design to construction, while adhering to the performance specifications.

Several project structures can assist the employer in this integration, including design-build, partnering and construction management. In general, each of these project structures allows the employer to integrate the services of architects, interior designers, engineers and constructors throughout design and construction. In response, many companies are growing beyond traditional offerings of design or construction services alone and are placing more emphasis on establishing relationships with other necessary participants through the design-build process.

The increasing complexity of construction projects creates the need for design professionals trained in all phases of the project's life-cycle and develop an appreciation of the building as an advanced technological system requiring close integration of many sub-systems and their individual components, including sustainability. Building engineering is an emerging discipline that attempts to meet this new challenge.

Financial advisors:

Construction projects can suffer from preventable financial problems. Underbids ask for too little money to complete the project. Cash flow problems exist when the present amount of funding cannot cover the current costs for labor and materials, and because they are a matter of having sufficient funds at a specific time, can arise even when the overall total is enough. Fraud is a problem in many fields, but is notoriously prevalent in the construction industry. Financial planning for the project is intended to ensure that a solid plan with adequate safeguards and contingency plans are in place before the project is started and is required to ensure that the plan is properly executed over the life of the project.

Mortgage bankers, accountants and cost engineers are likely participants in creating an overall plan for the financial management of a construction project. The presence of the mortgage banker is highly likely, even in relatively smaller projects since the employer's equity in the property is the most obvious source of funding for a construction project. Accountants act to study the expected monetary flow over the life of the project and to monitor the payouts throughout the process. Cost engineers and estimators apply expertise to relate the work and materials involved to a proper valuation. Cost overruns with government projects have often occurred when the contractor was able to identify change orders or changes in the project resulting in large increases in cost, which are not subject to competition by other firms as they have already been eliminated from consideration after the initial bid.

Large projects can involve highly complex financial plans and often start with a conceptual estimate performed by an estimator. As portions of a project are completed, they may be sold, supplanting one lender or owner for another, while the logistical requirements of having the right trades and materials available for each stage of the building construction project carries forward. In most of the countries in Europe and Asia, projects typically use quantity surveyors and the American continents typically use cost engineers or estimators.

Legal aspects:

A construction project must fit into the legal framework governing the property. These include governmental regulations on the use of property, and obligations that are created in the process of construction.

The project must adhere to the zoning and building code requirements. Constructing a project that fails to adhere to codes will not benefit the employer or the owner of that particular project. Some legal requirements come from considerations, or the desire to prevent things that are indisputably bad: bridge collapses or explosions. Other legal requirements come from *malum prohibitum* considerations, or things that are a matter of custom or expectation, such as isolating businesses to a business district and residences to a residential district. An attorney may seek changes or exemptions in the law governing the land where the building will be built, either by arguing that a rule is inapplicable (the bridge design will not collapse), or that the custom is no longer needed (acceptance of live-work spaces has grown in the community). However, it needs to be noted that exemptions or changes are pre-requisites to the project commencement.

A construction project is a complex net of contracts and other legal obligations, each of which must be carefully considered. A contract is the exchange of a set of obligations between two or more parties, but it is not so simple a matter as trying to get the other side to agree to as much as possible in exchange for as little as possible. The time element in construction means that a delay costs money, and in cases of bottlenecks, the delay can be extremely expensive. Thus, the contracts must be designed to ensure that each side is capable of performing the obligations set out. Contracts that set out clear expectations and clear paths to accomplishing those expectations are far more likely to result in the project flowing smoothly, whereas poorly drafted contracts lead to confusion and collapse.

Legal advisors in the beginning of a construction project seek to identify ambiguities and other potential sources of trouble in the contract structure, and to present options for preventing problems. Throughout the process of the project, they work to avoid and resolve conflicts that arise. In each case, the lawyer facilitates an exchange of obligations that matches the reality of the project.

Interaction of expertise:

Design, finance, and legal aspects overlap and interrelate. The design must be not only structurally sound and appropriate for the use and location, but must also be financially possible to build, and legal to use. The financial structure must accommodate the need for building the design provided, and must pay amounts that are legally owed. The legal structure must integrate the design into the surrounding legal framework, and enforce the financial consequences of the construction process.

The important aspects on appointing a sub-contractor are the following:

Privity of Contract: Privity of Contract holds good in a contract i.e.; under a claim situation, only the contracting parties can have a claim on the other.

This theoretically means that an employer cannot have any claim on a sub-contractor, although he can have a claim on the main contractor for any breach of the contract on the part of a sub-contractor.

A very important aspect of contract to understand here is the fact that though the main contractor is liable for the defective/faulty works of his sub-contractor, he in turn has got equal rights over a claim on his sub-contractor. Therefore, the risk is indirectly passed on to the sub-contractor executing a part of the main works.

Helping-Hand Concept: The concept of involving a sub-contractor is due to the requirement of a helping hand or the requirement of a Specialized Agency in the execution of a contract arose due to the ever increasing complexities of a construction projects. The demand from a contractor to complete quality work within a very tight schedule calls for the use of Specialized Agents (also called sub-contractors) on a contract such that he delivers the works to the client within the stipulated time and matching the quality needs per the contract i.e.; HVAC works, Ducts, Electrical, Installations, Special Systems, etc.

Risk Mitigation: A very important aspect of sub-contracting is the leveraging of the risk associated with a contract from the main contractor towards the sub-contractors. The benefits of this to the client is that this approach does not compromise his status, when compared against the main contractor due the concept of Privity of Contract, and at the same time he gets better quality of works by pulling in specialized agencies as the sub-contractor (without actually entering into a contract with this agency).

Back-to-Back Arrangement: Generally this is the norm of the sub contract arrangement on a construction contract. Back to Back arrangement passes on both, benefits/rewards or the claim/punishment to the sub-contractor in the ratio of the contractual arrangement between the main contractor and the concerned sub-contractor. However, this arrangement is not a recommended approach due to obvious reasons.

Time: It is easier and faster for a main contractor to get a specialized sub-contractor for a certain job than to hunt for the manpower and material for such a specialized job if he were to do it himself, which at times may be very difficult to find within the stipulated time frame to adhere to the contract period. This in the long term helps avoid any imposition of Liquidity Damages to the main contractor and helps the client to have his project within time that was originally envisaged. This becomes more relevant and important due to the insertion of contractual terms such as "Time if the essence of Contract," very commonly found in almost all forms of contracts used almost in any part of the world.

Project complexity: Complexity of modern projects together with the complexities of procedures, especially when new procedures from the government are introduced to maintain cost and quality. A sub-contractor with an understanding of local market and understanding of the rules and regulations of the local environment plays a vital rule in the execution of a contract.

New method and forms of Contract: Many new contract forms such as the Design and Build contracts envisages that one main contractor will be awarded with the responsibility of executing a contract right from the Schematic Design Stage to carry it to Detailed Design Stage followed by its execution and final handover to the client. This invariably requires input from various design and construction firms, which in turn will involve multiple firms to come together, join hands to deliver the project in the manner that a client expects.

Cost & Cost Benefits: Benefits of cost is a vital element in sub-contracting approach. A sub-contractor will definitely be preferred if he is able to provide the same quality of product at a better rate than the main contractor. This is normally done by a specialized agency having better economy of scales.

Process Adaptation: Adaptation of a new process or system will normally entail that the main contractor take advantage of an available and competent sub-contractor who may at one hand do the works and on the other also serve to train the main contractor to execute the works in the new and better process for the future works.

Minimizing Disputes: A sub-contracting arrangement also goes a long way in minimizing disputes and litigations on a contract, due to the proper delivery of products. A client may be used to a certain kind of product on a particular segment of the works. Here it may be prudent to have the nominated (or domestic sub-contractor) to carry out that particular bit of the overall contract, such that the delivery matches the expectation. This definitely will minimize a chance of budding of a dispute in between the contracting parties.

Therefore, the principle reason for the use of domestic subcontractors in construction is definitely more than to only allow the main contractor to pass on as much time, price and quality risk as possible to his sub-contractor. The following are some of the advantages of using a sub-contractor on a project:

> Sub-contractor enables the main contractor to use specialized agencies on carrying out certain kinds of jobs. Thereby having better quality

at optimum price and time. At times and at certain places this may be the only solace due to reasons such as remoteness of the project, resource requirements and the like.

➤ Liability of the main contractor is not dissolved. Therefore, Employer is not exposed to any additional risk due to this approach.

➤ The liability chain is reflected as Sub Contractor to Main Contractor to the Client (i.e.; the sub-contractor possess the risk for the part of the works under his domain and the main contractor is responsible for the overall contract).

➤ The benefits percolates from the Employer to Main Contractor to Sub Contractor (i.e.; the subcontractor passes on the part of the project to the main contractor, the main contractor passes on the project to the employer).

➤ The risk is taken by the specialized sub-contractor for the part of his job, thereby the actual party taking on the risk for which he should be responsible. Therefore this approach also leverages on the insurance and risk domain. Risk sharing is observed in this case.

➤ Goes a long way in the execution of complex projects through the main contractor, who in turn approaches a sub-contractor who may be locally available with the required skills.

➤ But for the sub-contracting approach, an employer would be required to enter into numerous contracts for a project and therefore managing the project would become a difficult task for any particular employer.

➤ Partnering approach to the execution of a contract is encouraged through this mechanism as all the entities can be productive towards the common goal of achieving the objective of the provision of quality and timely projects at reasonable cost to the employer.

➤ Under special requirement or in places where most of the specialized manpower or plant and machinery may not be available or made available in the stipulated time, it is in the interest of all parties to tie up and obtain delivery of a part of the main contact through a sub-contractor that may be locally available and who has got substantial working experience and knowledge of the local environment.

➤ Consideration of the factor such as "Economy of Scales" may also tempt a main contractor to have a part of the contract executed through a subcontractor, if in the opinion the main contractor it is felt that the quantity of the goods required for the part of the job dos not provide a good economy. Added to the fact that there may be a local contractor who may be specializing on that particular part of the contract and may be in a better position to pass on the benefits of the economy of scales the main contractor.

The professional team

In a traditional contracting, the task of designing the work is carried out by an architect. A Quantity Surveyor may also be found in larger works. New forms of contract have given rise to professional groups called Project Manager, Engineer, Engineer's Representative or Employer's Representative.

In this book and for the benefit of understanding we would assume all the above parties (other than contractor) to be a team member of employer (Employer) and the other party being the contractor (Contractor).

Engineer/Employer's Representative

A common feature of construction contracts is the provision of an independent third party to issue certificates signifying particular events and usually embodying administrative decisions. Generally this third party is referred to as Engineer or Employer's Representative. However, this book refers to the direct contracting parties (Employer or Contractor) and assumes that the delegated responsibilities shall be in accordance with the Agreement.

Implied terms:

In addition to the express terms, there may be other terms implied into a contract which, although not specified by the parties either in writing or orally, are nevertheless as binding as expressed terms within a contract.

Exclusion Clauses

It is very common in standard form of contracts for there to be terms excluding or limiting liabilities of one party in the event of breach. It is a good practice to limit the exclusion clauses to the minimum and have only for genuine exclusions i.e.; issues over which the parties do not have direct control.

Construction Contract:

An agreement entered into by two parties wherein one party pays the other a consideration for the provision of physical and tangible works is termed as a construction contract.

Examples of construction contract are building works, provision of goods and maintenance thereof, construction of roadways, railways, etc.

Forms of Contract

The classic nineteenth century definition of a contract is a promise or set of promises which is enforceable by the law of the land. That is to say that there is reciprocity of undertaking passing between the promisor and the promisee. In contract, the rights and obligations are created by the acts of agreement between the parties to the contractual arrangement.

In the procurement of construction contracts, there are different forms of contract as detailed below:

➢ Standard forms

➢ Modified standard forms

➢ Bespoke.

Fédération Internationale des Ingénieurs-Conseils (FIDIC)

Representative agreement

Conditions of contract for construction

Conditions of contract for plant and design build

Conditions of contract for EPC (engineering, procurement and construction)/ turnkey projects

Conditions of contract for design, build and operate projects

Conditions of subcontract for construction (Short form of contract)

FIDIC forms of contact remain by far the most popular forms of contract in Europe and Asia. It is therefore, used as the standard reference within this book. However, other forms have also been discussed, where applicable.

Joint Contracts Tribunal (JCT)

DB: Design and build contract

CD: Standard form with contractors design

CE: Construction excellence contract

CM: Construction management contract

IFC: Intermediate form of building contract

MC: Management contract

MTC: Measured term contract

MW: Agreement for minor work.

PCC: Prime cost contract

MP: Major project construction contract.

RM: Repair and maintenance contract

SBC: Standard form of building contract

JCT traditional forms of contact remain by far the most popular forms of contract within the United Kingdom.

The Association of Consultant Architects (ACA)

Form of building agreement

PPC: Standard form of contract for project partnering

SPC: Standard form of specialist contract for project partnering

Chartered Institute of Building(CIOB)

CPC 2013

CIOB Contract for use within Complex Projects.

The New Engineering Contract (NEC): Construction Contract

Option A: Priced contract with activity schedule

Option B: Priced contract with bill of quantities

Option C: Target contract with activity schedule

Option D: Target contract with bill of quantities

Option E: Cost reimbursable contract

Option F: Management contract

Option G: Term contract

Other Forms of Contract

Other less commonly used forms of contract are the following:

The GC Works suite of standard government conditions of contract

New Engineering Contacts, now in their third edition (NEC3)

IChemE (The Institution of Chemical Engineers) forms of contract

ICC Infrastructure conditions of contract

The ICE forms of contract (Institution of Civil Engineers), that have now been withdrawn in favor of NEC contracts

IMechE/IET (The Institution of Mechanical Engineers/The Institution of Engineering Technology) Model forms of General conditions of contract.

Contract Conditions:

Contract conditions set out the principal legal relationship between the parties to a construction project, determining the allocation of works, service, risks and consequently, the price.

Modified Standard Forms of Contract

Bespoke Contracts

Majority of the contract professionals indicate that they seldom use purpose-written bespoke contracts. In fact in most of the cases, there is a practice to use the bespoke contracts, but with modifications to suite the actual requirements of the employer and to shift the risks to the other party.

Not only is this is considered inadvisable because of the risk that bespoke contracts may not adequately or fairly make provision for all circumstances, and that they are not supported by a history of case law, but it is also a poor reflection of how inflexible and ineffective the industry perceives many of the standard forms of contract to be.

Consultancy Services:

An agreement entered into by two parties wherein one party pays the other a consideration for the provision of any non-tangible services is termed as a consultancy contract.

Examples of consultancy services are provision of design services, supervision services, management services, etc.

By appointments, we are referring primarily to the situation where the employer contracts designers (such as architects, engineers, specialist designers, specialist contractors, etc.) or other consultants (such as cost consultants, Construction Design and Management co-ordinators, independent employer advisor, site inspectors, project managers, employer's representatives, etc.).

The employer contracts contractor's through a well described process, called as the tender or bidding process or contracting. On publicly-funded projects, the consultant team will often be contracted along with the main contractor as part of a complete integrated supply team, and so appointments may be restricted to independent client advisers and project managers.

An integrated project delivery team that includes employer, consultant and the contractor's representatives is referred to as a Project Management Office (PMO) and is recently gaining popularity around the world due to the realization that a consolidated team approach may be the best for all parties who are joining hands to accomplish the task of completing a large project in the most efficient manner.

Below are a few institutions that may help an employer to find consultants for his project:

Chartered Institute of Architectural Technologists (CIAT)

International directory of RIBA chartered practices

RIBA chartered member's directory

Royal Institution of Chartered Surveyors (RICS)

Appointments may be made by a process of:

Recommendation, for example, one consultant may recommend others, which can save time for the employer or client and make it easier to establish collaborative working practices (it is important to set out requirements for collaborative practices during the appointment procedure to ensure that the consultant team works effectively together throughout the project).

Appointments by recommendation may be coupled with one or more of the following techniques of selection:

➢ Research and interview process of the proposed consultant.

➢ Open competition (with or without design).

➢ Selective competition (with or without design).

➢ An existing relationship or framework agreement.

A survey by the RIBA in 2014 (Refer RIBA Journal of February 2014) revealed that the most common methods of appointing architects/consultants were:

Direct appointment	50%
Competitive fee bid or financial tender only	21%
Framework agreement with or without further competition for specific projects	10%
Invited competitive interview (no pre-qualification questionnaire, PQQ)	4%
Expression of Interest/PQQ only (no design work)	3%
Expression of Interest/PQQ followed by competitive interview (no design work)	3%
Expression of Interest/PQQ followed by design competition	2%
Invited design competition (no PQQ)	1%
Open design competition	1%
Other	4%

Smaller project tends to appoint consultant mostly by direct appointment (61%), whereas this is less common for larger practices (25%).

Appointments for publicly-funded projects may fall under the requirements of specific established procurement rules in which case strict procedures must be adhered to, including advanced advertising of an appointment. This procedure can take some time and so should be initiated as soon as the employer has identified a possible need for an appointment.

Whatever the process of selecting potential consultants, agreeing the scope of services and fee for the appointment will generally require that the employer prepares some form of request for proposal (RFP).

A request for proposal (RFP) generally would include the following:

➤ A strategic brief describing the employer's assumptions, aspirations, budget and programme.

➤ A management structure of the organization of the project.

➤ Assumptions of the proposed procurement method to be adopted.

➤ The scope of services required.

➤ Guidance on how fees should be quoted and broken down against various stages of the project.

➤ A description of the form of appointment and conditions of engagement (such as the step-in rights and the level of professional indemnity (PI) insurance requirement).

- ➢ Employer's information requirements (through BIM or any other, as specified).
- ➢ Requirements of collateral warranties (for use where a warranty is to be given to a purchaser or tenant of premises in a commercial and/or industrial development.
- ➢ It should request details of resources and curriculum vitae (CV) of staff along with a summary of their relevant experience on similar projects.
- ➢ It should request references, together with contact details thereof.
- ➢ It should seek hourly rates to be applied to any work outside the proposed scope of services.
- ➢ It should request identification of any sub-consultants that the proposed consultant intends to use on the project.
- ➢ For the appointment of design consultants, it may include a request for design proposals. If so, it is good practice for the employer to offer a payment for the work involved in preparing designs. This eventually benefits the employer as it will encourage the invited consultants to prepare their proposal more carefully, and will also demonstrate to them that the employer is serious about the project and is likely to treat them fairly.

Some employers may feel that they need assistance from an independent client advisor to decide on the form of appointment, identify a short-list of potential consultants, prepare the request for proposals, assess submissions and negotiate the proposed fees.

It is employer's responsibility to take reasonable steps to assess the competence of those they appoint. The employer should also confirm the consultant's level of professional indemnity insurance before an appointment.

Some of the standard forms of appointment for consultants are the following:

RIBA Standard Agreement for the Appointment of an Architect 2010

ACA Standard Form of Agreement for the Appointment of an Architect

RICS Standard Form of Consultant's Appointment

Form of Appointment as CDM Coordinator

NEC Professional Services Contract

RIBA Standard Agreement 2010:Consultant

ACE Agreements

JCT Pre-construction services agreement

JCT Consultancy agreement

Other forms of appointment are also available, and in some circumstances appointment may be made by letter or by a bespoke agreement. Various surveys have indicated that approximately 40% of appointments are made using bespoke agreements. However, this may be inadvisable because of the risk that bespoke agreements might not adequately or fairly make provision for all circumstances, and that they are not supported by history of case law. It is also a poor reflection of how inflexible and ineffective the industry perceives many of the standard forms of agreement to be.

With all forms of appointment it is important that there is clarity about the scope of services being provided, particularly where a range of consultants is being appointment. There might otherwise be uncertainty about which consultant is responsible for which aspects of the project.

On any proposed RFP/Tender, areas where clarity is particularly important are the following (at the minimum):

➢ Interior design and artwork

➢ Landscape design

➢ Highways, fencing and gates

➢ Acoustics

➢ Vibration control

➢ Below and above ground drainage

➢ Fire protection and safety systems

➢ Lightning protection

➢ Process engineering

➢ Chemical handling

➢ Specialist design such as laboratories

➢ Security systems

➢ Information and communications technology

➢ Connections to statutory utilities

➢ Planning applications (in particular, outline planning applications)

➢ Furniture and equipment

- Fixtures and fittings
- Geotechnical surveys
- Topographical and setting-out surveys
- Demolition works
- Specification writing
- External lighting
- Alterations to existing buildings
- Lifts and escalators
- Models and mock-ups
- 3D modeling
- Building control submissions
- Supervision and inspection during construction
- Record drawings
- Provision of certificates
- Insurance requirements

In addition, some standard forms of appointment may consider certain tasks to be "additional services" that are not covered within the consultant's fee unless specifically requested by the employer. These might include one or more of the following:

- Acting as lead designer, contract administrator or lead consultant
- Detailed thermal modeling
- Environmental assessments
- Options appraisal
- Preparing or compiling the brief
- Post-occupancy evaluations (which might include both a post-project review to evaluate the project delivery process and performance in-use assessments)

It is noted that ideally the employer should commit to carrying out post-occupancy evaluation at the beginning of the project so that appointment agreements and briefing documents can include a requirement to test whether objectives were achieved. Therefore, the documents need to address:

- Outline of planning applications
- Planning appeals
- Assistance in applying for grants or other funding

- ➢ Post-occupancy advice on letting, rating, maintenance, energy consumption, insurance, tenant queries and facilities management
- ➢ Assistance in the preparation of tender documents for maintenance and operation contracts
- ➢ Preparing a building user's guide (a non-technical guide with information for users about environmental controls, access, security and safety systems, etc.)
- ➢ Provision of unusual visual representations or models
- ➢ Building information modeling (BIM)
- ➢ Preparation of marketing materials
- ➢ Preparation of as-built information
- ➢ Party wall services
- ➢ Site surveys
- ➢ Whole life costing studies (life cycle costing)
- ➢ Environmental and ecological studies
- ➢ Site selection
- ➢ Provision of site inspectors
- ➢ Assessment of alternative designs submitted by others, i.e.; designs submitted during the tender process for the main contractor
- ➢ Dealing with contractual claims and disputes
- ➢ Services in relation to legal agreements
- ➢ As-built drawings (many key systems will be shown 'as manufactured and installed' on specialist drawings and so general arrangement drawings may only be relevant as location drawings or for indicating zoning issues such as compartmentalization)

Key Performance Indicators (KPI):

Performance measurement is an integral part of business management, and construction industry is no exception. By championing key company and project aims, managers are more likely to achieve success. But the only way of knowing whether those goals are being delivered is by identifying indicators of their success and using them to keep an eye on the way the project is performing. These are referred to as Key Performance Indicator (KPI's).

KPIs are very efficiently used in contracts involving service to the employer i.e.; provision of hard services, provision of soft services, provision of IT services, etc.

It is a normal practice to link reward/penalty to the identified KPIs in order to reward or penalize the service contractor, thereby keeping a tab on the level of services provided.

Benchmarking:

Performance measurement demonstrates whether a project is achieving continuous improvement. But particularly when you're new to measurement, it can be hard to know whether the scores you're achieving are any good or not.

The tool can be used to benchmark a project KPI against the back drop of national or industry average, and against each other. Benchmarking provides a yardstick by which to judge a particular project's performance. KPI therefore, provides comprehensive support for collecting, reporting and analyzing data. The KPI allows a project to:

Can be used to:

- ➢ Monitor costs
- ➢ Track progress.
- ➢ Assess client satisfaction
- ➢ Identify strengths & weaknesses
- ➢ Compare performance across and between projects
- ➢ Assess specific areas of a project such as sustainability, safety, waste management etc.

It is important that KPI's are identified in tender documentation and that the regular provision of the information required assessing KPI is a requirement of the contract. This may require the provision of sub-contractor information where performance on specific packages is to be monitored.

Key Performance Indicators may be of particular importance where the contact stipulates that the contractor will be rewarded or penalized based on their performance relative to certain indicators.

Examples of KPI's that can be used on construction projects include:

- ➢ Cost compared against budget.
- ➢ Project progress relative to milestones.
- ➢ Number of complaints.
- ➢ Number of incidents/accidents.

> The number of working hours spent on different aspects of the works.

> The use of materials (for example the amount of concrete poured or reinforcement used).

> The number of defects/Non Conformance Reports (NCR).

> The amount of waste generated and the amount of recycling.

> The number of variations.

> Value of variation is also a means to help with the rapid comprehension of the current financial position. It summarizes the comparison of figures against the budgeted values and also industry benchmarks that are published from the result of inter-firm comparison reports.

KPI's used to track profitability may include:

> Turnover by director/partner.

> Turnover by fee earner.

> Profit by director/partner.

> Profit by fee earner.

It is a good practice that only genuinely important performance indicators should be monitored so that it does not simply become a time consuming paper exercise.

KPI's can also be used more broadly as part of a bench-marking exercise to assess the performance of one project relative to another, to assess businesses compared to others within the industry and to assess the performance of the industry as a whole relative to the rest of the economy.

Other Sample KPI's used in construction business are the following:

> Client Satisfaction

> Defects

> Construction Time & Cost

> Productivity

> Profitability

> Health & Safety

> Employee Satisfaction

> Staff Turnover

- ➢ Sickness Absence
- ➢ Working Hours
- ➢ Qualifications & Skills
- ➢ Impact on Environment
- ➢ Whole Life Performance
- ➢ Waste
- ➢ Commercial Vehicle Movements
- ➢ Gross financial turnover

Chapter 3

Contract Administration

Contract administration includes all actions undertaken by the administrator in relation to a specific Contract after the Contract award has been made (for all practical purposes the actual association of a contract administrator, however may precede the award of contract). Its purpose is to assure that the Contractor's and Employer's total performance is in accordance with the specifications/scope of work, terms and conditions of the contractual agreement.

After issuance of a formal contract award document, generally resulting from a Request for Proposal (RFP) or Invitation for Tender (generally facilitated by the Contracts and Procurement Department of an organization), the Employer or his Representative shall generally designate a Contract Administrator (CA) in writing.

The Contract Administrator shall generally be the end user of the Contract or one who has a vested interest in the procurement and who will be responsible for the proper adherence to all contract specifications by the Contractor. The contract administrator shall be responsible for ensuring that the goods or services are provided in accordance with the terms of the contract.

Role of a Contract Administrator:

The contract administrator is the individual responsible for administering a contract. Contract administrator may be the architect, lead consultant, the cost consultant, or the client's/employer's representative (for clarification of doubt, this book refers to the contract administrator as a client/employer representative). It is also noted that the New Engineering Contract (NEC) form describe the contract administrator as the "project manager".

A contract administrator is appointed by the employer, and he usually act as the employer's representative/agent for the purpose of the administration of the referenced contract. When certifying or giving an assessment or decision, the administrator has to act honestly and reasonably and his decisions are open to challenge via the dispute resolution procedures normally identified in a particular clause/article of the contract.

Functions of a contracts administrator can also be understood from the role (please refer to the following paragraph) that he undertakes on a project.

A Contracts Administrator's role will generally include:

- ➢ Inviting and processing tenders
- ➢ Preparing contract documents for execution
- ➢ Administrating change control procedures
- ➢ Seeking instructions from the client in relation to the contract
- ➢ Issuing instructions such as variations, or relating to prime cost sums or making good defects.
- ➢ Reviewing and assessing claims
- ➢ Chairing construction progress meetings
- ➢ Preparing and issuing construction progress reports
- ➢ Coordinating and instructing site inspectors
- ➢ Agreeing to the commissioning and testing procedures
- ➢ Agreeing defects reporting procedures
- ➢ Ensuring that project documentation is issued to the client
- ➢ Issuing certificates of practical completion (TOC) and interim certificates
- ➢ Collating and issuing schedules of defects
- ➢ Issuing the certificate of making good defects (NCR closure reports and defects liability certificate)
- ➢ Issuing the final certificate
- ➢ Issuing the final statement and the statement of discharge

It is important to note that on a construction management contract, the role of a contract administrator may be attributed to the work of a construction manager, and on management contracts (where the works contracts are placed by the management contractor, the management contractor shall perform the role of a contract administrator.

Therefore, at a minimum a contract administrator shall be responsible for ensuring that:

(i) the review and approval of any and all invoices submitted for payment by the Contractor for any and all services related to the performance of the contract,

(ii) the contract in use is valid as related to the contract term dates and any renewal clauses,

(iii) the Contractor (or Consultant) is providing timely goods and/or services in accordance with the contract requirements,

(iv) the contract file is complete,

(v) the contract renewals and extension of time is granted or is closed in accordance with the expressed contract terms, and

(vi) provides factual details of his project in case of a dispute, wherever asked, to the appointed Mediator/Arbitrator or the Court.

The designated contract administrator shall be responsible for ensuring that they and any staff members having duties related to administering the contract, adhere to the policies set forth within the companies manual on Ethics in Contracting.

Failure and/or violations on the part of the designated Contract Administrator to adhere to and follow the guidelines specifically defined and related to their role and responsibilities as Contract Administrator may result in innumerable damage to the company, including but not limited to:

➤ Claims,

➤ Direct and indirect losses,

➤ Loss of goodwill,

➤ Litigations and court proceedings, etc.

The Contract Administrator shall maintain a file containing, at a minimum:

➤ the contract administration designation letter from the Representative,

➤ a complete copy of the Contract,

➤ contract modifications/amendments,

➤ all related invoicing and payment records,

➤ all related variations records,

- ➤ all related claims records,
- ➤ vendor performance documentation,
- ➤ copy of completed Contractor Evaluation Survey,
- ➤ signed renewal forms, and
- ➤ any reports required per the contract terms.

Inspection Records:

Inspection Records are a close and critical examination of goods or services delivered to determine conformance with applicable contract requirements or specifications.

Project personnel shall be familiar with the Contract in order to appropriately inspect the works completed/services rendered by the Contractor/Consultant.

Raising Non Conformance Report (NCR's) is the responsibility of the Employer or his representative and hence the records serve as a basis of payment or penalty to a Contractor.

Rejection should generally occur whenever the goods or services do not comply with contract requirements.

Rejection of goods/services by the Employer due to no fault of the Contractor may be considered breach of contract, and restocking, storage and/or additional charges Direct, as applicable, may be assessed by the Contractor and lead to Contractual Claim issue.

Latent Defects:

Concealed damage or latent defects should be reported to the Contractor within a reasonable time of the Taking over Certificate (TOC) date. If latent defects are found, the Contractor is responsible for making good the defects within the Defects Liability Period (DLP).

It is the nature of construction projects that faults and defects caused by failures in design, workmanship or materials, may not become apparent or readily detectable (even with the exercise of reasonable care) until many years after completion of the project, long after the completion of the defects liability period (DLP). Such defects are known as latent defects (as opposed to patent defects which are apparent).

Examples of common latent defects include:

- ➤ Defective basement water tank allowing water penetration
- ➤ Inadequate wind-posts or wall ties causing movement damage to walls
- ➤ Under-strength concrete or misplaced reinforcement allowing movement damage to the structure
- ➤ Inadequate foundations causing subsidence of the building

It is also a feature of construction projects that the completed building will have a life-cycle of many years often with a succession of future owners who had no involvement in the original construction, but who have a liability to maintain the structure.

After the completion of the defects liability period the building owner cease to have a contractual right to insist that the contractor rectifies defects not notified during that period (as will often be the case with latent defects). The building owner must instead seek redress in an action for damages, for breach of contract, or for negligence.

These rights of action are not perpetual, actions for breach of contract are time barred after 6 years from the date of breach (usually the completion of the building although with a failure of design the breach may occur earlier). However, for a contract under seal, the period is 12 years. Although the time barred provisions quoted here apply to the UK, similar provision is seen in contracts in other parts of the world too, albeit with different durations.

Complex arguments arise in respect of economic loss. This may be many years after the completion of the building.

Commercial fixes for latent defects and successive owners include, collateral warranties, guarantees, building warranty schemes and latent defects insurance. Latent defects insurance that had its origin in Europe came to be adapted in UK as decennial insurance. It soon fell out of favor as a result of being over-hyped and overpriced. However, it is again making a comeback and many countries are either already requiring it or looking at the possibility of including it.

Patent Defects:

At any point up to and until the Taking Over Certificate (TOC) has been issued, defects that are discovered by inspection (patent defects) may be reported to the contractor, who should rectify them within a reasonable time.

In any event, such defects should be rectified before a certificate of practical completion (TOC) is issued. This generally puts the contract administrator in a difficult position, where both the contractor and the employer are keen to issue the certificate (so that the building can be handed/taken over) and yet defects (more than a de minimis, i.e.; at the minimum) are apparent in the works. Issuing the certificate under these circumstances could render the contract administrator liable for problems that this causes, for example, in the calculation of liquidated damages.

Once practical completion has been certified, the client has taken possession of the works and the defects liability period (or rectification period) begins.

During the defects liability period (DLP), the client may report any defects that arise to the contract administrator. The contract administrator needs to decide whether they are in fact defects in the works (i.e. works that are not in accordance with the contract), or whether they are actually maintenance issues. If the contract administrator considers that they are defects, then he may issue instructions to the contractor to make good the defects within a reasonable time. It needs to be noted that it is contractor's responsibility to identify and rectify defects, not the employers, so even if the employer does bring defects to the contractor's notice, he needs to make clear that this is not a comprehensive list of all defects.

At the end of the defects liability period, the contract administrator prepares a schedule of defects, listing those defects that have not yet been rectified, and agrees with the contractor the date by which they will be rectified. The contractor must in any event rectify defects within a reasonable time.

When the contract administrator considers that all items on the schedule of defects have been rectified, they issue a certificate of making good defects (or certificate of making good). This has the effect of releasing the remainder of any retention and will result in the issuing of the final certificate.

In case a defect becomes apparent after the certificate of making good defects has been issued, but before the final certificate has been issued, the contractor may be given the opportunity to rectify the defect anyway, but the final certificate should not be issued until this has been done.

If the contractor, having been given the opportunity to rectify defects, fails to do so within a reasonable time, they may be in breach of contract. In this situation others may be employed to rectify the defects, and the cost of such works deducted from the contractor's retention.

In particular circumstances where the cost of rectifying a defect is disproportionate relative to the impact of the defect on the works, the employer may agree to have the certificate of making good defects issued anyway, but only on agreement that the contract sum is reduced by an amount that reflects the deduction in the value of the works as a consequence of the defect.

Under runs or over runs:

On a re-measured Contracts, there needs to be a limit to the acceptance of under runs or overruns, it is a good practice to state this in the terms and conditions provided during the RFP stage of a contract so that a bidder is aware of the requirement in advance of the contract award.

In general, contracts based on the "Federation Internationale Des Ingenieurs Counseils (FIDIC), Conditions of Contract for Works of Civil Engineering Construction" makes reference to the adjustment of contractor's site and general overhead costs in the event of variations exceeding (additions or omissions) 15% of the effective contract price.

Therefore, a good practice is to restrict over runs or under runs so as not to exceed 15% of the contract proceeds, and are not to be processed through change orders. It is highlighted that this may be altered at the time of signing of the Contract by both parties. In such a case, the amended cap shall apply.

Prices for overruns shall not exceed the quoted base price per unit or the quoted price for additional units and whichever price is less will prevail.

Prices for under runs shall also be calculated at the quoted base price per unit.

Defects or impropriety in invoice:

When there is a defect or impropriety in an invoice, the Contracts Administrator shall notify the Contractor if such defect or impropriety would prevent payment by the payment due date. Examples of impropriety in the invoice includes missing contract number, changes in unit price, extension errors, totaling errors, incorrect BOQ references, incorrect formats, etc.

It is highlighted that the prompt payment date does not begin until such issues are resolved. It is therefore, recommended that a payment request format is consolidated at the time of contract award or immediately thereafter, but in no case after the request for the advance/first interim payment.

Failure to provide deliverables and/or Reports per Contract requirement may result in non-payment for any services provided and invoiced during the reporting period. Payment may be withheld until such reports are provided.

Variations:

Any request for change affecting price, quality, quantity, delivery or cancellation requires an amendment to the original contract, and shall be done after going through the contractual process of change/variation document.

All Change Orders shall need to be evaluated for contract validity and price reasonableness.

A Contract may not be renewed and additional consideration may not be paid unless specifically provided for in the original contract.

Extension of Time (EOT) and Acceleration:

Delays occur on most construction projects, and always have done due to the inherent complexity of the industry. At some point during a project, particular parts of the works, or the works as a whole, may not progress as quickly as planned, with the risk that the contractual completion date would not be met. Sometimes, the lack of progress may be due to events that are the employer's responsibility under the contract; sometimes, the lack of progress may also be due to events that are the contractor's responsibility. For example, where traditional methods of procurement have been adopted, most construction contracts provide that delays caused by labour shortages or late delivery of materials will be the responsibility of the main contractor (or the subcontractor under a subcontract agreement), while delays caused by variations and/or the late provision of design information will be the responsibility of the employer (or the main contractor under a subcontract agreement). If a delay has been caused by an event that is the employer's responsibility, then in general, the contractor would be entitled to an extension of time. An extension of time defers the contract completion date and thereby gives the contractor a longer period within which to complete the works. In order to decide whether a contractor is entitled to an extension of time, it is necessary to establish the cause of the delay and the period of delay. In some cases this would be very easy but in many cases it may be difficult and can be controversial. Few contracts expressly make the contracts administrator, quantity surveyor or the scheduler responsible for the assessment of an extension of time claim; the task more commonly falls on the architect, contract administrator, engineer or the project manager. However, in practice, it is likely that quantity surveyors/ scheduler would be asked at least to assist with the preparation or assessment of a delay claim. The quantity surveyor's/scheduler's analytical training and methods of working are well suited to dealing with the complexities of a construction delay.

Extension of Time provisions:

The need for comprehensive extension of time provisions in construction contracts has been illustrated by various judgments made by as many dispute resolution authorities.

There may be multiple cases warranting extension of time and, in the absence of an extension of time clause within the contract, we may be left with 'at large' stage. With time at large, the liquidated damages provisions are not enforceable.

Extension of time provisions helps the contracting parties to be able to manage their time and in case it may be needed.

An absence of such an important provision in the Contract may result in a "time at large" situation.

Costs of delay:

If a project is delayed, it is likely that both the employer and the contractor will incur additional costs. The employer may incur additional finance costs and/ or lost rent and/or additional fees for professional services and/or a variety of other additional costs. The contractor may incur additional costs of site supervision, site offices and facilities, site security, head office management and overheads, general plant hire, insurance and other costs. The contractor's delay costs are sometimes referred to as 'prolongation costs' or the 'time-related costs'.

In the vast majority of cases, the employer's additional costs will be estimated, prior to tender enquiries going out, and will be expressed in the contract as a rate for 'liquidated damages'. Damages are amounts awarded by a court as compensation for loss or injury suffered by one party due to a breach of contract or breach of duty by another party; liquidated damages are amounts for damages that are ascertained and fixed in advance. The benefit of having a set rate for liquidated damages is that the parties know, in advance, the level of damages that will be applied in the event of a project overrun.

This allows the contractor to assess risk, prior to submitting its tender for the works, and it allows the employer to recover damages without having to go to the time and trouble of proving the amount of damages actually incurred.

Contractor's additional delay costs are rarely included as liquidated damages in a construction contract. This is because the contractor's delay costs are generally more wide-ranging, more uncertain and more variable than the employer's costs. Therefore, most contracts provide express terms for the assessment and reimbursement of delay costs, where appropriate, to the contractor. In the standard contract forms , the contractor's delay costs are referred to by the term 'loss and expense'. . In order to recover delay costs and/or to avoid liability for liquidated damages, a contractor will generally have to show that the delay was caused by events that are the employer's responsibility under the contract. The contractor does this by applying for an extension of time under the contract.

Delay events:

Extension of time clauses within a contract provides that a contractor shall be entitled to an extension of time if the contractor is or will be delayed by:

- ➢ variations
- ➢ exceptionally adverse climatic conditions
- ➢ unforeseeable shortages in the availability of personnel or goods (as defined) caused by epidemic or governmental actions
- ➢ any delay, impediment or prevention caused by or attributable to the employer or to his or her personnel; and
- ➢ events that entitle the contractor to an extension of time under any of the other clauses of the contract.

The other clauses are spread throughout the contract and include, for example, delays due to late access to the site.

It is also made explicit from the wording of clauses contained within a contract that an extension of time will only be awarded if the delaying event causes completion to be delayed, rather than simply causing delay to the contractor's progress.

Delay notices:

A contractor's entitlement to an extension of time generally is subject to compliance with the notice procedure set out within expressed clauses of the contract.

Generally the procedure for request for an extension of time requires the contractor to:

➢ Notify the contract administrator and describe the event or circumstance giving rise to the claim. This notice must be given as soon as it may be practical, and not later than a specific number of days after the Contractor became aware, or should have become aware, of the event or circumstance.

➢ Provide to the contract administrator a fully detailed claim which includes full supporting particulars of the basis of the claim within a stipulated number of days of becoming aware of the claim.

➢ Keep such contemporary records as may be necessary to substantiate any claim. These records may be monitored and inspected by the contract administrator.

➢ Submit other notices, if required by the contract, as well as supporting particulars for the claim. If the event or circumstance giving rise to the claim has a continuing effect, then the contract includes additional reporting requirements, including making interim claims at monthly intervals.

On receipt of such notice, the contract administrator is required to:

➢ Respond to the contractor within a stipulated number of days of receiving a claim, or any further particulars supporting a previous claim. The response must either approve or disapprove the claim and must provide detailed comments.

➢ Proceed in accordance with the contract conditions to agree or determine any extension of time and/or any additional payment to which the contractor is entitled.

A contract would generally seek to make the requirement of notice a condition precedent to an award of an extension of time and/or additional payment. A contract would normally provide that if the contractor fails to give notice of a claim within a stipulated number of days, the contractor shall not be entitled to an extension of time or any additional payment and the employer shall have no liability in respect of such claims.

Given the significance of the notice requirement, it is important to know when the period actually starts, and accordingly, when it expires. It is clear that it does not run from the occurrence of the event or circumstance giving rise to the claim, but from when the contractor 'became aware, or should have become aware, of the event or circumstance' giving rise to the claim. It is for this reason that the question of whether the contractor had, or should have had, the requisite knowledge is an evidential issue that would need to be determined on particular facts around the event.

Assessments:

Clauses specific to the extension of time would entitle a contractor to an extension of time 'if and to the extent that completion is or will be delayed. The method of assessment shall depend on the specific facts, namely, whether the delaying effect has occurred (or whether it is likely to occur in the future). The parties will be bound by the contract administrator's assessment (subject to any challenge raised by the contractor at the time), unless the contractor makes a further extension of time claim or the delaying event has a continuing effect. If the contractor makes further claims for an extension of time, then the contract administrator may take into account whether the previous prospective assessments reflected actual events, but may only increase, and not decrease, the total extension of time awarded.

Submission of delay notices:

Most of the standard forms of construction contract require the contractor to formally notify the employer in writing of delays to the works, either in advance of the delay event or as soon as possible thereafter. In general, the contractor is required to say whether he thinks if the delay is likely to impact upon the contract completion date and, if so, by how much. In most cases, the written notice does not have to be in a specific format and, usually, it will be nothing more than a letter or e-mail (only if allowed by the contract) notifying the employer of the delay and providing any other information required under the provisions of the contract. Sending an employer a formal letter about a delay can seem an odd thing to do if those delays have been discussed in detail at formal site meetings, informal meetings and over the telephone. In these circumstances, a contractor may well feel that the employer is fully aware that the works are in delay and the reasons for and likely duration of the delay.

However, if the contract requires formal written notification to be provided, then a contractor should give that notice, even if this merely confirms what has been discussed. Arguments about a failure to provide proper notice of delay often crop up if a dispute develops. Sometimes, an employer may seek to avoid a claim due to a lack of contractual notices. Whether or not a "no notice defence" (an argument that a notice was not served in accordance to the requirement of the contract) to an extension of time claim will succeed is likely to turn on the precise wording of the contract and the state of the law at the time. However, it is to the contractor's advantage to remove the risk by issuing a notice as required by the terms of the contract, regardless of whether the notice merely repeats points already well-known to all those involved in the project.

A timely notice also makes sure that the employer is well aware of the developments and the likelihood of delays and/or the associated additional costs to the completion of his project.

Measurement of delay:

The measurement of delay to a project is the difference between the date of completion of the works and the current contract completion date. If the works have been completed, then this retrospective exercise will be simple. However, measuring the delay period is only part of the task. A contractor will only be entitled to an extension of time for the period of delay for which the employer is responsible under the contract. Therefore, once the delay period has been established, it is necessary to work out whether the contractor is entitled to all, some or none of the additional time taken to complete the works.

Furthermore, in many cases, the actual period of delay will not be known when an extension of time claim is being made and assessed, because extensions of time are often dealt with prospectively (that is, before the actual completion date is known). The delay period in these circumstances must be measured as the difference between the projected completion date and the current contract completion date.

A review and analysis of the programme for the works is usually carried out to resolve questions of culpability for delay and/or to estimate the likely delay period. Sometimes it can be difficult for parties to agree which programme should be used to carry out the review, as programmes often change and/or are updated during a project. It is important to agree a programme as the benchmark for assessing an extension of time, otherwise the chances of agreeing the cause and extent (or likely cause and extent) of delays to completion will be greatly reduced.

Methods of delay analysis:

There are a number of methods of analyzing and assessing delays. Some methods are simple and relatively superficial, while others are more detailed and complex.

One of the simpler methods is an overview of the facts. Another relatively simple method is to compare actual progress achieved with the planned progress shown on the programme for the works. More detailed, forensic, exercises can be undertaken by adopting Critical Path Analysis (sometimes abbreviated as CPA).

A further option would be to use one or more of the basic methods to review a narrow time period. This approach may produce a more focused and reliable analysis of delay events.

The following are the methods of delays analysis that are used frequently:

- Overview of the facts
- Comparing actual and planned progress
- Critical path analysis
- Review of the planned programme
- Review of the 'as-built' programme
- Focused methods of analysis
- Delay assessments using BIM

Overview of the facts:

The simplest way of assessing delay, either prospectively or retrospectively, is by undertaking a review of the facts. The facts will be evidenced by letters, emails, meeting minutes, progress records, photographs, instructions, drawings and other contemporaneous documents, and possibly by personal first-hand knowledge of the project. This approach is likely to be suitable for dealing with relatively straightforward claims, where the cause and effect are reasonably apparent. For example, if the commencement date for a project is deferred, or if the whole of the works are suspended, it is highly likely that there will be a corresponding delay to the completion date. Similarly, if a significant variation is instructed as the works are being completed, then it is likely that any subsequent delay will be the result of the variation instruction.

In these types of case, the cause and extent of delay will generally be apparent and uncontroversial and the extension of time will not require any detailed analysis. A claim may comprise little more than a brief narrative statement, setting out dates, events and consequences. An overview of the facts may also be used to assess less straightforward claims, particularly where the difference between the claim and assessment is not great.

Comparing actual and planned progress:

This method of analysis is often referred to by programmers as the as-planned versus as-built method. As the name suggests, it is the technique of comparing the planned timings of the various programme activities with the actual or as-built timings.

It is a simple method to use and understand and does not require any specialist programming knowledge or computer software. Quite simply, the duration of the work activities, as actually carried out on site, are plotted on the planned programme, thereby illustrating discrepancies.

With this form of analysis, the work activities that commence and/or finish later than planned are likely to be the focus of attention. The reasons for any late commencement or completion of work activities will be reviewed, to ascertain why actual progress was not as planned. If, on review, it appears probable that the delay was due to an employer event, such as an instruction to vary the work, an extension of time will usually be appropriate, providing that the delay was considered likely to have an impact upon the completion date. Like the first method (Overview of the facts), this method relies upon a review of contemporaneous documents, and may make use of first-hand knowledge of the project. In this method, however, attention is particularly focused on discrepancies between planned and actual progress. A claim based on this method would include the programme comparing the planned and actual progress and a narrative explanation of the discrepancies. The explanations may be supported by references to contemporary documents.

Critical Path Analysis:

The primary purpose of a critical path analysis is to show which activities on a programme of works are critical to completion and which are non-critical. A critical path analysis can be produced manually but, due to the number of calculations required, it is in practice only feasible using specialist software uploaded onto a computer. The calculations made by the computer to establish the critical path are based on 'logic links' between activities. Logic links are input by the programmer that acts as ties or constraints between the various programme activities. For example, a link may well be inserted between the end of the load-bearing superstructure brickwork activity and the commencement of the roof construction. If the superstructure brickwork is delayed, and the programme is altered to show this delay, the link would cause the commencement date of roof construction works automatically to be pushed back when the programme is rescheduled by the software. If the logic link between the completion of superstructure brickwork and commencement of roofing was not made, the programme would not be rescheduled logically. Therefore, the revised programme might thus end up showing the roof commencing before the external walls had reached full height.

Once programme activities and the necessary logic links for all activities have been fed into the computer the software will be able to calculate the critical path. A delay to an activity that is on the critical path will have an impact upon completion and any delay to an activity that is not on the critical path will (at least initially) have no impact upon completion.

An example of a non-critical activity might be, say a fencing to rear gardens on a housing estate that was planned to be carried out in four weeks, commencing at week 30 of a 50-week contract. If the fencing is the last activity of external work, it will only become critical to completion if it is commenced after week 46. Any delay to commencement from week 30 to week 46 will not prevent the entire works being completed by week 50.

The time period during which an activity can be deferred, without having any impact upon completion of the project, is usually referred to as "float". In the above example, the fencing activity has a period of 16 weeks float (from week 30 to week 46).

Therefore, once the float is used up, the activity moves onto the programme's critical path. In contrast, a delay to a critical activity will have a direct knock-on effect on completion of the project. Therefore, critical activities must (at least in theory) start and finish at the planned start and finish times in order to prevent delay to overall completion. Critical path analyses can be used to review the impact of delay events on either the planned programme or the as-built programme.

Review of the planned programme:

This method of analysis is often referred to by programmers as the "planned impacted" method. The idea is that delay events are added to the computer generated planned programme to analyse what impact, if any, those events will have upon the completion date.

The method works by adding activities, or amended durations of existing activities, to reflect the impact of delay events. For example, if additional work is instructed, the time required to do this work can be input and the programme rescheduled to see what effect, if any, the additional work has upon the planned programme completion date. Any delay to overall completion will represent the critical delay associated with the instruction. If, for instance, the time taken to carry out instructed additional works is added to the planned programme, and the completion date moves, on rescheduling, from 14 June to 28 June, that would indicate that the event results in a delay to completion of two weeks.

However, it may also be that adding additional work would produce no change to the programme completion date. This would indicate that the additional work does not impact on the critical path and that no extension of time is required to complete the project.

One of the attractions of this method is that once the new data has been input and the programme rescheduled, the system will not only provide an explanation of the cause of the delay to completion, but will also provide a precise period of delay. This method can be used before, during or after delay events have occurred, but it is unlikely to be used retrospectively. Once delay events have occurred, it is likely that "as-built" information will be used to assess and measure the impact of delay events. A claim using a 'planned impacted' method may well include an electronic version of the programme, showing the logic links and the changes made. The claim should explain both the methodology adopted and the results of the exercise. It should also include a narrative explanation of the programmes and the delays.

Review of the 'as-built' programme:

This method of analysis is, in some respects, the opposite of the '"planned impacted" method referred to above. Instead of adding delay events to the planned programme, the delay events are removed from the "as-built" programme. Provided that the as-built programme has been prepared using computer software, and the activities have been "logic-linked", taking out delay events will cause the programme to shorten or "collapse" when rescheduled.

The difference between the original completion date and the rescheduled date represents the delay period that would have been avoided, but for the events removed from the programme. This method of analysis is often referred to by programmers as the 'collapsed as-built" or the 'as-built but for' method. If, as is likely, there are a number of delaying events, each event should be removed from the programme sequentially, usually starting with the last event, and the programme rescheduled each time to see whether the completion date changes. If the completion date is shown as being earlier, after rescheduling, this would indicate that the delay event was critical and causative of the delay to the completion date.

For example, if a delay event is removed from the as-built programme and the completion date moves from 28 of a month to 14 of that month that would indicate that the event caused a delay to completion of two weeks. As each successive event is removed, the programme collapses backwards to show when the works would have finished, had it not been for the delay events.

As with the "planned impacted" method, this method produces an explanation of the cause of the delay to completion and gives a precise delay period attributable to that cause. However, it can only be used retrospectively, as it is based on the progress that was actually achieved.

A claim using a "collapsed as-built" method will usually include an electronic version of the as-built programme, showing the logic links and the changes made, and details of the data used to create the programme. The claim should explain the methodology and should include a narrative explanation of why, and by how much, the programme collapsed when rescheduled.

Focused methods of analysis:

The basic methods of programming analysis referred to above usually considers the project as a whole. Such analyses may lack focus. Programmers have therefore developed ways of considering delays in more detail over shorter time periods.

One such method is usually referred to as "time impact analysis" (TIA). With this method, only the period of time in which the delay event is likely to have an impact is reviewed. If the delay event is an instruction to carry out additional work, the analysis may focus on the period from the date of the instruction to the date the additional work is likely to be completed. As with the "planned impacted" technique described above, this method involves adding (or impacting) delays onto the programme. However, instead of using the original planned programme as a starting point, this method uses an updated programme, showing the progress actually achieved at the start of the review period. In the example given above, this would be at the time the instruction was given.

Time impact analysis is essentially a prospective technique, in that it seeks to predict the likely future delay based on progress achieved prior to the delay event. This technique is prescribed by certain new forms of contract for the analysis of delays due to a "compensation event".

An alternative, but similarly focused approach, would be to restrict the analysis of delays to particular periods of time. Programmers usually refer to this method as a window or time slice analysis. A window or time slice is a particular period of time. It might run from one monthly progress report to the next. As with time impact analysis, the planned programme is updated to reflect actual progress achieved up to the commencement of the period, any delay in the period is then analyzed.

"Windows" analysis requires as-built information to review the delays. This method is thus used retrospectively. The adoption of a method of analysis that focuses on a relatively short period of time should produce a more sophisticated review and one that is more closely related to the realities of what was actually happening on site. It should also remove or reduce the complexities of trying to review the project as a whole. As with other claims, a claim using one of these more focused methodologies should include narrative explanations, along with electronic versions of the programmes.

Delay assessments using BIM:

Building information modelling (BIM) seeks to provide detailed information about a building, not just in terms of its three physical dimensions, but also with regard to time and cost issues. Time is usually referred to as the fourth dimension.

By linking a 3D model of a building to the programming software, it is possible to create a model comparing planned and actual progress of the works. Such a model will not necessarily illustrate the cause of a delaying event, but may prove to be invaluable in helping to understand and illustrate, in detail, the consequences of a delay event, or for the comparison of planned and actual progress. In the future, BIM is likely to become a very important tool in the analysis of delays on construction projects.

Choosing the most optimum method of delay analysis:

There are a number of different methods of delay analysis. Therefore, it is one of the important tasks of a contracts administrator to choose which of these needs to be adopted when preparing or assessing a delay claim.

The contracts administrator therefore, would have to take this important decision based on the answers that he would get from the following:

- ➤ terms of the contract
- ➤ type of works being undertaken
- ➤ nature of the delay
- ➤ information available; and
- ➤ timing of the delay analysis.

The terms and conditions of most contracts allow any delay methodology to be used, providing it produces a fair and reasonable assessment of any additional time to be allowed to the contractor to complete the works. However, the contract terms needs to be checked as soon as a delay occurs, as they may prescribe procedures that need to be followed.

It is therefore, recommended that a contract administrator, if he is involved at the pre-contract stage, to provide for adequate clause and language to ensure that the provisions within the agreement is clear and unambiguous for the project team to understand the delay methodology to be applied for a particular project.

One example of a contract condition that prescribes assessment is the NEC3 form of contract. This form prescribes that the assessment and measurement of delays must be carried out by impacting the delay events onto the latest version of the agreed planned programme. The type of work undertaken may govern the methodology adopted, as some methods of delay analysis are more suited to some types of construction than others. For example, the use of critical path analysis generally works well when analyzing delays during the construction of a structure on a new-build project, where links between programme activities are likely to reflect the reality of the works being undertaken. Delays to the construction of structural columns and beams on one floor, for instance, are likely to have a direct and corresponding impact on the construction of the rest of the structure. The links on a computer-generated programme should reflect this. Critical path analysis is, however, likely to work less well on a refurbishment of a large building, where delays to work in one part of an existing building may well have little or no direct impact on works in the rest of the building, and where activity links on the programme may not reflect the reality and flexibility of the actual programming of works on site.

The choice of the most suitable method of analysis will also depend to an extent, on the nature of the delay event. If the delay and its consequences are relatively straightforward, then a simple review may well suffice. If the situation is more complicated, a critical path analysis may be the best choice. Regardless of other factors, the information available may constrain the methodology that can be used. For example, if the as-built information is incomplete, contradictory or intermittent, then it will not be possible to use delay methodologies that are based on the use of as-built data.

The timing of the analysis will also influence the method that can be used. Most contracts require extensions of time to be awarded during the works. In these circumstances, the methodology will have to be one that allows for predicting the likely completion date, which would rule out a methodology relying solely on as-built data. In contrast, where the extension of time is being reviewed retrospectively, which is usually the case in adjudication, arbitration and litigation, the methodology is likely to rely on as-built data.

Therefore, there is no single method of delay analysis that is best to use in all circumstances. Instead, the method chosen to prepare or assess a delay claim will depend on a variety of project-specific factors.

Ultimately, if a dispute is referred to adjudication, arbitration or litigation, it will generally be decided on the facts. Hence, any programming analysis carried out must be logical to the factual background. Whichever method is used, it is important to recognize its inherent strengths and weaknesses. If the cause and duration of the delay to completion cannot be agreed, it is likely that the parties will expend considerable time and effort criticizing the method of analysis used by the other party. If an agreement is to be reached, it must be accepted that all methods have some fundamental weaknesses, and strengths.

Strengths and weaknesses of delay analysis methods:

The methods of delay analysis discussed above have got their inherent strengths and weaknesses. Some of them are discussed as below:

Overview of the facts:

An overview of the facts is a simple approach and is particularly suitable for dealing with relatively straightforward claims. It is likely to be one of the quickest and least costly methods of making and/or assessing a delay claim. However, it is also likely to be with the least analytical approach, with the final conclusion dependent on a broad judgment as to whether the delay events impacted (or were likely to impact) on the completion date.

When a judgment of the facts and their impact is made, the parties will frequently reach different conclusions, each viewing the situation in a manner most favourable to their own side. This may lead to disagreements and disputes, which the lack of analysis will make difficult to resolve, other than by a commercial compromise or by referring the matter to an adjudicator, arbitrator or judge. If a formal dispute does ensue, an analysis based on an overview of the facts may not be considered to be sufficiently robust. To reduce the risk of disagreements, it is important that a review of the facts should be carried out logically and methodically. The assessment of delay should not be speculative or impressionistic.

Comparing actual and planned progress:

The attraction of an analysis comparing the as-planned and as-built programmes is that it is simple to understand and does not require any specialist programming knowledge or specialist computer software to produce. A review of significant discrepancies between planned and actual programme durations may well highlight delay areas, and the causes of delays may already be known to the parties and/or easily explained. This is a more analytical method than the overview procedure and allows the parties to focus on problem areas.

However, in isolation, an "as-planned versus as-built" programme analysis may indicate nothing more than that the original planned start dates and durations were too optimistic (or pessimistic) and/or that the contractor used more (or less) resources than planned, causing the works to be carried out at a different speed to that envisaged. By itself, this method will not provide an analysis of the cause and effect of delay events. It may, however, be possible to show the cause and effect of delay events by combining the programme analysis with a review and summary of the key facts.

Critical Path Analyses (CPA):

In a critical path analysis, a programme is generated by computer software showing the critical path activities. When updated, this programme can react dynamically to show the impact of delay events upon the completion date of the works. Delay events can be impacted onto a planned programme, or removed from an as-built programme, to illustrate the cause and effect of the events.

This analytical and precise methodology can be impressive and captivating but, in order for it to work properly, someone must link the programme activities, and these links may, at times, be more subjective than objective. As even reasonably minor changes to the logic links can have a relatively significant impact on the results of the exercise, these links can become a source of controversy and may lead to concern that the analysis has been manipulated to produce a desired result. The planned impacted technique may also be criticised as being theoretical, particularly where a contractor departs from the planned sequence and/or resourcing levels and carries out the works in a significantly different way to that shown on the planned programme.

The as-built collapsed method avoids allegations of being based on theory, as it relies on the facts of what actually took place, but it can only work if the as-built records are sufficiently detailed and accurate. Even with good records, this method can still run into difficulties if there are questions as to when precisely an activity actually commenced and was completed. There may also be arguments about the links created between as-built activities and, as stated above, minor changes in links can result in major changes in the results of the exercise.

While a critical path analysis may look precise and detailed, it may therefore be based in part on subjective logic links, on a programme that does not reflect what actually happened or on the subjective interpretation of as-built data. Critical path analyses are also likely to be expensive to produce, as they require specialist programmers and a significant investment of time.

Focused methods of analysis:

Time impact analysis (TIA) is one of the more focused types of delay analysis as this method uses an updated programme to show progress actually achieved at the start of the review period, it avoids one of the potential key weaknesses of the planned impacted method, in that it is not based on a theoretical programme, at least up to the point of the commencement of the review. It also has the advantage of being a technique that can be used during the currency of the works. However, it remains at least partially theoretical, in that the assessment of delay caused to the completion date is based on the future planned programme and not on what actually has happened on site. This method could therefore produce an extension of time award at odds with the reality of what ultimately would have transpired.

The alternative of analysing delays in windows of time also has the advantage of a starting point based on actual progress achieved, with the added benefit of being a review of what actually happened. However, this retrospective approach may not suit the terms of a contract requiring extensions of time to be awarded in advance.

As with the critical path techniques, these focused methods of delay analysis are likely to require specialist programmers and a significant input of time, making them expensive to produce.

Concurrent liability for delays:

It has been a contract administator's wish that if the contract procedures had been properly applied and an appropriate method of analysis agreed and adopted, the problems of delay analysis would be completely dealt with to the satisfaction of all contracting parties. However, a general residual problem relates to concurrent delays and how to deal with them.

It is not unusual to find a number of separate identifiable delay events occurring at any one time on a busy construction project. Common sense will tell us that some of these events are trivial and cannot sensibly be attributed to the delay, or a likely delay to the completion of the entire project. However, that may still leave some delay events that are the responsibility of the employer (typically due to design choices, variations and works by statutory undertakers) and some that are the responsibility of the contractor (typically, supply of materials, labour productivity and subcontractors' works). One important question that needs to be answered would be "when such concurrent causes of delay exist, is the contractor entitled to an extension of time?

Extension of Time (EOT) to a Contract is primarily required to cater to the following contractual needs:

> To prevent Liquidated Damages
> To prevent a Contract slipping into Frustration doctrine (Contract at large)
> To safeguard the Contracting parties due to Force Majeure

It is generally argued by a party requesting EOT that the requirement for additional time is mandated due to such and such reason and that any person can apply a little common sense to understand and grant the requested EOT.

However, a common sense is a very general terminology and shall definitely not be the basis on which an Extension of Time shall be evaluated. A common sense, if applied to arrive at the Extension of Time, would entail that evaluation of all able minded individuals is identical. However, this is not the case when professionals arrive at the Extension of Time. Before an EOT is granted, the Employer (Architect/Contract Administrator) needs to satisfy himself of the relevant event that has occurred but also that it is likely to cause a delay to the completion of the whole of works. Any effect needs to have a cause. Here we need to understand the issue of Causation. "Causation is understood as a mental concept, generally based on inference or induction from uniformity of sequence as between two events and there is a casual connection between them, however it is not concerned with the philosophical speculation, but is only concerned with the everyday life, thoughts and expressions".

Although the concept of causation appears straightforward, i.e.; event A caused a delay to event B. Construction Contract is more complex than this simple analogy. This is so because the nature of construction operations is such that there are often numbers of potentially causative factors involved in any delay. For example, the employer's instruction to carry out additional works took longer than envisaged due to labor difficulties, and thereafter there was a spell of bad weather to worsen this already delaying situation. These complex set of delay causing factors have to be analyzed under to arrive at the proper and justified extension of time. Therefore, it will have to be assessed whether any of the relevant events has caused delay to the progress of the works and if so, by how much. Employer must then apply the result of his assessment to the amount of delay caused by the relevant event by extension the contract period for completion of the works, and by postponing the completion date.

It is a question of fact whether progress of the works has been or is likely to be delayed by a particular relevant event. In making this enquiry as to the effect of the event, the employer can arguably consider other competing and concurrent causes of delay, if they are relevant to the circumstances of the case. The employer is therefore not limited to consideration of the impact of a particular relevant event on which the contractor has based his claim for additional time.

It is important to note here that generally the ***burden of proof*** to establish the extension of time entitlement is on the Contractor. Also, because of the complexity of most construction contracts, the evidence from the Contractor should include some or all of the following:

- ➢ Cause and effect schedules
- ➢ As-built records
- ➢ Programmes showing planned and actual progress
- ➢ Critical path analysis
- ➢ Expert evidence
- ➢ Evidence of fact from persons involved with the project

Time but no money, Apportionment or responsibility based on critical path delay analysis.

Time but no money principle tracks back to the early 1900s when a strict rule against apportionment was applied.

Concurrent delay:

Concurrent delay is commonly used to describe circumstances where different causes of delay overlap during a period of time (between two dates in a schedule). As such, concurrent delay could occur if a delay that was caused by the Employer is on the same activity path or a parallel activity path as a delay that was caused by the Contractor. If the employer-caused delay and the contractor-caused delay affect the same activity or affect different activities on parallel activity paths which are equally critical, and as such the employer-caused delay and contractor-caused delay would each have delayed the completion date of the project, the delays are said to be concurrent.

Within the construction industry, ***Concurrent delays*** cause the severest difficulties in connection with causation. These are two or more delays the competing causes of which impinge of the progress of the project at the same time and with approximate equal efficacy. The issue of concurrent delay has exercised many engineers, architects, judges and commentators over the years, and it has to be said that they are not all of one mind as to the most appropriate way to deal with it. Four broad ways can be identifies as below:

- ➢ Apportionment
- ➢ The tortuous solution
- ➢ The Dominant Cause approach

➢ The Delvin approach

Apportionment:

It is generally recognized that any one delay of period might be attributable to more than one cause, but is also accepted nevertheless that any one of these causes affords grounds for an extension of time; the contractor is entitled to an extension of time.

Also, issue of concurrent events should be addressed together with *Supervening events* i.e.; what is the position where a delay is first caused by one event, but that delay is then wholly or partly overtaken by a delay the result of another cause? This requires that the employer decide whether his logical analysis should be done on a first cause or ultimately critical basis.

We can thus observe that, if a building was delayed by two successive events, one (the first) the responsibility of the employer, the other (and second in time) the responsibility of the contractor, the employer is still responsible for the delay he caused because the supervening event did not prevent the delay being incurred.

For example, if an employer delays in providing approval for a substantial drawing on a project and at the same time the contractor also delays in appointment of a specialist sub-contractor, there is a legitimate claim for an extension of time as the delay by employer would have impacted the project progress even if the specialist sub-contractor was available to commence the part of the project works assigned to him.

An important point to note is that Liquidated Damages shall not be applied for periods encompassing concurrent delays.

Thus an international industry primarily has adopted that for periods of concurrent delay, the contractor would not have entitlement to recover its delay costs and likewise, the employer would not have entitlement to recover its liquidated damages.

It would seem that the most commonly used approach to delay analysis is to contrast the as-planned with the as-built programme and then to seek to explain the variance. This is a form of ultimate critical analysis. A point frequently overlooked by those who use this method is that it is still necessary to justify the reasonableness of the original works programme. Also, although the method is simple and useful in identifying where the main delay periods probably arose, it arguably lacks the rigor necessary for complex projects with many activities and many competing delay events. For such projects, a more sophisticated methodology such as impacted as-planned, collapsed as-built or time impact analysis might be required.

The Tortuous Solution:

The tortious solution involves envoking the "But For" question. Proponents of the As Built But For method of analysis seems to require a vast logic linked as-built programme of everything which needs to be analyzed minutely on a "but for" basis (more of a torture solution). However in discrete scenarios asking yourself what if X had not happened [i.e. but for] can be useful to understand the relative impacts of events.

In an attempt to improve the efficiency and consistency of the administration of extension of time claims, the Society of Construction Law has proposed the adoption of protocol for dealing with both extensions of time and compensation for delay and disruption. Some of the points to be addressed while evaluating Extension of Time are the following:

➢ Should the evaluation be based on net or gross method (i.e.; contractual date of completion or when the effect of an instruction began to bite).

➢ Who does the float (in the programme) belong to, or who is the owner of the float within a programme.

Dominant Cause Approach:

Dominant cause approach to resolving the concurrent delay issue suggest that when concurrent delay occurs, one an owner risk event and the other a contractor risk event, only one of the delays is the dominant cause for the delay to the project and prevails over the other cause of delay. Difficulties with this approach include:

1. The tiers of fact must make a decision as to which of the delays is dominant, which may be inherently difficult,

2. Requires the relaxation of the but-for test, and

3. May conflict with the preventive principle.

The Delvin Approach:

The Delvin approach for the concurrent delay analysis for an extension of time is by far the most widely used approaches and sometimes considered to be the most appropriate for concurrent delays. It states that when there are two competing events, one caused by the employer and the other caused by the contractor, each causing a delay (concurrently) then the contractor is entitled to an extension of time for the extent of the delay caused by the employer caused event.

Concurrent liability for delays:

It is not unusual to find a number of separate identifiable delay events occurring at any one time on a busy construction project. Common sense will tell us that some of these events are trivial and cannot sensibly be attributed to the delay (or likely delay) to the completion of the entire project. However, this may still leave some delay events that are the responsibility of the employer (design, variations and works by statutory authorities) and some that are the responsibility of the contractor (supply of materials, labour productivity and subcontractors' works). The important question that needs to be answered is "when such concurrent causes of delay exist, is the contractor entitled to an extension of time?"

The fact that the contract administrator has to award a fair and reasonable extension does not imply that there should be some apportionment in the case of concurrent delays. This would appear to provide a clear answer to the question. However, it will often remain difficult to decide whether delays are indeed concurrent.

Summary:

When delays are likely to occur on a project, the first thing the parties should do is to check their contract. It would generally set out a procedural requirement in terms of notices, provision of information and time periods for making claims and/or assessments. These procedural requirement needs to be followed. Consideration must then be given to the most appropriate means of assessing the delay. Assessments must identify the cause of delay, the period of delay and whether the delay event will have or would have had an impact on the completion of the project as a whole. Under most contracts, the method of assessment will not be prescribed and so a decision will have to be made as to what method should be used. The decision may not be easy as all methods are open to criticism.

The quicker and simple methods may be criticized for being too superficial, the more sophisticated, computer-generated methods may be criticized for being impenetrable or manipulated to achieve the desired result. Methods using planned programmes may be dismissed as theoretical and methods using as-built data may be dismissed as being artificial or false.

However, unless the cause and effect of a delay event is unusually straightforward, a choice of delay assessment must be made and, in any given set of circumstances, some methods will prove to be more suitable than others. In the vast majority of cases, a delay assessment will have to include a written statement explaining the legal basis (usually the terms of the contract that provide for the completion date to be amended) and the facts (the events that caused the delay and the impact of those events on the completion date).

If the assessment is based on an analysis of programmes, the purpose of and the conclusions to be derived from those programmes should be clearly explained. It should be made clear when producing written statements that the references to days and weeks are references to calendar days and weeks or working days and weeks. The two should not then be mixed up. In case of concurrent causes of delays, generally the contractor will still be entitled to a full extension of time. However, there may be difficulties of defining, with precision the amounts of a concurrent delay.

Delay assessments can be very difficult but it should be borne in mind that the test as to whether a claim should be allowed is generally on the balance of probabilities. The claim does not have to be proved beyond all reasonable doubt. This is important to keep in mind because absolute precision will be difficult or may even be impossible to achieve when making or assessing a delay to a project. A degree of flexibility may have to be adopted if an agreement is to be reached. Therefore, a reasonable delay claim is generally entitled for an extension.

It is therefore, evident that every construction contracts usually provide for Extension of Time (EOT) to be granted by the Employer (or Engineer, if appointed) on a variety of specified grounds. However, where the ground of extension would otherwise be the contractor's risk, the extension is purely a concession, such as for inclement and adverse weather. In cases, where the extension is based on some act or default of Employer, for example, ordering of variations or late instructions, the Contractor may be entitles to extra time and may also include payments.

Employer may extend the term of an existing contract to allow completion of any work undertaken but not completed during the original term of the contract, subject to the approval of the EOT.

Acceleration:

It is generally observed that it is the employer who requires acceleration of construction works. An employer might be anxious that its building be handed over earlier than is set out in the contact or, where the contractor has been allowed extension of time, earlier than the revised completion date. In the latter case, an acceleration agreement can be used as a "wrap up" agreement removing or obliterating all outstanding claims for extension of time and loss and expense.

It may also happen that acceleration is requested at the behest of the employer at an agreed consideration and embedded into the contract or agreed as a variation to the existing contract.

A contractor may also at times, request for acceleration to a part of his works or the whole of works. This requirement may come up due to the changed business or strategic circumstances of the contractor who may wish to re-locate some or all of his plant and machinery to another location or project.

Contractor's Acceleration Proposal:

Before instructing the contractor to accelerate the works, there is generally a negotiation period, sometimes within a time frame stipulated within the construction contract.

The contractor is required to put together a proposal that needs to include the following as a minimum:

- Additional resources of manpower, plant and materials directly employed or subcontracted.
- The revised methodology and actions to be taken to achieve the accelerated date. This might include off-site prefabrication, extra scaffolding, temporary weatherproofing, etc.
- A revised programme with target intermediate dates by which progress can be measured. This might include proposals for phased completion if this is advantageous to the employer.
- A statement on working hours on and off site, including weekends, holidays, night working and shift working (if applicable).
- Additional supervision and any other increased costs for items categorized as preliminaries.

> - Any concessions made by the employer to assist the programme which might include, changes to design or specifications (for example standardization by replacing bespoke requirements).
> - Reduction in scope (for example transferring part of work to a separate post-contract agreement under occupational works).
> - The terms of settlement of all outstanding claims. This will include payment that might be linked to achieving the revised programme milestone dates.

Employer's Assessment of the Acceleration Proposal:

The employer's consultant team needs to be asked to prepare a report on the contractor's acceleration proposals, including a risk assessment of matters that may impede the contractor in achieving the revised programme.

The cost consultant in particular should comment on the validity of the detailed prices set out in the contractor's proposal. The design team should be requested to comment on any proposed changes to the design or specification.

The employer and consultant team might want to re-assess exactly how risk needs to be allocated in the work to be undertaken and whether any changes to the original contract might be appropriate. For instance a reduction in the first month of liquidated and ascertained damages might lead to a reduction in the sum of money the contractor has put in their price for risk in case of failure to meet the revised completion date. At the opposite extreme, a set of one-off bonus payments for each milestone achieved can encourage the contractor to go flat out, spending contingency money to collect the bonus payments.

In the end, only the employer (through his contract administrator) can weigh up whether or not the proposal represents value for money within the context of its business plan for the development.

The Agreement:

It is advisable to have an agreement drawn up by a lawyer reflecting the outcome of negotiations. It is usual for acceleration agreements to be treated as an addendum to the construction contract. As such it is advisable to have it drafted by the legal team that had put together the original contract documents so that inconsistencies and ambiguities are avoided.

The agreement must also include details of:

➤ What happens if the contractor fails to implement some or all of the measures in it's proposal.

➤ What happens if the contractor fails to meet intermediate targets and/or the completion date.

➤ The points at which each payment is due and the payment terms.

➤ Changes required to the existing contract documents to accommodate the acceleration agreement including any changes to design or specification.

➤ The treatment of retention (if any) in respect of acceleration, claims and bonus payments.

Termination or suspension:

Termination/Suspension of a Contract may only be done in accordance with the provisions of the Contact, after providing written notice to the party (or parties) of such an action.

Complaints and/or discrepancies on Contractor performance should be reported as they occur using the Contractor's feedback and performance Form.

Contractors are required to respond within a stipulated time normally expressed within the Contract document. Failure to respond within the prescribed time may result in written notifications and subsequent cancellation of the Contract, suspension or termination of the Contract.

Most forms of contract will include termination clauses, setting out the circumstances under which a contract may be terminated. When a contract is terminated, the parties to the contract are no longer obliged to perform their obligations under the contract.

Terminating a contract can be complex, and it is very important that the correct procedures are followed. This may involve issuing notices setting out the grounds for termination, allowing warning periods, and giving the opportunity to remedy breaches.

There are a number of reasons why one or both parties to a contract may seek to terminate the contract.

Breach of Contract:

A Contract is a binding Agreement between parties with an expectation that all will honor its commitment towards the other. However, if one party does not fulfill its contractual promise, or indicates through his action or words that he shall not perform his obligations as mentioned within the Contract, he is said to be in the breach of contract.

Law allows the Contractor/Consultant incidental damages arising out of Employers breach. It should be noted that both the Employer and the Contractor may be guilty of breach of Contract should they be responsible for violation of the terms and conditions of the contract.

A Contractor or Employer is considered in default/breach if they fail to perform in accordance with the terms and conditions of the contract.

In a Contract, if one of the parties fails to perform in accordance to the requirement of the contract, the relevant action may constitute a breach of contract. A breach of contract may entitle the innocent party to make a claim for damages for the losses it has suffered.

If the breach of contract is serious (a material breach), then the innocent party may also consider that it is discharged from any further obligations under the contract.

If the breach is less serious (a non-material breach, sometimes referred to as a default) the innocent party may make a claim for damages, but may not consider it is discharged from any further obligations under the contract. This prevents the innocent party from excusing their performance because of a minor breach of just one part of the contract.

This is generally the position on construction contracts, where some works are likely to have been carried out, but one or more may remain not done, incomplete or defective. As construction contracts are usually divided up in to parts and include a series of separate payments, this sort of partial failure would not allow the innocent party to excuse their performance, i.e.; a failure in one part will generally only mean that the employer is not liable to pay for that part. Furthermore, if the works have been substantially performed, then the employer must pay for those, subject to a claim for the parts that have not been performed.

On construction contracts, it is generally in the interests of both parties for the contract to continue with the progress of works irrespective of minor problems that may be evident. Whilst damages for breach of contract may seek to put the innocent party in the position it would have been in, had there not been a breach of contract, the delay and disruption caused by having to appoint a new contractor can far outweigh the difficulties of proceeding, albeit under difficult circumstances.

Construction contracts generally make provisions for the contact to be varied without there being a breach. Variations, extension of time, claims for loss and expense, liquidated damages, and the defects liability period, all provide for the contract to be varied or for problems to be rectified.

Where one party behaves in such a way that it indicates it no longer intends to accept its obligations under the contract, this is considered to be a repudiatory beach (or fundamental breach) allowing the innocent party to terminate the contract and to sue for damages. Generally the contract will set out what those breaches are, but they might include:

➢ Refusal to carry out work.

➢ Abandoning the site.

➢ Removing plant from the site.

➢ Failure to make payments.

➢ Employing others to carry out the work.

➢ Failure to allow access to the site.

➢ Failure to proceed regularly and diligently.

➢ Failure to remove or rectify defective works.

Where repudiation is considered to have occurred, the innocent party can either affirm that the contract will continue or accept the repudiation and so terminate the contract. In either case, they will have the right to claim damages. Either way, it is important that there is some sort of response, as inaction may be considered to be an affirmation of the contract.

Assessing the seriousness of breaches of contract depends on the particular circumstances and terms of the contract. For example, if a contractor has failed to carry out the work to an agreed timetable, this might be considered a relatively minor issue on some projects, whilst on others it could be an extremely serious breach. The innocent party must be careful therefore to establish that there has actually been a material breach before considering that the contract is terminated, otherwise they might find themselves in breach of contract. This can lead to disputes, where for example, the employer refuses to make payment, claiming that the contractor has failed to perform, whereas the contractor contends that they are not performing because the employer has refused to make payment.

An anticipatory breach (or anticipatory repudiation) occurs when one of the parties to the contract declares to the other that they do not intend to perform their obligations under the contract.

A contract may also allow termination under other circumstances, such as frustration or insolvency. It may also allow termination for 'convenience', but this may leave the terminating party open to significant claims by the other party.

Frustration:

Frustration occurs due to circumstances that are not the fault of either party, meaning it is impossible to continue with the contract. The contract will come to an end without any party being considered to be in the breach thereof. However, parties need to be certain that a frustration event has occurred so as not to be in breach of contract.

It is highlighted that force majeure provisions might provide for circumstances that could otherwise be considered frustration events, and so result in termination of the contract. Force majeure (for example exceptionally adverse weather conditions) is generally considered a relevant event in construction contracts which will allow for an extension of time and a claim for loss and expense rather than termination. This may be in the interests of both parties.

Convenience:

Contracts may allow termination for 'convenience'. This can be useful for example if the employer fails to secure sufficient funding for the project to proceed. However termination for convenience can leave the terminating party open to significant claims by the other party.

Termination for convenience is only provided for in some forms of contracts and is often only available to the employer, although it may be made available to the contractor if both parties agree to the clause before signing the agreement.

Others:

Contracts may also allow termination under specific circumstances peculiar to a particular project. They may also allow termination for insolvency or bankruptcy.

Rescission:

Rescission is a process of returning both parties to the position that they would have been in, had they not entered into a contract. This might be appropriate for example if there is a serious error in the contract.

Suspension of Performance:

Contracts may also allow suspension of performance. The circumstances allowing suspension are generally similar to those allowing termination. Suspension can be useful, for example, if the employer has difficulty in raising funds to pay for the work to proceed at the speed anticipated by the contract. Furthermore, the contract may also give the right to suspend performance for failure to make payment that has been notified as due.

Either party may have the right to terminate at the end of a suspension period, or if a suspension becomes prolonged with no prospect of work re-commencing.

Suspension:

Construction contracts will generally require that the contractor progresses the works regularly and diligently. However, there are contractual and statutory provisions under which the contractor may suspend performance.

Amongst other provisions under common/civil law around the world, The Housing Grants, Construction and Regeneration Act 1996 (in United Kingdom) is intended to ensure (amongst other things) that payments are made promptly throughout the supply chain.

Its provisions include:

- ➤ The right to be paid in interim, periodic or stage payments.
- ➤ The right to be informed of the amount due, or any amounts to be withheld.
- ➤ The right to suspend performance for non-payment.

The Act applies to all contacts for 'construction operations', including construction contracts and consultants' appointments.

Parties under a contract also have the right to suspend performance of any or all contractual obligations when a required payment of a notified sum has not been made. This includes suspension of part or all of the works and other contractual obligations such as the provision of insurance. They will also be entitled to payment for reasonable costs incurred in exercising their right to suspend performance, and to have the period of suspension disregarded when calculating the competition date.

The right to suspend relates only to the contract for which payment has not been made and the party must not suspend statutory duties. Notice of seven days (or as agreed within the contract) must be given of the intention to suspend performance and the right ceases if the payment is made during this period.

In some forms of construction contracts, there are express terms allowing suspension for failure to make a payment by the due date. There may also be other circumstances in which the contract may allow suspension of the works. Clauses dealing with suspension tend to be similar in nature to those dealing with termination. In addition, there may be a right to terminate at end of the period of suspension or if the suspension becomes prolonged, with no prospect of re-commencing. Suspension may be permitted due to a breach of contract by the employer, the employer becoming insolvent, as a result of force majeure, or by agreement between the parties, for example if circumstances make proceeding with the works temporarily impossible, if there are difficulties in determining how to proceed with a project or if the employer has difficulty in raising funds to pay for the work to proceed at the speed anticipated by the contract.

The provisions of extension of time clauses also allow the construction period to be extended where there are delays that are not the contractor's fault. For more information, please refer to extension of time details discussed earlier in this chapter.

It is important to be certain that the circumstances do allow the works to be suspended, and that the correct procedures are being followed. If the employer has exercised some right under the contract to withhold or reduce payment, then wrongfully suspending the works could possibly amount to a repudiatory beach, where one party behaves in such a way that it indicates it no longer intends to accept its obligations under the contract, allowing the innocent party to terminate the contract and to sue for damages. However, this is not automatic and needs to be substantiated by the party intending to terminate the contract.

The complexity of the situation therefore makes it necessary to obtain legal advice before suspending performance.

Irremediable Breach:

The term irremediable breach refers to a situation where there is a defects in the works for which the cost of rectification is unreasonable relative to the nature of the defect. Under these circumstances the contractor administrator may issue a certificate of making good defects, with a deduction relative to the amount by with the value of the works has been reduced due to the defect.

Contract Interpretation:

Interpretation may be defined as an act or the process of explaining the meaning of something. However, it has been observed in many practical cases that two parties to a contract may carry fundamental differences in their understanding of a term defined within the agreement.

Interpretation of a contract therefore relies very heavily on experience and knowledge of the persons interpreting. However, it is assumed that the two parties to a contract have the same interpretation, and therefore this issue takes precedence over others.

It should be assumed that no article of the contract is void of any meaning or superfluous but must have some purpose. It is only where no clear alternate interpretation is available to remove absurdity or ambiguity from an article, that the court will void an article of a contract.

When this issue reaches a court, generally it will try to discover the intentions of the contracting parties using the plain, ordinary and popular meanings of the words used. A court generally does not try to re-write a contract using interpretation rules but, rather use these rules to pinpoint the intentions of the parties at the moment of signing the contract.

There are guidelines and best practices to proper and just interpretation. A few guidelines are discussed as under.

The Seven Guidelines of Contract Interpretation:

➢ Read the Contract as a whole

➢ Understand the definitions of key Contract terms

➢ Apply the Order of Precedence Clause

➢ Understand the Extrinsic Evidence

➢ Apply the Parol Evidence Rule

➢ Apply the Interpretation against the drafter

➢ Understand and practice the duty to seek clarifications

The cardinal rule of contract interpretation is to seek to ascertain a single interpretation of the contract that reflects the parties' intent.

"Well-written Contracts that are easily understood, effectively managed, and successfully executed do not occur by accident, but is a result of focused approach of individuals who are trained and experienced enough to see the end, even before the commencement of a project".

The Start or Commencement:

Conduct a Post-Award Contract review before the start of work. Project Managers shall typically refer to such a post-award contract review before the start of work as a project kick-off meeting.

The specific nature and extent of Contract Administration varies from contract to contract. It can range from the minimum acceptance of a delivery and payment to the Contractor to extensive involvement by project, audit and procurement officials throughout the Contract Term. Factors influencing the degree of Contract Administration include the nature of the work, the type of contract and the experience and commitment of the personnel involved. Contract administration starts with developing clear and concise performance based statements of work to the extent possible and thereafter, preparing a contract administration plan that cost effectively measures the contractor's performance and provides documentation to pay accordingly.

Post award orientation, either by conference, letter or some other form of communication, should be the beginning of the actual process of good contract administration. This communication process can be a useful tool that helps Employer and Contractor achieve a clear and mutual understanding of the contract requirements, helps the Contractor understand the roles and responsibilities of the Employer's personnel and it's representative, who shall administer the contract and reduces future problems. It is helpful to have a pre-meeting with applicable project and contracting officials prior to the post award orientation conference so that there is a clear understanding of their specific responsibilities and restrictions in administering the contract. Items that should be discussed at the pre-meeting include such things as the authority of Employer's personnel who will administer the contract, quality control and testing, the specific contract deliverable requirements, special contract provisions, Employer's procedures for monitoring and measuring performance, contractor billing, voucher approval, and payment procedures.

Where appropriate, an alternate dispute resolution (ADR) technique should be included within the Contract to help avoid future contract administration problems. It involves Employer's and Contractor's management staff mutually developing a "plan for success", usually with/or without the assistance of a neutral facilitator. The facilitator may help the parties establish a non-adversarial relationship, define mutual goals and identify the major obstacles to success for the project, in case needed. Potential sources of conflict are identified, and the parties seek cooperative ways to resolve any disputes that may arise during contract performance. The process results in the parties developing a partnership charter, which serves as a roadmap for contract success. Many agencies have successfully used partnering on construction projects and are now beginning to apply these principles in the automated data processing/information resources management area.

"Partnering" is a technique that is recently being preferred over traditional procurement routes with an intention to prevent disputes from occurring. It involves Employer's and Contractor's management staff mutually developing a "plan for success".

Good contract administration assures that the end users are satisfied with the product or service being obtained under the contract. One way to accomplish customer satisfaction is to obtain input directly from the customers through the use of customer satisfaction surveys. These surveys help to improve contractor performance because the feedback can be used to notify the contractor when specified aspects of the contract are not being met. In addition, the contracting and program officials can use the information as a source of past performance information on subsequent contract awards. Customer satisfaction surveys also help to improve communications between the procurement, program, and contractor personnel.

Distinct Stages of a Contract:

Any Contract typically has two distinct stages, Pre-Contract Stage and Post-Contract Stage.

Although appointment of a Contract Administrator (CA) is recommended immediately after the award of a Contract, it is a good practice to involve him from as early as possible so that he is aware of the actual requirements and has the visibility to the outcome of the intended project.

We shall therefore, explore the complete life cycle of a project in this book with an intension to get the best out of an efficient contract administration practice.

Contract administrators are appointed by the Employer and usually act as the Employer's agent. When certifying or giving an assessment or decision, the administrator has to act impartially, honestly and reasonably and their decisions are open to challenge via the dispute resolution procedure unless the contract makes their decisions final and conclusive, which is very rare within construction contracts.

For example, on certain contracts the assessments, notifications and certificates of the project manager can be reviewed under the dispute resolution procedure as a result of "any action or inaction of the project manager/contract administrator".

A contract administrator's role generally includes:

- ➢ Inviting and processing tenders
- ➢ Preparing contract documents for execution
- ➢ Administrating change control procedures
- ➢ Seeking instructions from the client in relation to the contract
- ➢ Issuing instructions such as variations, or relating to prime cost sums or making good defects
- ➢ Reviewing or considering claims
- ➢ Chairing construction progress meetings
- ➢ Preparing and issuing construction progress reports
- ➢ Coordinating and instructing site inspectors
- ➢ Agreeing commissioning and testing procedures
- ➢ Agreeing to the defects reporting procedures

- ➤ Ensuring that project documentation is issued to the client
- ➤ Issuing certificates of practical completion and interim certificates
- ➤ Collating and issuing schedules of defects
- ➤ Issuing the certificate of making good defects
- ➤ Issuing the final certificate

It is highlighted that on a construction management contract, the role of a contract administrator might also be attributed to the construction manager. On management contracts (where the works contracts are placed by the management contractor) the management contractor will perform the role of a contract administrator.

Chapter 4

<u>Contract (Pre-Award Stage)</u>

Pre-Contract award is a distinct phase under the procurement process which precedes the actual agreement between the contracting parties.

As a minimum, the following are the typical works involved in this phase of a Contract:

- Tender vetting (identification of onerous conditions of contract)
- Detailed examination of contractual and programming obligations to help minimize tender risks
- Detailed analysis of the proposed method statement and the resource/technical capabilities proposed by the bidders
- Analysis of proposed rates and prices for lump sum contracts, thereby increasing confidence factors on the tender sums
- Taking off BOQ and providing budget prices to facilitate speedy tendering and increased accuracy

Confidentiality:

Strict confidentiality regarding the procurement process needs to be maintained by all stakeholders, notwithstanding whether involved in the procurement activities or not. Dissemination of information regarding the procurement process to individuals not involved in the procurement process needs to be avoided.

Archiving:

Archiving and retention of documents related to procurement activities shall be in compliance with statutory requirements and company's document retention policy. Without prejudice to the foregoing, key documents related to procurement activities generally, needs to be maintained for a minimum period of 10 years (or such periods recommend/required by the law of the land's retention and archiving policy) after the date of completion of the relevant Contract unless they relate to a pending issue or an issue that may end up in dispute at a later date. In such cases the documents shall be retained beyond the minimum period of 10 years or such periods recommend/required by the law of the land's retention and archiving policy, until the issue is conclusively resolved.

The key documents shall include but may not be limited to the following:

- Tender documents
- Technical Bids
- Commercial Bids
- Bid evaluation reports
- Commitment approvals
- Contract documents
- Correspondence with Bidders/Contractors

Tendering Activities

Initiation of Tendering Process:

The requirement for a project/Works is generated with the End-user (the department intending to procure the referenced Project/Services who is by far the most important stakeholder). Hence, typically the end user initiates the tendering process by submitting to the Contracts/Procurement department a request (generally referred to as a Works or Purchase Request) complete with scope of works or services required for the initiation of the Tendering Process along with bill of quantities, specifications, drawings, service levels and key performance indicators and all schedules that is needed to be included within the tender (RFP) package. Technical evaluation criteria shall include all details of evaluation, including the details of the technical evaluation committee and approved budget in order to initiate the Tendering Process.

Tendering Process

Open tendering:

A tender is a submission made by a prospective supplier in response to an invitation to tender (ITT). It makes an offer for the supply of goods or services. In construction, the main tender process is generally the selection, by the employer/client/owner, of a contractor to construct the works. However, as procurement routes have become more complex, so tenders may now be sought for a wide range of goods and services.

Irrespective of the nature of the goods or services that are being sought, securing tenders generally follows one of a number of basic procedures:

- ➤ Open tendering
- ➤ Selective tendering.
- ➤ Negotiated tendering.
- ➤ Serial tendering.
- ➤ Framework tendering.

Open tendering:

Open tendering allows anyone to submit a tender to supply the goods or services that are required. Generally an advertisement will be placed giving notice that a contract is being tendered, offering an equal opportunity to any organization to submit a tender (Request for Proposal or RFP).

On larger projects, there may then be a pre-qualification process that produces a short-list of suitable suppliers from the respondents expressing interest in the contract (Expression of Interest or EOI). This short list will then be invited to prepare tenders. The selection of a short list can include pre-qualification questionnaires and interviews. This sort of pre-qualification process is not the same as selective tendering. Selective tendering only allows suppliers invited from a pre-selected list to take part in the tender process.

Open tendering has often been criticized for being a slow and costly process, attracting tenders or expressions of interest from large numbers of suppliers, some of whom may be entirely unsuitable for the contract and as a result it can waste a great deal of time, effort and money. However, Open tendering offers the greatest competition and has the advantage of allowing new or emerging suppliers to try to secure work and so can facilitate greater innovation. The number of firms tendering for a work can be reduced (ideally to around ten in numbers) by a pre-qualification process, and if this uses a standard pre-qualification questionnaire, then the time wasted by unsuccessful applicants can be minimized.

On public projects, or projects that include an element of public funding, it may be necessary to advertise contracts as a requirement of the Public

Contracting Regulations of the land. This is intended to open up public procurement within the country (or group of countries) and to ensure free movement of supplies, services and works.

Open tendering can be either single stage or two stages. Two stage tendering is used to allow early appointment of a supplier, prior to the completion of all the information required to enable them to offer a fixed price. In the first stage, a limited appointment is agreed allowing them to begin work and in the second stage a fixed price is negotiated for the contract.

Selective tendering:

Selective tendering allows suppliers to submit tenders by invitation only. A pre-selected list of possible suppliers is prepared that are known by their track record to be suitable for a contract of the size, nature and complexity required. They might then be asked if they would be interested in tendering for the contract, and then based on the responses received, a number of them are invited to tender (generally around ten bidders). From the tenders received, a preferred tenderer is selected based on criteria such as price and quality and may be negotiated or otherwise.

Consultants or experienced clients may maintain an approved list of prospective suppliers appropriate for particular types of contract and then regularly review performance to assess whether they should remain on the list.

Selective tendering may be particularly appropriate for specialist or complex contracts, or contracts where there are only a few suitable firms. Selective tendering will tend to be faster than open tendering and can be seen as less wasteful as there is no pre-qualification process as part of the tender procedure itself, and only suppliers that are known to be appropriate for the proposed contracts are invited to prepare tenders. It can also give clients/ owner greater confidence that their requirements will be satisfactorily met.

However, it can exclude smaller suppliers or those trying to establish themselves in a new market, it can reduce the potential for innovation and can be seen to introduce bias into tendering as firms may be excluded from approved lists for unknown reasons, because of a lack of awareness or because of personal preferences. It can also result in prospective suppliers continually contacting clients and consultants to check that they are on the appropriate lists.

Negotiated tendering:

Negotiated tendering occurs when the employer approaches a single supplier based on their track-record or a previous relationship and the terms of the contract are then negotiated.

Negotiating with a single supplier may be appropriate for highly specialist contracts (where there may be a limited number of potential suppliers), or for extending the scope of an existing contract. It can give the employer the confidence of working with a supplier they already know, can reduce the duration and costs of tendering and can allow early supplier involvement.

However, unless the structure of the negotiation is clearly set out there is potential for an adversarial atmosphere to develop, even before the contract has been awarded. Carrying out negotiations in the absence of competition so that both parties feel the outcome is fair can be complex and time consuming.

Negotiated tendering can be seen as anti-competitive and exclusive, with the potential for unhealthy relationships to develop between the employer and the supplier. Negotiated tendering may not be permitted by some organizations due to the perceived lack of accountability. On public projects or projects that include a publicly-funded element it may be necessary to advertise contracts and hence this approach cannot be used.

Serial tendering:

Serial tendering generally involves the preparation of tenders based on a typical or notional bill of quantities or schedule of works. The rates submitted can then be used to value works over a series of similar projects, often for a fixed period of time following which the tender procedure may be repeated.

Serial tendering may be used where the employer has a regular programme of works that they would like to be undertaken by a single contractor often minor works and repetitive in nature such as housing or maintenance works. The tender document will generally define the buildings that will be covered by the works, the term over which works may be required (often between one and five years), an estimate of the likely total value of the works that will be required over the term and an estimate of the likely size of individual orders.

Appointment is based on an agreed schedule of rates related to the categories of work that are likely to form part of the programme.

When individual works are required, the employer issues an instruction (or order) to the contractor which may include a written description of the works, drawings if appropriate and a valuation agreed by the employer and contractor. Payments are then calculated based on the agreed schedule of rates (SOR).

Serial tendering can reduce tender costs, and may encourage suppliers to submit low rates to secure an on-going programme of work. However, it may be seen as anti-competitive and exclusive. It can be argued that it both encourages innovation (by giving contractors the confidence to invest in continuous improvement) and discourages investment (by preventing other contractors from submitting alternative proposals).

Framework contract:

Employers that are continuously commissioning construction work might want to reduce timescales, learning curves and other risks by using framework agreements. Such arrangements allow the clients to invite tenders from suppliers of goods and services to be carried out over a period of time on a call-off basis as and when required.

The framework contract document should define the scope and possible locations for the works or services likely to be required during the defined period of time.

The contract document should describe the contract conditions that will be used for pre-construction services (such as design) and/or the contract conditions that will be used to execute the works. Depending on the size and complexity of the anticipated projects, the supplier/contractor might provide a pricing mechanism or risk adjustment mechanism for different types of contract that might be used, for example a minor works contract, a cost reimbursable contract, a design and build and so on. The options would then be selected by the employer depending on the nature of the projects that emerged.

Framework tender documents are likely to include:

➢ The starting and completion dates of the agreement

➢ Requirements and obligations regarding insurance, bonds and warranties

- ➢ A description of the contract conditions to be used and assumptions regarding preliminaries
- ➢ A description of how the project will be managed in its various stages and the basis of remuneration
- ➢ A description of the tender selection procedure and assessment procedure to be employed by the client
- ➢ A description of inflation, interest and retention percentages to be applied
- ➢ A description of incentive mechanisms to be applied
- ➢ A description of dispute resolution procedures
- ➢ Rates for travel and subsistence expenses
- ➢ A request for schedules of rates and time charges to be submitted and a breakdown of resources and overheads to be applied to design, or manufacture and installation (including any proposed sub-contractor or sub-consultant details)
- ➢ Any other criteria required from tenderers in order that the employer can properly assess their suitability

One or more suppliers are then selected and appointed. When specific projects arise the employer is then able to simply select a suitable framework supplier and instruct them to start work (usually done through Task Orders).

Where there is more than one suitable supplier available, the employer may introduce a secondary selection process to assess which supplier is likely to offer best value for a specific project. The advantage to the employer of this process is that they are able to instigate a selection procedure for individual projects without having to undertake a time consuming pre-qualification process. This should also reduce tender costs.

The advantage to the supplier is that the likelihood of them being awarded a project when they are already on a framework contract should be higher than it would be under an open procurement process. Some suppliers however complain that having already been appointed on a framework agreement; they may then have to bid for individual projects anyway, and after a great deal of time and effort may not be awarded any projects.

Process of Invitation to tenders:

➢ Limited Tender or Open Tenders

➢ Competitive Tendering or Single Sourcing Procurement Process

Limited Tender or Open Tenders:

The choice of going ahead with the limited or open tender process lies with the contracts/procurement process of the organization. In general, for an average value tender, procurement shall be performed using a limited tender process. Bids shall be accepted only from Bidders who have been invited to submit a Bid. In order to have a healthy competition amongst bidders and to obtain the overall best bid, the contracts/procurement department may also wish to seek Expression of Interest (EOI) from the prospective bidders. This EOI stage is followed by inviting bidders to formally go through the tendering process.

A company may also like to procure through open tender process by advertising in the print or electronic media.

Competitive Tendering or Single Sourcing Procurement Process:

Competitive Tendering process is defined as a process where more than one Bidder is invited to Bid for a tender.

Single sourcing is defined as a process where only one Bidder is invited to Bid for a tender.

It is a good practice to have all procurement activities to be generally based on a competitive tendering process. Where available in the Commercial Directory, it shall be endeavored to have sufficient number of bidders in the list of bidders with the objective of obtaining sufficient technically acceptable bidders. It is recommended to invite anywhere between 5 to 10 Bidders for the tendering process (after having been through the Expression of Interest and/or Prequalification process).

Single Sourcing is not a mechanism intended to circumvent a competitive tendering process and shall only be applied in case of a specialized nature of the project requirement. Also, it needs to be treated as an exception and approved by a Competent Authority. It is further noted that the existence of single source procurement must not prevent the contract administrator from enforcing all contract terms.

Soliciting Tenders:

Tenders (including Technical Bids and Commercial Bids) are recommended to be obtained in two separate sealed envelopes. A good practice is to also have a separate sealed envelope for the submission of a Bid Bond. It is also recommended to appoint a Tender Opening Committee, who shall at the first instance, only open the Technical Bid and pass that on to the pre-selected Technical Evaluation Committee. The Commercial Bids shall only be opened after the Technical Bids evaluation has been concluded and a Technical Evaluation Report obtained from the Chairperson of the Technical Evaluation Committee.

After the opening of the Commercial Bids, the Tender Opening Committee, through the contracts/procurement department shall pass that on to the Commercial Evaluation Committee. This committee shall thereafter, complete the commercial evaluation and the Chairperson of the Commercial Evaluation Committee shall submit its Report to the Procurement department, who will then consolidate the two reports and do a consolidated Report with a recommendation for the award of Contract.

While consolidating the report, the Procurement department shall make sure that the evaluation committee has followed the Contract Strategy at the first instance. Any deviations noticed needs to be highlighted to the senior management/Competent Authority.

However, if the nature of the scope requires evaluation of both the Technical Bids and Commercial Bids together, then subject to approval of the Competent Authority, both the Technical Bids and Commercial Bids may be obtained together in a sealed envelope.

Tender for construction contracts:

A tender is a submission made by a prospective supplier (bidder) in response to an invitation to tender. It makes an offer for the supply of goods or services.

An invitation to tender might be issued for a range of contracts, including equipment supply, the main construction contract (including design by the contractor), demolition, enabling works, etc. Generally, tendering refers to the construction works (rather than securing consultancy services which are referred to as 'appointment' and are done through 'Request for Proposal').

Invitation to Tender (ITT):

An invitation to tender may follow the completion of a pre-qualification questionnaire (PQQ) in response to an advertisement posted by the employer and perhaps a pre-tender interview. The purpose of a pre-qualification questionnaire and pre-tender interview is to enable the employer to produce a short list of suppliers that are likely to be most appropriate for their particular project who will then be invited to tender. This helps reduce inefficiency and wasted effort in the tender process.

An invitation to tender generally includes the following:

- ➢ A letter of invitation to tender
- ➢ The form of tender
- ➢ Preliminaries (including pre-construction information and site waste management plan)
- ➢ The form of contract, contract conditions and amendments
- ➢ A tender pricing document (or contract sum analysis on design and build projects)
- ➢ A drawing schedule
- ➢ Design drawings
- ➢ Specifications

Ideally, a tender document shall be broken down into a series of packages (even if there will only be one main contract) each with its own design drawings and specifications suitable to be issued by the main contractor to potential sub-contractors. This makes the tender easier to price for the contractor and easier to compare with other tenderers for the employer. It is important when this is done to ensure that the interfaces between packages are properly identified and clearly allocated to one package or another. Having too many packages increases the number of interfaces and so the potential problems. The cost plan (pre-tender estimate) should also be re-assembled package by package to allow easy appraisal of tenders received.

Clarification:

While tender bulletins and addendum are general clarification tools at the tendering stage, mid-tender interviews may also be arranged to allow clarification of matters that might otherwise lead to an inaccurate tender being submitted, they can also give the employer insights into potential problems or opportunities in the project as it is described by the tender documentation.

Responses to queries raised during the tender process can lead to clarification or amendment of the tender documentation which may also result in an extension of the tender period. It is better to allow sufficient time during the tender process to investigate opportunities and clarify problems, as the resulting tenders will then be better prepared and will be likely to save time and money later.

It is important that any clarification, additional information or changes to the tender documents are circulated to all of the tenderers to ensure a level playing field. However this should not give away a particular contractor's proposed methodology, commercial proposals or programming advantages, which may have been divulged to the employer or his representative in interviews. Such information must be treated as confidential.

Submission:

In response to an invitation to tender, invited tenders will submit their tender (proposal), which will include their price for supplying the goods or services along with proposals for how the employer's requirements will be satisfied if these have been requested.

The precise content of tenders will vary considerably depending on the procurement route, however they might include:

> - A tender return slip, with details of the contract, return address, tender checklist etc.
> - A completed tender pricing document (or contract sum analysis on design and build projects)
> - Schedules of rates
> - An initial construction phase plan
> - Any design proposals or method statements (maybe both) that have been requested
> - Alternative or non-compliant proposals. These should only be submitted if they have been requested and should be accompanied by a mandatory compliant proposal
> - Programme of work
> - Procedures to be adopted such as procurement procedures, cost management procedures etc.

- Demonstration of capability, for example design capability, systems used etc.
- Key project personnel (generally requested to include their updated curriculum vitae)
- Management organization
- Plant and labour resources and availability
- Prior experience
- References

Settlement Meeting:

Once the employer has identified the preferred tenderer (or bidder, this may involve further interviews) they may hold a tender settlement meeting to enter into negotiations. This may result in further adjustment of the tender documents and the submission of a revised tender.

Public Projects:

On publicly-funded projects the procurement processes preferred by the Government Construction Strategy are all generally based on inviting tenders from an integrated supply team (including designers, suppliers and contractors) to design, build and sometimes operate and finance the development. On private finance initiative (PFI) projects, the process of securing offers from integrated supply team is referred to as "bidding" rather than "tendering".

It is noted that a public project or publicly-subsidized projects may be subject to specific Government's procedures, enacted under the law of the land.

In many countries, public contracts are regulated by the respective public works departments who work on guidelines enacted by specific government bodies.

Two Stage Tendering:

Two-stage tendering is used to allow early appointment of a contractor, prior to the completion of all the information required to enable them to offer a fixed price.

In the first stage, a limited appointment is agreed allowing the contractor to begin work and in the second stage a fixed price is negotiated for the contract. It can be used to appoint the main contractor early or more commonly as a mechanism for early appointment of a specialist contractor, such as a cladding contractor. A two-stage tender process may also be adopted on a design and build project where the employer's requirements are not sufficiently well developed for the contractor to be able to calculate a realistic price. In this case, the contractor will tender a fee for designing the building along with a schedule of rates that can be used to establish the construction price for the second stage tender.

Construction Management:

As a construction manager performs a consultancy and management role (unlike a traditional contractor) their appointment may be on similar terms to the consultant team, and collaborative working with the consultant team will be vital to the success of the project.

Management Contracts:

The agreement between the employer and management contractor is likely to cover both pre-construction and construction activities, with a notice to proceed between the two, before which works contracts cannot be let. The terms of the appointment must be clear about what is to be provided by the management contractor (such as the provision of site facilities, etc.) and whether activities constitute pre-construction or construction services.

Emergency Procurement:

An emergency is a serious or urgent situation requiring immediate action to protect Employers property and resources or where immediate safety or regulatory compliance is required. An organization may need to do an Emergency Procurement when an urgent situation arises and the particular need for goods or services cannot be met through normal Procurement routes. It is therefore, recommended that a provision for the procurement of such an emergency requirement is made within the Procurement procedure and a senior executive of the company assigned with the responsibility to authorize such emergency procurement.

However, it is a good practice that all documents and details pertaining to such procurement be formally submitted to the contracts/procurement department after the event.

Emergency procurement requests shall only be permitted for immediate and unplanned requirements, and backed by documentary evidence for such an action. The intention behind circumventing an established procurement process for an emergency procurement is to help facilitate procurement of emergency items for an organization resulting in eventual savings and the resultant goodwill to the company.

Bidders Lists:

An organization may not always go for open tenders by advertising and soliciting tenders. One general route of procurement is to invite pre-selected or registered vendors/contractors to participate in the bidding process. This is also referred to as closed tendering.

One of the important challenges that a contract administrator face at the on-set of such a tender (close tender) is the selection of bidders from the list of registered companies (or companies that are registered with government/ industry directory) looking forward to provide such a service that the Employer intends to procure.

A Bidders list is the selected list of bidders that an Employer wishes to invite for the collection of tender documents and the subsequent submission of Bids to participate in a particular RFP/tender.

The Bidders List shall comprise a list of pre-qualified entities either from the commercial directory or entities which have been specifically pre-qualified for a particular procurement activity. It shall be endeavored to have Bidders of comparable commercial and business standing in the Bidders List to ensure a level playing field.

Standard Tender Documents:

It is recommended that all procurement activities be conducted using standard forms of Contracts as the basis. The choice of the form of contract shall be based on the nature of the tendered scope and the risks involved. Such standard forms shall be procured from the likes of FIDIC, JCT, RIBA, PPC 2000 etc.

Exceptions proposed by Bidders to the terms and conditions of the standard forms of Contracts shall be dealt with on a case-by-case basis. Where necessary, contracts/procurement department shall coordinate with other stakeholders in this regard. Legal department's review and acceptance is the key to such a modification to the terms and conditions of contract forms.

It is highlighted that any exception to the terms and conditions of the Contract shall not be entertained as otherwise; the expectation of a "level playing field" from all Bidders is very likely to be compromised in favor of a particular Bidder requesting such an exception. In case the exceptions raised have a definitive merit, it is recommended that it is passed-on to all Bidders with a request for a formal response from all.

As we have seen earlier, a tender is a submission made by a prospective supplier in response to an invitation to tender (ITT). It makes an offer for the supply of goods or services. Tender documents are prepared to seek tenders (offers). Generally, tendering refers to the construction works, rather than consultancy services which are referred to as appointing (generally procured through Request for Proposal or the route).

Tender documents may be prepared for a range of contracts such as; equipment supply, the main construction contract (including design by the contractor), demolition, enabling works etc.

Ideally, tender documents should be broken down into a series of packages (even if there will only be one main contract) each with its own design drawings and specifications suitable to be issued by the main contractor to potential sub-contractors. This makes the tender easier to be priced for the contractor and easier to compare with other tenderers for the employer. It is important when this is done to ensure that the interfaces between packages are properly identified and clearly allocated to one package or another. Having too many packages increases the number of interfaces and so the potential problems. The cost plan (pre-tender estimate) should also be re-assembled package by package to allow easy appraisal of tenders received.

Tender documents may include:

- ➤ A letter of invitation to tender.
- ➤ The form of tender.
- ➤ Preliminaries: including pre-construction information and site waste management plan.
- ➤ The form of contract, contract conditions and amendments.
- ➤ A tender pricing document (or contract sum analysis on design and build projects).
- ➤ A drawing schedule.
- ➤ Design drawings.

> ➢ Specifications.

Copies of the tender documentation should be kept for records and archived in line with the statutory requirements.

It is good practice to send relevant documents direct to sub-contractors who have been named in the bills of quantities and to inform the tendering contractors that this has been done, so they know they do not have to.

Communication with Bidders:

It is highly recommended that all communications between Employer and Bidders shall be conducted through a centralized department that has the responsibility of procuring goods and projects for the organization i.e.; its Procurement department, and through the person authorized to do so. Generally the persons authorized to procurement are the Procurement Managers or Contracts Managers.

Other than the authorized persons, no one should communicate with the Bidders during the Tendering Process. All communications with the Bidders shall be formal and written either though letters, email or fax. The intention of such a requirement is to provide equal opportunity to all Bidders and to obtain the best Bids for the product/services that the Employer seeks through the tendering process. Establishment of clear lines of communication is a very important task.

Information Management:

Ensuring that the appointed consultants sign up to the use of compatible systems and adopt agreed document and drawing standards will help facilitate collaboration.

Systems might include:

> ➢ Computer aided design (CAD).
> ➢ Specialist modeling tools such as building information modeling (BIM).
> ➢ Common document management systems.
> ➢ Common E-document management systems (these can be in-house, or externally hosted, i.e.; a project extranet)
> ➢ A consistent approach to computer aided design (CAD), both the CAD system, version, drawing standards and file formats are very

important for design projects and will avoid duplicated effort and errors. Drawing standards are particularly important and might include:

➢ Layering standards

➢ Zoning strategy

➢ Grid strategy

➢ Origin and orientation

➢ Naming protocols

➢ Agreed standards for dimensions, abbreviations and symbols

➢ Standard templates (for example drawing titles)

➢ Standard page sizes and scales

➢ Distribution protocols

➢ Change control procedures

Standardization procedures also apply to the production of other forms of project documentation. The creation of a document matrix outlining key documents that will be required in the development of the project, their format and distribution can be beneficial.

Establishing a common data environment (CDE), within which the creation of information such as drawings and specifications can be shared between the consultant team can improve efficiency, avoid duplication and enhance co-ordination.

A common data environment requires:

➢ Systems for describing information.

➢ Checking and approval procedures.

➢ Version, revision and status control.

➢ Folder structures.

➢ Methods of exchange.

➢ Storage and archiving procedures.

Bid Opening:

Generally Technical Bids and Commercial Bids are received in two separate sealed envelopes and are opened by a pre-appointed Tender Opening Committee.

Late submissions generally should not be allowed, unless this has been authorized by a Competent Authority who must also authorize the late submission without compromising the positions of any bidder. The authorization thus needs to be on a reasonable ground and not for normal delay attributable to the bidder's direct delay. The basic rule to be followed is the requirement of a tendering to be equal for all bidders with respect to time constraints imposed within the bid process, and that all bidders are on the same level playing field.

Commercial Bids of only the technically acceptable bidders needs to be opened. It needs to be made sure that in no case, the Commercial Bids of technically unacceptable Bidders is opened for comparison purpose. This ensures the sanctity of the tendering process and ensures that non-compliant bids are not used for commercial advantages to any particular party.

Tender Documents Collection Fee:

Tender collection fee is an optional provision that may be used by an Employer who wishes to provide Tender documents only to the serious Bidders. In case an Employer wishes to go ahead with the tender document collection fee, it is recommended that it shall charge the Bidders a onetime non-refundable fee for the collection of the tender documents.

Where re-bid is sought, the Bidders who had initially purchased the tender documents after the payment of fee shall not be required to pay the fee again for the collection of re-bid Tender documents.

The requirement stipulated within the Tendering Process for collection of Tendering fee is to provide tendering documents to serious bidders only and not to generate any revenue for the employer organization and therefore, the tender fee needs to be set to an optimum value to keep interested parties into the tendering process while at the same time keeping out the bidders who many not be very keep on the kind of the referenced tender.

Tender Bond:

A Tender Bond is a bank guarantee requested to be provided by all Bidders and is generally equivalent to 5% to 10% of the estimated contract price or the bid price. It is recommended that it is drawn on a registered bank within the region/country.

In order not to divulge information of the sealed Commercial Bid, it is recommended that the Employer requests the Bidders to provide a Tender Bond equal to a fixed percentage of its Bid Price and is either included within the Commercial Bid or in a separate envelope, clearly marked as "Tender Bond" (but definitely not within the Technical Bid package. An Employer may request for a statement from the bidders, to be included with the Technical Bid package stating that they have enclosed a Tender Bond in accordance with the Tender requirements. Another preferred way is to request for a stipulated value of the tender bond to be submitted by all bidders. Since the value of the bond is stipulated by the Employer, any likely chances of the bid price getting divulged is minimized.

Tender Evaluation Criteria:

It is highly recommended that the Bid evaluation criteria is finalized, endorsed and approved by the Competent Authority within the Employer organization prior to issuing the invitation for Tender. No change thereafter needs to be allowed to an approved evaluation criteria after opening of the Bids. An evaluation of the Bids other than in accordance with the pre-approved Bid evaluation criteria shall require approval of an authority equal or higher than the Competent Authority with explanations backing such a decision.

Technical Bid Evaluation:

Scope evaluation of the Technical Bids needs to cover all technical as well as un-priced commercial aspects of the tender submissions, with the sole exception of the pricing information contained within the Commercial Bid.

Some general Technical Bid Evaluation Criteria for evaluation are as follows:

- ➤ Company experience in the required scope of work (internationally and in the local market)
- ➤ Approach and methodology
- ➤ Overall scalability of the proposed solution/workmanship
- ➤ Support capabilities
- ➤ Ability to deliver the required technical requirements
- ➤ Manpower/resources within the company
- ➤ Manpower/resources that the company can mobilize within a short notice
- ➤ Company's health and safety record in the past 5 years (or 10 years)
- ➤ Company's financial health, etc.

Evaluation Process:

Evaluation of the Technical Bids shall be performed strictly on the basis of the documents submitted by the Bidder against the approved Technical Bid Evaluation Criteria. The importance weighs down to the fact that the selection of the optimum provider is the key for which a robust evaluation process was drafted at the first place. The importance weighs down to the fact that the selection of the optimum provider is the key for which a robust evaluation process was drafted at the first place. The evaluation team shall not consider any external information including prior personal knowledge or experience in the evaluation process. In case the Technical Bids contain any Bidder's qualification related to conditions of contract, this shall be clarified with the Legal or other Stakeholders and accordingly resolved through the post tender clarification with the Bidders prior to opening the Commercial Bids.

Rejections (technical):

Rejection of a Bidder shall be based on demonstrated non-compliance with the Technical Bid Evaluation Criteria. Before rejection, a clarification needs to be sent at least once to each Bidder in respect of the non-compliant portions of their Technical Bid.

Commercial Bid Evaluation:

Scope Evaluation of the Commercial Bids shall be limited to evaluation of the pricing information only. All other aspects of the offer shall have been evaluated as part of the evaluation of the Technical Bid.

It needs to be clear to the Commercial Evaluation Committee members of their actions in case of an anomaly that they may notice in the price of a Bidder within the Form of Tender and the BOQ.

It is very important to note that commercial submissions of only the technically qualified bidders are opened. Contracts administrator shall ensure that under no circumstances commercial submissions of bidders not qualified in the technical evaluation are opened, and that the unopened submissions are returned back to the bidders as-such. This is to maintain the sanctity of the procurement process and also to culminate the feeling of missing out on a "better offer" which may not have always been the case, had the overall evaluation to be taken into consideration.

Evaluation Process:

Evaluation of the Commercial Bids shall be performed strictly on the basis of the pricing information submitted by the Bidder against the approved Commercial Bid Evaluation Criteria. Should the pricing be qualified in any manner, it should be recorded and clarified with the Bidder. In any case the evaluation results shall be concluded in a manner that the evaluation results reflect an equitable comparison of the received Offers, which shall be duly recorded and taken into consideration in the final recommendation. Equitable comparison may require correction of mathematical errors or normalization.

Commercial evaluation shall make sure that all prices submitted by the bidders are in line with the requirement and the amount contained within the Form of Tender and the BOQ is equal. Commercial evaluation and the clarification of all rates and prices is the last opportunity available to the employer's team to consolidate the BOQ and the contract price. Once locked and a contract is awarded, all future valuations and variations shall be in accordance with these rates and prices until the contract close-out (unless if the contract says otherwise).

Rejections (commercial):

Rejection of a Bidder shall be based on demonstrated non-compliance with the Commercial Bid evaluation criteria. Before rejection, clarifications should be requested at least once from each Bidder in respect of non-compliant portions of their Commercial Bid, in order to dispel any unclear items from the proposal.

Final Selection & Award:

Selection of the successful Bidder shall in all cases be made from amongst the technically acceptable Bidders. Depending on the nature of the tender, the following guidelines shall be adhered to in selection of the successful Bidder from amongst the technically acceptable Bidders:

Low-bid selection: This selection focuses on the price of a project. Multiple construction management companies submit a bid to the owner that is the lowest amount they are willing to do the job for. Then the owner usually chooses the company with the lowest bid to complete the job for them.

Hence, the quoted Contract price shall be used as the basis for final selection where there is no consideration other than the quoted Contract price.

Lowest Evaluated Price: The evaluated price shall be used as the basis for final selection where the quoted Contract price itself may not necessarily reflect the total cost to the Employer, such as cost of potential changes, operating costs, etc. and provided further that there is no other consideration.

Techno-Commercial selection of the successful Bidder may be performed on a techno-commercial basis where the technical rating of a Contractor is an important factor as well as the price. Criteria suitable for the tendered scope shall be defined and approved by Competent Authority.

Best-value selection: This selection focuses on both the price and qualifications of the contractors submitting bids. This means that the employer chooses the contractor with the best price and the best qualifications. The owner decides by using a request for proposal (RFP), which provides the owner with the contractor's exact form of scheduling and budgeting that the contractor expects to use for the project.

Qualifications-based selection: This selection is used when the employer decides to choose the contractor only on the basis of their qualifications. The employer then uses a request for qualifications (RFQ), which provides the owner with the contractor's experience, management plans, project organization, and budget and schedule performance. The employer may also ask for safety records and individual credentials of their members.

Contracts based on Payment mechanism:

Lump-sum: This is the most common type of contract. The construction manager and the employer/owner agree on the overall cost of the construction project and the employer/owner is responsible for paying that amount whether the cost of construction project exceeds or falls below the agreed price of payment.

Cost-Plus-Fee: This contract provides payment for the contractor including the total cost of the project as well as a fixed fee or percentage of the total cost. This contract is beneficial to the contractor since any additional costs will be paid for even though they were unexpected for the owner.

Guaranteed Maximum Price: This contract is the same as the cost-plus-fee contract although there is a set price that the overall cost and fee do not go above.

Unit-Price: This contract is used when the cost cannot be determined ahead of time. The owner provides materials with a specific unit price to limit spending.

Tender Negotiation:

In response to an invitation to tender (ITT), invited tenderers will submit their tender, which will include their price for supplying the goods or services along with proposals for how the employer's requirements will be satisfied if these have been requested.

Once tenders have been received, tender negotiation might proceed with two (or more) preferred tenderers prior to selection of the successful bid. There is an opportunity to agree or clarify matters regarding the pricing and quality of the proposed works, conditions/terms of contract and the programme. This is the last chance the employer and the consultant team will have to negotiate with tenderers while they are still subject to the pressures of competition.

Tender Negotiations may involve:

➢ Tender qualifications to the proposed contract conditions.
➢ Anomalies or clarification in the tender pricing document.
➢ Alternative offers to the design or specification.
➢ Resolution of provisional sums.

The record of the agreements reached needs to be carefully drafted and signed off by both parties as it will form part of the contract documents.

Generally, the contract administrator co-ordinates negotiations with the tenderers, but negotiations may be led at different stages by the cost consultant, contract administrator, lead designer or architect, or by an employer's representative such as a project manager.

Notification of Award/Letter of Award:

Award of Contract to the successful Bidder shall be notified either by issuing a Notification of Award (also called Letter of Award) or by issuing the Contract documentation for execution by the successful Tenderer/Bidder (and the Employer/Owner).

Starting the tendering work stage:

The lead consultant co-ordinates a start-up meeting with the consultant team and the employer to agree to the programme and procedures that will be adopted for tendering. The employer gives any instructions necessary regarding lists of approved bidders/tenderers, statutory requirements, and preferred form of contract, contract conditions, allocation of risk and the appointment of the contract administrator.

The contract administrator agrees with the employer their delegated limit for issuing instructions in relation to the tendering process.

The lead consultant and employer prepare selection criteria for bidders and if appropriate, pre-qualification questionnaire. If it is necessary and has not already been done, advertisements are prepared although and ideally, in order to avoid serious delays, this should have been done when planning approval was received.

The employer takes advice from the lead designer and decides whether to appoint, or arrange for the appointment of site inspectors.

Preparing the tender documentation:

Throughout the stage of preparation of tender documentation, the lead designer co-ordinates completion of statutory approvals and other approvals and negotiations (such as negotiations with insurers, etc.).

The lead consultant co-ordinates advice from the consultant team on the form of contract and contract conditions and advises the employer.

The employer considers advice on the form of contract and contract conditions and instructs the lead consultant.

The lead designer co-ordinates the preparation of tender documentation and any other information required for the preparation of the pre-tender estimate, cash flow projection and tender pricing document.

The cost consultant prepares the pre-tender estimate, cash flow projection and tender pricing document.

The Construction Design & Management (CDM) coordinator shall co-ordinate the preparation of pre-construction information.

The employer may develop, or arrange for the consultant team to develop a site waste management plan.

The lead consultant co-ordinates a review of the tender documents and issues instructions to make amendments, if necessary.

The employer considers the tender documents (including assessment of the pre-tender estimate in relation to the budget) and issues instructions to make further amendments if necessary.

The lead consultant instigates a change control procedure for the tender documents and the lead designer or a nominated person/department arranges printing of the tender documents.

Identifying potential bidders/tenderers:

From responses received to any advertisements placed or from recommendations received, the contract administrator co-ordinates the preparation of a long list of potential tenderers (the client/employer may wish to include particular tenderers on the list).

The contract administrator issues pre-qualification questionnaire to the long list of potential tenderers.

The contract administrator receives completed pre-qualification questionnaire from the long list of potential tenderers.

The cost consultant needs to carry out financial checks on potential tenderers (ideally the estimated contract value should not be more than 20% of the annual turnover of the potential tenderers).

The CDM co-ordinator advises on potential tenderers competence as principal contractor.

The contract administrator prepares a short list of tenderers for the employer's comment or approval.

The employer accepts or alters the initial short list of tenderers and instructs the contract administrator to arrange pre-tender interviews with the initial short list of tenderers.

If necessary, following the comments received during the pre-tender interviews, the contract administrator may be required to co-ordinate amendments to the tender documentation.

Following the pre-tender interviews, the contract administrator co-ordinates any amendments to the initial short list of tenderers and agrees the final short list of tenderers with the employer.

Identifying the preferred bidders/tenderers:

The cost consultant collates tender documents for the main contract and arranges dispatch and return to and from the tenderers.

The contract administrator compiles queries from tenderers and co-ordinates responses, which should be issued to all tenderers.

If necessary, the contract administrator arranges mid-tender interviews or site visits for the tenderers.

If queries from the tenderers or discussions during the mid-tender interviews result in significant clarification or changes to the tender documentation, the contract administrator may recommend to the employer that the tender period is extended.

After the employer receives the tenders. They may follow a formal procedure for opening and recording tenders.

The contract administrator co-ordinates the assessment of the tenders (this may include further interviews).

The lead designer needs to co-ordinate assessment of any contractor's proposals submitted by tenders.

The CDM co-ordinator assesses any initial construction phase plans submitted by the tenders.

The employer receives the tender appraisals from the consultant team, and instructs the contract administrator to enter into negotiations with the preferred tenderer(s). A reserve tenderer may be retained in the event that negotiations with the preferred tenderer is unsuccessful.

Entering into negotiations with the preferred bidder/tenderer:

The contract administrator shall be responsible for the co-ordination of negotiations (if any) with the preferred bidder/tenderer. Negotiations may be led at different stages by the cost consultant, contract administrator, lead designer, architect or by an employer's representative such as a project manager.

Note: It is very important in any negotiation that the individuals at the negotiating table either have authority to fully negotiate terms or make it clear from the start the limits of their authority. This may mean re-convening with the right people empowered to make decisions.

Contract administrator co-ordinates the preparation of a tender report. The employer considers the tender report and if necessary instructs changes to the tender document.

If instructed the contract administrator co-ordinates adjustments to tender documents and requests a revised tender from the preferred tenderer/ tenderers.

Deciding to appoint the preferred bidder/tenderer:

Before a decision is made to appoint the preferred tenderer, the employer must ensure adequate funding is in place so that the execution phase is free of road-bumps

Contractor's appointment:

The contract administrator (or sometimes the cost consultant) collates the contract document and arranges for the execution (engrossment) of two copies, one for the employer and one for the contractor. Alternatively, the employer might retain one executed contract, with certified copies being issued to the contractor, this can avoid potential errors in preparing two contract document for execution. The contractor may be required to provide a performance bond, warranties and evidence of insurance cover in accordance with the ones stipulated in the terms and conditions of the contract.

The contract administrator also arranges for copies of the contract documentation (or relevant parts) to be issued to the consultant team.

The CDM co-ordinator notifies the Health and Safety executives of the principal contractor's contact details, and the contract administrator is needed to officially inform all other tenderers that they have been unsuccessful, while thanking them for their interest and participation for the project.

Pre-Construction:

The pre-construction stage begins when the owner (or client/employer) gives a notice to proceed to the contractor that they have chosen through the bidding process. A notice to proceed is when the owner gives permission to the contractor to begin their work on the project. The first step is to assign the project team which includes the project manager (PM), contract administrator, superintendent, and field engineer.

During the pre-construction stage, a site investigation must take place. A site investigation takes place to discover if any steps need to be implemented on the job site. This is in order to get the site ready before the actual construction begins. This also includes any unforeseen conditions such as historical artifacts or environment problems. A soil test must be done to determine if the soil is in good condition to be built upon.

Due diligence when selecting contractors or subcontractors:

Financial failure of a contractor or a key supplier can be catastrophic to a construction project.

In order to reduce exposure to risks it is important to have a thorough grasp of both the capability and financial status of a prospective organization before appointing them.

Reliance on credit checks involving accounts filed with the Registrar of Companies (or Company House) can be useful, as can assessments of past track record, but they have their limitations. It is important to understand where the organization might be exposed to risks through commitments to or reliance on third parties, and how secure and well-resourced they are given the size of the proposed contract and their other commitments.

The following issues should be evaluated against the proposed scope of works to be undertaken:

History:

➢ Track record and appropriate references.

➢ Audited accounts.

➢ Tax returns.

Current Status:

➢ Main customers (each expressed as a percentage of total turnover to reveal where there may be significant dependencies).

➢ Current contracts in progress including project programmes and values (to assess where there may be significant overlaps that would put the organisation under pressure).

- Staff resources and CV'S of senior management.
- Organization chart.
- Current debt position with debt expiry dates.
- Current direct labour resource, including comparisons with previous years.
- Current subcontractors and suppliers.
- Details of current warrantees, guarantees, encumbrances, liens, performance or on-demand bonds or charges held by third parties.

Future position:

- Works in Pipeline (under tender or under negotiation).
- Current unaudited annual accounts in progress.
- Proposed subcontractors and suppliers.

Legal Position:

- Litigation, claims and other disputes in progress.
- Ownership of intellectual property, patents, licenses and certification required to carry out the work.
- Insurances in place.
- Partnerships or joint ventures with other organisations.
- Ownership of machinery and facilities required to execute the work.

Technical capability:

- Examination of past or current similar work.
- Competency, qualifications and certificates.
- Subcontractor and supplier capability.
- Building Information Modelling (BIM) or other software capability.
- Overall capacity to undertake the work.
- Disaster planning in the event of a catastrophic occurrence such as fire, earthquake, etc.
- Health, Safety and Environmental issues related capabilities.

Other indicators:

- The cost of performance bonds.
- Reputation in the insurance market.

- ➢ Time taken to pay subcontractors and suppliers.
- ➢ Bid/no-bid decision of the bidders.

Bid/No-Bid Decision:

A bidder's bid/no-bid decision also needs to be taken into consideration in the overall analysis of the bids. It has to be acknowledged that all costs of a bidding process is borne by the bidders, and only one bidder will eventually be awarded with the Works.

It is therefore, evident that a contractor who participates in many bids would not be offered a contract for all of them. As a general practice the strike rate is in the range of 5-10 percentage of the overall participation of a contracting company.

Therefore, a bidder who participates in any bid would in general include a cost of bidding for other (related or un-related) projects into a particular bid.

A contract administrator has therefore, to understand this concept of cost apportionment by a contracting company to better understand the costs allocation within any tendering process.

Mid-tender interview:

Mid-tender interviews may be offered to tenderers after they have been invited to participate in a tender and they have had time to consider the tender documentation, but before their tender has been submitted. Pre-tender interviews may have already been held, however on large or complex projects, mid-tender interviews can be beneficial both to the employer and to the tenderer as they not only allow for clarification of matters that might otherwise lead to an inaccurate tender being submitted, they can also give the employer an insights into potential problems or opportunities in the project as has been described within the tender documentation.

Issues that emerge during mid-tender interviews may be dealt with by issuing clarification notes or an addendum, however if significant changes are made to the tender documentation, it may also be necessary to extend the tender period to ensure that accurate tenders may be prepared for submission. Where clarification or additional information is given, it should be given in writing and made available to all tenderers. However this should not give away a particular contractor's proposed methodology, commercial proposals or programming advantages, which may have been divulged to the employer or its representatives in interviews. Such information must be treated as confidential.

Mid-tender interviews should be carefully managed so that tenderers are not made aware of who the other tenderers are, as this may impact on the competitiveness of the tenders they submit. This may include arrangements in relation to timing, car parking, waiting rooms and signing in books as well as the removal of any materials left at the interviews by the tenderers.

Pre-tender interview:

Following an assessment of the pre-qualification questionnaires submitted by prospective tenderers, an initial short-list of prospective tenders may be invited to attend pre-tender interviews before they are invited to tender.

A Pre-tender interview is an opportunity to:

> ➤ Assess the tenderers understanding of the commission.
> ➤ Assess the tenderers likely approach to the project.
> ➤ Assess the tenderers current workload.
> ➤ Assess the tenderers enthusiasm.
> ➤ Clarify ambiguities on either side.
> ➤ Verify that the proposed timescale for the tender process is achievable.
> ➤ Verify that the proposed nature of the tender process will obtain the best results.
> ➤ Price does not feature in the pre-tender interviews as tender documents have yet to be issued.

Discussions held during the interviews may result in changes being made to the tender documents or to the length of the tender period. It can be in the interest of an employer to make these changes as it ensures that they get the best value and most accurate tenders possible.

The interviews will normally be arranged by the contract administrator. They may include presentations by prospective tenderers, followed by questions from a small panel. The panel should agree in advance the nature of questions to be asked from each representative/consultant based on an assessment of their pre-qualification questionnaires. Answers may be scored and weighted, and sufficient time allowed between interviews for scores to be compiled and considered. This allows an objective appraisal to take place and also allows a consensus opinion to be formed, rather than having decisions driven by a single person.

Pre-tender interviews should be carefully managed so that tenderers are not made aware of who the other tenderers are, as this may impact on the competitiveness of the tenders they submit. This may include arrangements in relation to timing, waiting rooms and signing in books as well as the removal of any materials left by at the interview rooms by prospective tenderers.

If the pre-tender interviews reveal that one or more prospective candidates are unsuitable, the initial short list may be reduced and the remaining candidates invited to tender.

It may also be appropriate to hold mid-tender interviews to enhance the quality of tenders.

Tendering Stages:

A tendering may be single stage or two stages, depending on the contract strategy that needs to be followed, this needs to clarified in the tender documentation.

A single stage tendering is one wherein the commercial and technical submissions may be included within the same envelope and assessed as-such. The resultant is that the evaluations are faster and price of all bidders are simultaneously observed by the same evaluation committee.

Two stage tendering is the one where the technical proposal is evaluated before commencing with the opening of the commercial bid. The resultant is that commercial offer of only the bidders who pass the technical evaluation stage are opened by the commercial committee. Although this consumes a little more time when compared against the single stage tendering, the advantages outweighs this additional time consumption. As a result, almost all public tendering go for two stage tendering.

Two stage tenders would generally consist of the following forms:

Tender Submission Forms: Technical

- ➤ Tender Submission Letter
- ➤ Financial Statements
- ➤ Bidder's License, Registration Document and Power Of Attorney
- ➤ Statement of Compliance to Base Tender (and Alternate Tender)

- ➢ Statement of Non-Collusion
- ➢ Conflict of Interest
- ➢ Statement of Confidentiality and Copy Right Undertaking
- ➢ Bidder's Organisation, Ability to Respond and Experience
- ➢ Bidder's Authorised Representative(s) and Key Personnel
- ➢ Method Statement/Proposed Work Plan
- ➢ Plant and Equipment Schedule
- ➢ Manpower Table
- ➢ Contract Programme
- ➢ Quality Assurance
- ➢ Environmental, Health and Safety Plan
- ➢ List of Proposed Sub-Contactor(s)/Vendors for Major Purchase Orders
- ➢ Workload Statement
- ➢ Insurances
- ➢ References
- ➢ Any other information relevant to the project

Tender Submission Forms: Commercial

- ➢ Form of Tender
- ➢ Price Proposal for Base Tender (Mandatory)
- ➢ Price Proposal for Alternate Tender (Optional)

Chapter 5

Contract (Post-Award Stage)

Post-award stage is a distinct phase in a contracting process. This phase follows an Agreement (Signed and executed Contract) between the Contracting parties.

The Agreement between the contracting parties resulting into a valid Contract needs to include a detailed execution plan submission and its approval. It is recommended that the submission of break-down of the Bill of Quantities (BOQ) and the submission of estimated cash flow (facilitating time bound progress and realization of payment) is completed within the time stipulated within the Contract.

Interim valuations and final accounts need to be dealt with speed and accuracy. A Contract needs to have Procedures for issuing, valuing and managing variations to a Contract. Identifying extras and preparing star rates would avoid missed opportunities. Notification of claims protects and secures the contractual position of the parties. Claim preparation and negotiation prevents losses and maximizes profits. Sub-contractor financial and contractual management eliminates claims and maintains pre-determined margins.

Construction:

The construction stage begins with a pre-construction meeting brought together by the contract administrator and the consultant. The pre-construction meeting is meant to make decisions dealing with work hours, material storage, quality control, and site access. The next step is to move everything onto the construction site and set it all up.

At this stage, construction monitoring and supervision is of great importance to ensure that a project is completed on time and within budget, while meeting all relevant regulations and quality standards in accordance with the terms and conditions of the Contract.

Contract Administration Activities:

Generally the following activities are associated with the post-award stage:

- Facilitator of the kick-off meeting
- Interim applications and payment certificates
- Claims for additional payments, i.e.; prolongation cost, escalation, etc.
- Contractual correspondence
- Extension of time entitlement and its valuation
- Milestone achievement
- Dayworks

The Contract Administrator's role will generally include:

- Inviting and processing tenders
- Preparing contract documents for execution
- Administrating change control procedures
- Seeking instructions from the employer in relation to the contract
- Issuing instructions such as variations, or relating to prime cost (PC) sums or making good defects
- Considering claims
- Chairing construction progress meetings
- Preparing and issuing construction progress reports
- Coordinating and instructing site inspectors
- Agreeing commissioning and testing procedures
- Agreeing defects reporting procedures
- Ensuring that the project documentation is issued to the employer
- Issuing certificates of practical completion and interim certificates
- Collating and issuing schedules of defects
- Issuing certificate of making good of defects identified within Non Compliance Reports or the Snag List
- Issuing of the Final Certificate and Statement of Discharge

Advance Payment:

An advance payment is stipulated within a Contract to facilitate cash flow to the Contractor such that he is able to mobilize his resources at site in a timely manner. The Contractor therefore, needs to request for the advance payment as soon as the Contract is signed by both parties.

However, while the Employer fulfills his obligation to release the advance payment, the Contractor needs to help the Employers Contract Administrator by providing the necessary back-up documentations with the request for advance payment. Minimum requirements stipulated to release this payment is the requirement of a valid Bank Guarantee from an approved bank that shall be in accordance with the proforma included within the Contract documents.

The advance payment shall be progressively recovered from payments due under the Contract such that the entire amount is recovered at the time or before the final payment is made to the Contractor.

There also may be special circumstances where the entire payment or a portion thereof may have to be made upfront without any subsequent recovery or without an Advance Payment Bank Guarantee. This may be applicable for special types of requirements. This may be approved on a case-by-case basis by the Competent Authority for award considering the specific circumstances, and specific provisions needs to be made in the Contract to safeguard Employers interests.

If the employer agrees to make an advance payment (sometimes also referred to as a down payment) to a supplier, a bond may be required to secure the payment against default by the contractor. This is referred to as an Advance Payment Bond (APB), advance payment guarantee or advance stage payment.

Typically on a construction project an advanced payment bond will be required by the employer if the contractor requests advance payment to help them meet significant start up or procurement costs that may have to be incurred before construction begins i.e.; where the contractor has had to purchase high-value plant, equipment or materials specifically for the project. The bond will protect the client in the event that the contractor fails to fulfill its contractual obligations, for example if the contractor becomes insolvent.

An advance payment bond will normally be an on-demand bond, meaning that the bondsman (the bank) pays the amount of money set out in the bond immediately on demand, without any preconditions having to be met. This is as opposed to a conditional bond (or default bond) where the bondsman is only liable if it has been established that there has been a breach of contract.

Advance Payment Bonds must be very carefully drafted to set out the circumstances for payment and to make clear that they are on-demand bonds.

Interim Payments:

Interim payment is stipulated within a contract to facilitate cash flow for the continuity of the project works.

Provision of interim payments is an important provision of any contract. Generally, an interim payment is requested on a monthly basis and is paid to compensate the contractor for the works done until the month end, thereby maintaining a consistent cash flow.

Contractor is supposed to raise a payment application, together with all pertinent details (proof of progress, insurance certificates, material at site, sub-contractor payment applications, etc.) and submit to the Employer as prescribed within the Contract.

The Contract Administrator (with or without the help of Engineer, depending on the nature of contract) is expected to review the payment application for its merit & accuracy and advise the contractor to raise an invoice for the value that is payable within the stipulated time.

Thereafter, the Contractor shall raise a corresponding invoice that shall be processed by the Contracts Administrator in the form of a Payment Certificate that includes details of the contract and cumulative payments to the most recent Payment Certificate. A format a standard Payment Certificate is enclosed within the Chapter on Valuations (Chapter 6).

Interim certificates provide a mechanism for the employer to make payments to the contractor before the works are complete. In the construction industry, if a contract generally exceeds 45 days, a contractor is entitled to interim or stage payments.

Interim payments can be agreed in advance and paid at particular milestones, but they are more commonly regular payments the value of which is based on the value of work that has been completed (this is the actual value of the work completed, taking into account variations, claims, etc.). The amount of these payments is entered onto an interim certificate (generally valued by the cost consultant, perhaps having taken advice from the lead designer/consultant) and the employer must honour the certificate within the period stipulated within the contract.

If the employer intends to pay a different amount from that shown on the interim certificate, then they must give notice to the contractor of the amount they intend to pay and the basis for its calculation. This is also referred to as a Pay less Notice.

The value of interim certificates is the value of the work completed, less any amounts already paid, less retention. Half of this retention shall have to be released on certification of practical completion (Taking over Certificate) and the other half upon issue of the certificate of making good defects (Defects Liability Certificate).

Interim certificates should make clear the amount of retention and a statement should also be prepared showing retention for the nominated sub-contractors, if there are any. The contract may require that retention is kept in a separate bank account and that this is certified. In this case, the employer will generally keep any interest paid on the account.

There may be particular provision to include the value of particularly costly materials that the contractor has not yet delivered to site. This allows the contractor to order items in good time, without incurring unnecessary long-term expense, but does put the client at some risk if the contractor becomes insolvent.

On design and build projects, the amounts certified as payable may be based on a contract sum analysis. An important aspect of interim payments within construction contracts is the ability thereof to be adjusted within successive certificates. In other words, a recommendation for payment contained within an interim payment certificate is to facilitate cash flow and does not in any way confirm or certify the works that is being recommended to be paid to a contractor, and hence, the employer has the right to adjust an over-payment within the next interim payment certificate of the contractor.

Final Payment:

Final payment is the last payment that is done to the Contractor and signifies the completion of the Contract.

It is therefore, one of the most important activities that a Contract Administrator does while performing his duties. The accuracy of this particular payment is evident more so, due to the fact that there may not be any chance of correction of the Final Payment Certificate.

After completion of all obligations within the Contract, a Contractor is supposed to raise the final payment application, together with all pertinent details (copies of DLC, TOC, Final Statement, etc.) and submit to the Employer as prescribed within the Contract.

The Contract Administrator (with or without the help of Engineer) is expected to review the final payment application for its content, merit & accuracy and advise the Contractor to raise an invoice for the value that is payable within the stipulated time.

Thereafter, the Contractor shall raise a corresponding invoice that shall be processed by the Contracts Administrator in the form of a Final Payment Certificate that includes details of the Contract and the cumulative payments to date.

Construction contracts generally provide some mechanism for the final payment to be made to the contractor on completion of the works described in the contract. Generally this payment will be made at the end of the defects liability period providing that all patent defects have been rectified.

Preparing the final account is the process of calculating and agreeing any adjustments to the contract sum (the amount originally set out in the contract to be paid to the contractor for completion of the works) so that the amount of the final payment can be determined. The amount of the final payment is then set out in the final certificate (or final statement). It is possible for the final certificate to show that money is owed to the employer, rather than due to the contractor.

Construction contracts may in fact not require the preparation of a final account , although they generally do require the contractor to provide all documents necessary for the adjustment of the contract sum within a specified time, and set out the time scale for and consequences of issuing the final certificate.

The contract sum may need to be adjusted for a number of reasons, including:

➢ Variations
➢ Fluctuations
➢ Prime cost sums
➢ Provisional sums
➢ Payments to nominated sub-contractors or nominated suppliers

- Statutory fees
- Payments relating to the opening-up and testing of the works
- Loss and expense
- Liquidated and ascertained damages
- Contra claims imposed as a result of the contractor's operations (such as a third-party claim resulting from contractor negligence or contractual breach, for example, flooding a neighbour's property)
- The release of any balance of the retention

Agreeing the final account can be a complicated, time consuming and adversarial process, often resulting in disputes. The process can be made easier if adjustments to the contract sum are agreed as the project progresses rather than saving them up for the end. It is also beneficial if the employer's quantity surveyor and the contractor's quantity surveyor work together on drafts of the final account before agreement it sought. It is preferable that a draft copy of the final account is signed off by the contractor as an "in full and final settlement" prior to issue.

Agreement of the final account will allow the contract administrator to issue the final certificate. The final certificate is conclusive that all patent defects have been remedied, all adjustments to the contract sum have been agreed and all claims settled. Latent defects may still become apparent after completion of the contract and these may give rise to action for damages, for breach of contract or negligence.

Where proceedings have begun in relation to a dispute, the conclusiveness of the final certificate is subject to the findings of those proceedings.

In addition, the final certificate itself can be disputed (usually within 28 days). Adjudication, arbitration or other alternate dispute resolution procedures may then be necessary to resolve the dispute. The final certificate is then only conclusive in relation to matters that are not disputed.

If the employer intends to pay a different amount from that shown on the certificate, they must give notice to the contractor of the amount they intend to pay and the basis for its calculation

Variations:

FIDIC Conditions of Contract defines Variation as any change to the Works, which is instructed or approved as a variation under clause "Variations and Adjustments".

Variations to an existing Contract may come about as a result of one or more of the below mentioned factors:

- ➢ Revision to Original Plans and Specifications
- ➢ Unforeseen Field Conditions
- ➢ Plan Deficiency
- ➢ Specification Conflict or Ambiguity
- ➢ Industry Regulations
- ➢ Contractor Proposed Change
- ➢ Execution of Provisional Sums
- ➢ Stakeholder Changes
- ➢ Extra work or unanticipated need
- ➢ Design Criteria Changes
- ➢ Works executed through Day Work rates

Processing of Variations is one of the important tasks of a Contract Administrator and the details are discussed in a separate chapter dedicated to this topic.

Variation within a construction contract:

A variation (sometimes also referred to as a variation instruction or variation order) is an alteration to the scope of works in a construction contract in the form of an addition, substitution or omission from the original scope of works.

Almost all construction projects vary from the original design, scope and definition. Whether small or large, construction projects will have inevitably departs from the original tender design, specifications and drawings prepared by the design team. This can be because of technological advancement, statutory changes or enforcement, change in conditions, geological anomalies, non-availability of specified materials or simply because of the continued development of the design after the contract has been awarded. In large civil engineering projects variations can be very significant, whereas on small building contracts they may be relatively minor.

Variations may include:

- ➢ Alterations to the design
- ➢ Alterations to quantities

➢ Alterations to quality

➢ Alterations to working conditions

➢ Alterations to the sequence of work

➢ Variations may also be deemed to occur if the contract documents do not properly describe the works actually required.

Variations may not (without an expressed consent of both parties):

➢ Change the fundamental nature of the works

➢ Omit work so that it can be carried out by another contractor

➢ Be instructed after practical completion

➢ Require the contractor to carry out work that was the subject of a prime cost sum

➢ In legal terms, a variation is an agreement supported by consideration to alter some terms of the contract. No power to order variation is implied. Hence there should be express terms in contracts which give the power to instruct variations. In the absence of express terms in the contract the contractor may reject instructions for variations without giving rise to any legal consequences.

Standard forms of contract generally make express provisions for the contract administrator (generally the architect or engineer) to instruct variations. Such provisions enable the continued, smooth administration of the works without the need for another contract. Variation instructions must be clear as to what is and is not included, and may propose the method of valuation.

Valuation of Variations:

Variations may give rise to additions or deductions from the contract sum. The valuation of variations may include not just the work which the variation instruction describes, but other expenses that may result from the variation, such as the impact on other aspects of the works. Variations most likely require adjustment of the completion date. However, it may also be possible that this is not always the case.

Variations may be valued by:

➢ An Agreement between the contractor and the employer

➢ The cost consultant

> ➤ A variation quotation prepared by the contractor and accepted by the employer

> ➤ By some other method agreed by the contractor and the employer

> ➤ Valuations of variations are often based on the rates and prices provided by the contractor in their tender, provided the work is of a similar nature and carried out in similar conditions.

> ➤ By using the concept of star rates i.e.; using the rates contained with the contract to build the rates for works involved for a varied work resulting in the determination of a fair and reasonable cost of variation

In some contracts, when rates are applied to the valuation of variations, the contractor is not able to claim for additional payments in relation to profits and overheads.

If similar types of works to those instructed by a variation cannot be found in the drawings, specification or bills of quantities, a fair valuation of the contractor's direct costs, overheads and profit is necessary. Thus becoming a very important task of the contracts administrator to take care of this aspect. Any deviation from a fair price will render a party to the agreement in an adverse situation. If the variation and associated cots are substantial, this issue can also lead to a major dispute.

However, there are contract conditions that differ from the approach discussed above. Certain contracts may recommend assessment of compensation events on their effect on a defined cost plus a fee. This approach is different from our above discussion wherein variations are valued using the rates and prices in the contract as a basis.

Variation: A source of conflict:

Conflict may arise when work is not mentioned in the bills of quantities, drawings or specifications. Generally, this silence does not mean the contractor has an automatic right to claim for extra payment. The employer is not bound to pay for things that a reasonable contractor must have understood were to be done but which happen to be omitted from the bills of quantities. Where there are items that, whilst they are not expressly mentioned, are nonetheless required in order to complete the works the contractor should have included them in their price. The bills of quantities and specification do not necessarily have to include for each and every small works that has to be done by the contractor. For example in fixing GRC façades it is necessary to have steel supports, and a reasonable experienced contractor must make provision for this in the contract price. Unless expressly excluded, such supports are not paid for as a variation.

Conflict can also arise when a sub-contractor qualifies (after an Agreement has been in-place) that "Supply & Fixing of Door is included" but "Supply & Fixing of Ironmongery is excluded". A reasonable sub-contractor should foresee that a door cannot be fixed without hinges (which is a part of the ironmongery), so even if ironmongery is excluded, the sub-contractor cannot expect a variation for any of the items required to fix the doors.

Also under the pretext of variation, the contract administrator cannot change the nature of works. For example, if the contract provides for secant pile shoring, they cannot ask for diaphragm wall shoring as it will entirely change the nature of the work. Further, if the contract administrator omits work from contractor's scope, such an omission must be genuine, i.e.; the work omitted must be omitted from the contract entirely, it cannot be used to take work away from the contractor to give it to another.. Similarly, the contract administrator is not empowered to order variations to a contractor if the contracted works are proving too difficult or expensive for them.

A sound contract administrator is expected to adhere to a sound and reasonable approach to his job without being partial to a particular party within a Contact.

Limitation or putting a cap to variations:

FIDIC forms of contract put limitations on variations that can be instructed. If the value of the contract increases or decreases by more than 15% of the net contract sum (excluding provisional sums and day works), the contract administrator can add or deduct from the contract sum a determined value upon consultation with the contractor, having due regard to their site expenses and other general overheads. It needs to be noted that this 15% increase or decrease is not for a single item of work, but the total contract sum at completion.

Other forms of contract may have different limitations and hence a contracts administrator needs to act in accordance to his referenced contract.

Conclusion:

Variations may very often be a source of dispute (either in the valuation of the variation or to agreeing whether part of the works constitutes a variation at all, i.e.; in form or in quantity) and may cost a lot of time and money during the course of a contract. Whilst some variations are unavoidable, it is wise to minimize potential variations and subsequent claims by ensuring that uncertainties are eliminated before awarding the contract. Therefore, and while we may say that variations are necessary evil, we can minimize them by adhering to the following good practices:

- ➤ Thorough site investigations and condition surveys
- ➤ Ensuring that the project brief is comprehensive and is supported by stakeholders
- ➤ Ensuring that the legislative requirements are properly integrated into the project
- ➤ Ensuring that risks are properly identified
- ➤ Ensuring that designs are properly coordinated before the tender
- ➤ Ensuring the contract is unambiguous and explicit
- ➤ Ensuring the contractor's rates are clear
- ➤ Preparing concise drawings, bills of quantities and specifications, providing for all situations which are reasonably foreseeable

Claims:

A Claim may be defined as a legitimate request for additional compensation (cost and/or time) on account of a change in the terms of the contract.

A Claim may arise under any form of construction contract. There are specific steps to be followed in dealing with a claim situation and is addressed separately in Chapter No. 8 of this book. A Contract Administrator plays a very pivotal role in an effective management of a Claim situation.

Claims may comprise costs resulting from disruption to the works or from delays to the works (prolongation).

The contractor must give written notice of a claim as soon as it becomes reasonably apparent that the regular progress of the works is being materially affected. This need not necessarily result in a delay to the completion date, and so claims for loss and expense and claims for extensions of time do not necessarily always run together.

It is worth noting that claims are restricted to 'direct' *loss and expense* and so the 'consequential losses' (i.e.; lost or missed production) are generally excluded. Direct losses are those that flow naturally from the breach of contract. There is disparity between contract types about whether items such as head office overheads can be included in claims for loss and expense. While there may be instances wherein such claims would have been allowed, this is generally not the norm. If there are specific consequential losses which the parties to the contract wish to exclude, it may be prudent to state these explicitly within the contract.

Guarantees

Performance Bank Guarantee:

It is a good practice to have the provision of Performance Bank Guarantee from a recognized and approved bank for a certain percentage of the Contract value from the Contractor. Generally this is kept at around 10% of the Contract value, but increased when there is a corresponding increase in the Contract value due to variations to the contract, in order to maintain the value at around the originally envisage 10%.

Parent Company Guarantee:

Contractor need to provide Parent Company Guarantee for high value Engineering, Projects & Construction (EPC) Contracts or Construction Contracts, if the financial capability of a potential Contractor has been assessed on the basis of the financial strength of its parent company.

Collateral Warranties:

Collateral Warranties takes its place due to the doctrine of *Privity* of Contract, which states that only the parties to a contract can sue on that particular contract. Privity of contract, therefore almost always causes the problem for an affected third party, who is not a party to the contract (third party is denied an opportunity to sue another party to enforce an obligation towards the former).

One way of creating Privity of Contract where it would not normally arise is by Collateral Warranties. These documents should mirror the main contract. In other words, when an employer enters into a contract with a main contractor, he requires that the main contractor also enters into a collateral contract for the benefit of the future purchaser of the building. The same exercise can be carried out to create contractual links between a future purchaser and the design team, the employer and any subcontractors, and so on.

In an instance, a construction contract was between a bank and a contractor. After a while, the bank transferred the property to another owner. Now if it so happens that the building is found to be defective, and unless there is a Collateral Warranty, the new owner of the building cannot sue the bank or the contractor (provided that the bank had not warranted to the condition of the premises when it was transferred to the new owner). Also, since the bank had not suffered any loss, so technically it could not recover more than the nominal compensation.

In a similar situation arising in UK resulted in the formulation of the Contracts (Rights of Third Parties) Act 1999 which in various forms are under use in other countries too. The following are the general provisions of the Act:

Right of Third Party to enforce a term of the contract: The promisor is the party to the contract against whom the term is enforceable by the third party. The promisee is the party to the contract by whom the term is enforceable against the promisor.

Variation and rescission of contract: The parties to a contract cannot by agreement rescind the contract or vary it so as to extinguish or alter the third party's rights, without the third party's consent, unless they have reserved the right to do so in the contract. Also, the variation clauses in construction contracts vary the Works, not the Contract, so they can still operate without consent being required.

Defences available to the promisor: This section allows the promisor to rely on any defence or set-off that would have been available had the claim been by the promisee (not the third party).

Enforcement by the promisee: This section preserves the rights of the promisee against the promisor, i.e.; the original parties to the contract.

Protection from double liability: Where the promisor has compensated the promisee for the breach because they have suffered due to the fact that they have made good a loss to the third party, then such payment will be taken into account when any claim is brought by the third party.

It is noted that there are exceptions to this act and that this act does not apply to contracts such as: Negotiable Instruments, between a company and its members, Employment contracts and Carriage of goods by sea, road, rail or air.

Supplementary provisions relating to third parties: The act does not affect any other remedies that might be available to the third party. The third party cannot use Unfair Contract Terms. The third party is not regarded as a party to the contract for the purposes of any other legislation.

Arbitration Provisions: The third party will be treated as a party to any arbitration agreement contained in the contract which contains the term that they are attempting to enforce for their benefit.

In cases that there is a clear intention of the contracting parties not to confer any benefits to the third parties, it must be very clearly spelled out in the contract documents.

Therefore, Contracts (Rights of Third Parties) Act tends to cater to the requirements of a Collateral Warranty by extending the risk coverage to the third parties too (who are not the contracting parties) under a breach of contract.

Insurances:

Provision of insurances is included in almost all modern day Contracts, and is rightly done to safeguard against the foreseen and un-foreseen risks associated with the complexities associated in construction contracts.

A Contract needs to make sure that an adequate provision of insurance is built within the Contract, and Contract Administrator shall ensure that all insurances are provided for by the Contractor and kept up-to-date at all times.

Certain insurances may also be Employer provided. Therefore, the Contract Administrator shall be aware of these requirements and ensure that these too are kept updated at all times.

Some of the common types of insurance used within the construction industry are as follows:

➢ Insurance of Works and Contractor's Equipment
➢ Professional indemnity (PI) insurance
➢ Accident or injury to Workmen
➢ Automobile Liability and Other insurance
➢ Third Party Liability

Collateral warranties:

Collateral warranties are agreements which are associated with another 'primary' contract. They provide for a duty of care to be extended by one of the contracting parties to a third party who is not party to the original contract.

They came into being as a result of the courts deciding that defects in buildings were not recoverable in tort (an infringement of right of a party), as they were an economic loss which was only recoverable through a contractual relationship. Collateral warranties therefore create direct contractual relationships between parties that would not otherwise exist.

A typical example would be where an architect of a new office development owes a duty of care to an occupier of the development in so far as any subsequent defects which may arise are concerned. Privity of contract (relation between parties in a contract that allows them to sue each-other but prevents others from doing so) rules would prevent any liability arising between the architect and occupier without the existence of a collateral warranty.

There may also be a contractual requirement for parties to obtain further warranties, for example there may be an obligation for the main contractor to obtain collateral warranties from sub-contractors.

Collateral warranties may include 'step-in' rights allowing the beneficiary to step-into the role of the employer. This can be important, for example to banks providing funding for a project, enabling them to ensure that the project is completed if the employer becomes insolvent.

There are a number of standard forms of collateral warranty, however there can be some dispute about their specific terms, with employers often claiming that industry standard warranties favour contractors and designers. There can also be difficulties with onerous terms that designers or contractors are unable to agree to as their insurers will not provide cover. As a consequence many collateral warranties are bespoke.

One of the disadvantages of collateral warranties is the difficulty in actually completing them. On large projects with many consultants and sub-contractors and multiple occupants, there can be a great number of warranties. The Contracts (Rights of Third Parties) Act can offer a way around this difficulty by allowing the primary contracts to confer benefits upon third parties even though they are not a party to that contract.

Retention:

It is not mandatory to have retention clauses in every Contract. However, a retention clause may be included in high value Contracts to safeguard against possible errors in estimating status of completion and/or hidden defects in works or services. Retention may either be in the form of a Retention Bank Guarantee or physical retention from invoices.

Liquidated Damages:

Liquidated Damages clauses shall be written into Contracts where delay in delivery/completion is likely to cause material damage to the Employer (Time is of the Essence Clause). The appropriate rate of liquidated damages may vary. However, each situation needs to be reasonable and based on expectation of possible losses.

As liquidated damages are not a penalty, they must have been based on a genuine calculation of damages when they were set. If they are not genuine, they may be considered a penalty by the courts and so will be unenforceable

Liquidated damages are not penalties, they are pre-determined damages set at the time that a contract is entered into, based on a calculation of the actual loss the client is likely to incur if the contractor fails to meet the completion date. They might include, rent on temporary accommodation, removal costs, extra running costs and so on. They are generally set as a fixed daily or weekly sum. There could very well be more complicated formulae where the works are phased, or where there will be partial possession. It is important that the method of calculation is formally documented.

It is a recommended practice that a cap to the limit of Liquidated damages is expressed within the Contract.

Communication with Contractors:

It is highly recommended to have all communications with the Contractor in a formal manner, written and in the name of the Authorized Representative identified within the Contract. Email communications may also be used for expediting purposes. Exceptions to this policy may be permitted depending on the specific circumstances of the Contract.

However, as a general rule it needs to be emphasized that communication is the key to the success of a Contract and hence the cardinal rule is the all relevant requests, instructions, approvals or consents needs to be traceable.

Relationship with Contractors:

Responsibility of Contract Administration needs to be assigned to capable and responsible personnel of the Employer organization, who shall ensure Contractors' compliance with the terms of the Contract.

It shall also be necessary to ensure timely performance by the Employer's personnel of its obligations under the Contract such as approval of Contractor's submittals and payment of Contractor's invoices.

Termination of Contract:

It is a good practice for all Contracts to include provisions for termination of the Contract, both for convenience as well as for default (by both parties). A general rule is that this clause needs to facilitate and be in the best interest of the contracting parties.

A Contract shall not be terminated without following the contractual notification requirements and shall be subject to endorsement by the Competent Authority.

Not all construction projects end happily, and sometimes it's best for the owner and contractor to part-company. But when a contractor's contract is terminated, a project can suffer delays and cost overruns. Careful planning, however, can soften the effects of termination. Before terminating a contractor's contract, consider and re-consider the following six questions:

1. Terminate for convenience or for cause

2. Does the Bond have any Pre-Termination requirements

3. Is the Contract being closed out properly

4. Have all claims been preserved

5. What does the project designer think/Designer's view

6. Prepared for Litigation

Terminate for convenience or for cause:

Many construction contracts allow the owner to terminate the contract for its convenience: in other words, without needing to find the contractor in default. Terminating for convenience can be an attractive option, but there are potential downsides.

For example, some standard contract forms require an owner that terminates for convenience to pay profit on unperformed work, so the owner could wind up paying both the terminated contractor and its replacement to complete the project. The employer, therefore needs to carefully compare the pros and cons of terminating for convenience and for cause, and determine which option best fits the circumstances.

A few important questions that need to be asked at this stage would be:

Does the Bond have any Pre-Termination Requirement?

It's common for employers to purchase performance bonds in which a surety stands behind the contractor's work. If there is a performance bond for the project, the employer should carefully review the bond's requirements. Performance bonds sometimes contain steps that an employer must take before terminating the contractor's contract.

Is the Contract being closed out properly?

Construction contracts often contain detailed terms for wrapping up the contract, and the employer should review these terms and ensure compliance. For example, the contract may require the terminated contractor to assign its subcontracts to the employer, or to protect and preserve its work.

At the same time, the contract may require the employer to take certain actions upon termination; for example, when terminating for convenience, the employer may have to pay the contractor within a set number of days. Proper close-out should help avoid issues from lingering after termination.

Have all claims been preserved?

The employer should assess its claims against the terminated contractor and take actions to preserve them. For example, to help avoid a fight over what work the terminated contractor is responsible for, the employer should document the status of the work:including all known defects:before the replacement contractor takes over.

Also, the replacement contractor should document the costs for correcting defective work and performing work outside of the terminated contractor's scope of work:for example, by using separate cost codes.

These steps won't stop an argument over responsibility for work or how much the terminated contractor is owed, but they should make it easier for the owner to assert its claims and defend against the terminated contractor's.

What does the project designer and consultant think?

An employer who determines that the contractor's work has defects should consider asking the project designer for an assessment. It is highlighted that the project designer would most likely play a vital role in any future litigation between the employer and contractor.

Prepared for litigation?

If it's possible that termination will lead to litigation, there are other questions to consider. How are disputes to be resolved under the contract? Does a selected lawyer have the right experience for the job? Do experts need to be hired? Is there understanding of the risks involved in pursuing claims or defending against the contractor's? If the employer and contractor do end up in litigation, the employer should not be caught flat-footed.

No matter what the situation, terminating a contract can be a difficult and risky decision. Proper preparation, though, can reduce the risks and losses of termination.

Contract Close-out

A Contract that is physically complete and administratively closed is termed as a closed Contract.

Contract closeout begins when the Contract has been physically completed, i.e., all services have been performed and products delivered. Closeout is completed when all administrative actions have been completed, all disputes settled, and final payment has been made.

Contract Closeout requires close coordination between various departments of Employers office and the Contractor. Contract closeout is a very important aspect of Contract Administration.

Generally full and complete performance is required to discharge contractual obligations. However, in a construction contact the purpose of signifying completion is not only to release the Contractor, but to permit the Employer in taking possession of the Works and to allow the Contractor to leave the site.

Discharge of Contracts:

Discharge is a general term for release of contractual obligations. Contracts do not end automatically, unless by becoming statute barred. Once a contract is discharged neither party can rely on its terms. They can only enforce whatever rights may arise from the discharge itself.

Discharge of a contract is brought about in the following four ways:

- ➢ If the parties complete all obligations under the contract (discharge by performance)
- ➢ If the performance becomes impossible to achieve (frustrated)
- ➢ Serious breach by one party
- ➢ One party commits breach and the other party recovers damages in satisfaction of the failed performance.

Chapter 6

<u>Valuations</u>

A Contract generally provides for a tangible product to the Employer in return for a consideration to the Contractor. Furthermore, there is a specified duration (Contract Term) within which the Contract Works are expected to be completed. Contracts within the construction industry may have term ranging from a few days to a few years. It is therefore a necessity that the overall consideration to be paid to the Contractor is split into multiple payments.

Generally (and specifically in UK the Housing Grants, Construction and Regeneration Act 1996 (HGCRA 1996)) it is required that for all contracts with a duration exceeding 45 days, interim payments shall be paid and contracts with duration of 45 or fewer days can be paid as one lump sum payment.

One of the important observations of most modern-day construction projects are that they are of high value involving multiple agencies and runs into millions of dollars. It is therefore, a requirement that a Contract shall include for regular payments to the Contractor to maintain steady cash flow in accordance with the progress or Work at site. Optimum payment mechanism is one that takes best care of the interests of both the Employer and the Contractor at any point of the Contract Term.

Periodic payments are therefore an essential part of all modern day contracts. These payments assist a contractor in overcoming their cash flow interruptions and provide for a self-financing support in respect of the main contractor's own commitments to the sub-contractors and suppliers, besides of course taking care of his own overhead costs and other direct and indirect expenses of every business entity.

Regular payments are therefore a necessity in all contracts (lump sum as well as re-measured contracts). Holding regular payments of a contractor shall be viewed as a breach of contract by the Employer.

It is generally required that all construction contracts include payment provisions which are at least equal to the following:

- Payment by installments for all contracts of more than 45 days duration

- The contractor should be informed of the amount to be paid, how it was calculated and when it is due for payment

- The contractor to be given notice if the employer intends to withhold any payment

- The contractor to have right to suspend performance of the contract if payment is not made within a specified period

- Under this act, 'pay when paid' types of clauses are declared "unenforceable"

The concept of Interim Payments for construction contracts is rooted in history. Accuracy in interim valuation cannot be over-emphasized and is essential from both the employer's and the contractor's viewpoint:

- If there is overvaluation, an employer may lose the over value is a contractor becomes insolvent during the progress of the work.

- If there is undervaluation, the strain on a contractor's limited capital reserves may prevent the contractor from proceeding efficiently, thus inducing a state of insolvency. Important aspect to bear in mind here is that a contractor's cash flow needs to be maintained for the employers works too.

If an employer fails in his duty to honour interim certificates within the stipulated time frame of the Contract, most standard forms of contracts provide a mechanism whereby the contractor can either exercise his statutory right to suspend performance or terminate his employment, provided that he follows the appropriate procedure (i.e.; specific clauses mentioned within the Contract Conditions).

A sound payment terms within a contract document needs to address the following recommended practice (these provisions are used widely across many Forms of Contract used around the world):

- Where the contract duration is more than 45 days, the contract must provide for payments by installments.

- The contracting parties are free to agree payment amounts and intervals.

- There must be an adequate mechanism for determining what is due and when and the final date for payment of sums of money that is due.

> The parties are free to agree the period between the due date for payment and the final date for payment.

> The payer must issue a notice stating the amount to be paid and how it was calculated within five days of the date of payment.

> The payer cannot withhold payment of an amount due beyond the final date for the payment unless an effective notice of intention to withhold payment has been served. The notice must specify the grounds for withholding and the amounts in question. The parties are free to agree how long before the final date for payment the payer can serve a notice of intention to withhold payment.

> If the payee is not paid in full by the final date for payment and no effective notice of intention to withhold payment has been served, the payee can suspend performance. The right to suspend performance cannot be exercised without first giving the defaulting payer at least seven (7) day notice of intention to suspend performance.

Mediation is the preferred route to any dispute resolution as per HGCRA 1996 and this approach has been recommended in almost all partnering contracts. However, a need for adjudication may arise due to a breach to the contract by either of the contracting parties. In matters concerning payments as we saw above, route to mediation takes a back seat if an employer dies not hour interim payment certificates in time without notifying the contractor or if a contractor intends to overvalue and demand that to be paid by the client.

Breach may be client (employer) driven or contractor driven. The following are some common examples of breach by the Employer:

> Failure to give possession of the site to the contractor.

> Wrongful ejection the contractor from the site.

> Non-payment of monies due to the contractor.

> Withholding payments beyond the due time period with a notice conveying employer's intention to do so.

> Deliberate hindrances to contractor's contractual works.

The following are some common examples of breach by a Contractor:

> Unjustified abandonment or suspension of works.

> Defective works.

> Failure to comply with health and safety requirements.

➢ Delay to an extent that it harms employer's interest.

Whether or not an employer's or contractor's breach of contract is sufficiently serious to justify termination by the employer is always a question of facts and degree.

When all means to sort out disputes by Mediation is lost, one may resort to Adjudication. It is a summary process by which disputes between parties to a contract are decided by a third party. In most circumstances, the decision is binding on the parties if and until the matter is settled by legal proceedings, arbitration or agreement.

Advance Payment:

An advance payment is stipulated within a Contract to facilitate cash flow to the Contractor such that he is able to mobilize his resources at site in a timely manner. The Contractor therefore, needs to request for the advance payment as soon as the Contract is signed by both parties.

However, while the Employer fulfills his obligation to release the advance payment, the Contractor needs to help the Employers Contract Administrator by providing the necessary back-up documentations with the request for advance payment. Minimum requirements stipulated to release this payment is the requirement of a valid Bank Guarantee for an approved bank that shall be in accordance with the proforma included within the Contract documents.

The advance payment shall be progressively recovered from payments due under the Contract such that the entire amount is recovered at the time or before the final payment is made to the Contractor.

There also may be special circumstances where the entire payment or a portion thereof may have to be made upfront without any subsequent recovery or without an Advance Payment Bank Guarantee. This may be applicable for special types of requirements. This may be approved on a case-by-case basis by the Competent Authority for award considering the specific circumstances, and specific provisions needs to be made in the Contract to safeguard Employers interests.

Interim Payments:

Interim payment is stipulated within a contract to facilitate cash flow for the continuity of the project works.

Provision of interim payments is an important provision of any contract. Generally, an interim payment is requested on a monthly basis and is paid to compensate the contractor for the works done until the month end, thereby maintaining a consistent cash flow.

Contractor is supposed to raise a payment application, together with all pertinent details (proof of progress, insurance certificates, material at site, sub-contractor payment applications, etc.) and submit to the Employer as prescribed within the Contract.

The Contract Administrator (with or without the help of Engineer, depending on the nature of contract) is expected to review the payment application for its merit & accuracy and advise the contractor to raise an invoice for the value that is payable within the stipulated time.

Thereafter, the Contractor shall raise a corresponding invoice that shall be processed by the Contracts Administrator in the form of a Payment Certificate that includes details of the contract and cumulative payments to the most recent Payment Certificate. A format a standard Payment Certificate is enclosed herewith.

The elements to be included within an interim certificate can be summarized as below:

- Preliminaries (time related & method related charges)
- Measured works
- Valuation of variations
- Measurement for provisional items, prime cost (PC) sums and provisional quantities
- Valuation of nominated subcontractors and suppliers
- Unfixed material on site, and where allowable, materials off site (with or without a vesting certificate and insurances)
- Fluctuations, where allowed for in a contract

Final Payment:

Final payment is the last payment that is done to the Contractor and signifies the completion of the Contract.

It is therefore, one of the most important activities that a Contract Administrator does while performing his duties. The accuracy of this particular payment is evident more so, due to the fact that there may not be any chance of correction of the Final Payment Certificate.

After completion of all obligations within the Contract, a Contractor is supposed to raise the final payment application, together with all pertinent details (copies of DLC, TOC, Final Statement, etc.) and submit to the Employer as prescribed within the Contract.

The Contract Administrator (with or without the help of Engineer) is expected to review the final payment application for its content, merit & accuracy and advise the Contractor to raise an invoice for the value that is payable within the stipulated time.

Thereafter, the Contractor shall raise a corresponding invoice that shall be processed by the Contracts Administrator in the form of a Final Payment Certificate that includes details of the Contract and the cumulative payments to date.

Payments of Retention Money:

Generally all construction contacts make provision for the retention of a fixed percentage (5% to 10% of every pay-out) from all interim payments to the contractor. Monies so retained are released in two different stages. One-half of the retention is released upon the issue of the Taking-Over Certificate (TOC).

The second half of the retention money is released upon the expiration of the Defects Liability Period for the Works, as confirmed by the issuance of the Defects Liability Certificate (DLC).

Correction of Certificates:

The Engineer may by any Interim Payment Certificate make any correction or modification in any previous Interim Payment Certificate which shall have been issued by him and shall have authority to omit or reduce the value of such work in any Interim Payment Certificate.

Final Statement:

After the receipt of Defects Liability Certificate (DLC), the Contractor shall prepare and submit to the Employer a draft final statement with supporting documents showing in detail:

> ➤ the value of all work done in accordance with the Contract, and

> ➤ all other sum of money that the Contractor considers to be due to him under the Contract or otherwise.

If the Employer disagrees with or cannot verify any part of the draft final statement, the Contractor shall submit such further information as the Employer may reasonably require and shall make such changes in the draft as may be agreed between them. Thereafter, the Contractor shall prepare and submit the final statement as agreed.

Discharge:

Upon submission of the Final Statement, the Contractor shall also give to the Employer, a written discharge confirming that the total of the Final Statement represents full and final settlement of all monies due to the Contractor arising out of or in respect of the Contract (provided that such discharge shall become effective only after payment due under the Final Payment Certificate).

Time for Payment:

The amount due to the Contractor under an Advance Payment Certificate, Interim Payment Certificate or the Final Payment Certificate needs to be paid by the Employer within the time stipulated within the Contract (normally expressed within the Particular or General Conditions).

Approval only by Defects Liability Certificate:

Defects Liability Certificate (DLC) is the only document that shall signify the completion and approval of the contracted Scope of Works.

Unfulfilled Obligations:

Generally within all construction contracts, Defects Liability Certificate is the document that signify the contract completion, hence all unfulfilled obligations under the provisions of the Contract prior to the issue of the Defects Liability Certificate, shall be deemed to remain in force between the parties to the Contract.

Payment Certificate (PC)			
			PC No.:
Contract No.:		Contract Type:	
Contract Reference:		Payment Type:	
Project Reference:		Period Ending:	
Employer:		Invoice No.:	
Contractor:		Invoice Date:	
Work Description:		Interim/Final:	
	AED		
Contract Value:		Progress in %:	
Provisional Sums:		Contract:	
Dayworks:		Variations:	
Contingencies:			
Effective Contract Value:		Commencement Date:	
Est. Variations/Claims:		Completion Date:	
Est. Final Contract Value:		Revised Completion Date:	
Performance Bond:		XXX Insurance Details:	
Advance payment Bond:		XXX Insurance Details:	
XXX Insurance Details:		XXX Insurance Details:	
This certificate for payment is issued under the terms of the above referenced Contract:			
(Appendices):		AED	AED
Cumulative value of work done			
Value of Material On-Site			
Approved Variations			
Dayworks			
Claims (approved in principle)			
Sub Total: (Total Work to Date)			
Advance Payment (outstanding)			
Sub Total: (Gross Amount to Date)			
Deduct:			
Retention			
Liquidated Damages/Penalties			
Other Deductions			

Sub Total: (Payment Application)		
Previous Payment Certified		
Amount to be Paid in this Certificate		
Authorized Signatory	Signed	Date
Authorized Signatory	Signed	Date

Employer
Engineer

Consultant
Contractor

Contract No
Contract

Interim Payment Application No
Period Ending

CUMULATIVE VALUE OF WORK DONE

Bill No.	Description	Contract Ammount (AED)	Value of Work done (AED)			Percentage to Date
			Previous	This Month	Cumulative	
	Bill Total					
Add	Contingency Allowance					
	Sub-Total					
Add/Delete	Adjustment Items					
	Total					

Total Contract Value
Total Certified to Interim Payment Certificate No.

Consultant/Engineer's Representative
Date

Engineer
Date

Employer
Engineer

Consultant
Contractor

Contract No
Contract

Interim Payment Application No
Period Ending

Original Contract Value
Current Contract Value

Estimated Final Contract Value

CONTRACT CERTIFICATE LEDGER

Certificate No.	Date Certified	Value of Work Done	Value of Advanced Payment	Gross Valuation	Retention	Net Valuation Cumulative	Less Liq. Damages or Other Deductions	Less Previous Certified Amount	Net Payment on This Certificate	Cumulative Amount	Remarks

Consultant/Engineer's Representative
Date

Engineer
Date

Employer
Engineer

Consultant
Contractor

Contract No.
Contract

Interim Payment Application No.
Period Ending

VALUE OF MATERIALS ON SITE (SUMMARY)

BOQ No.	Description	Unit	Material Status (Monthly)					Rate (AED)	Amount (AED)	Remarks
			Previous	This Month	To Date	Qty. Used	Balance Qty.			
Total Value of Material										
____ % Value of Materials carried to Interim Payment Certificate No. (Percentage as indicated in Appendix to Contract)										

Consultant/Engineer's Representative
Date

Engineer
Date

Employer
Engineer

Consultant
Contractor

Contract No.
Contract

Interim Payment Application No.
Period Ending

VARIATIONS

VR No.	VO No.	Description	Variation Instruction Ref.	Estimated Amount (AED)	Value of Work Done (AED)			Remarks
					Previous	This Month	Cumulative	
		Total carried to Interim Payment Certificate No.						

Consultant/Engineer's Representative
Date

Engineer
Date

Employer
Engineer

Consultant
Contractor

Contract No
Contract

Interim Payment Application No
Period Ending

DAY WORKS

S.No.	Description	Instruction Reference	Date	Estimated Amount	Amount Certified (AED)		
					Previous	This Month	Cumulative
Day works carried to Interim Payment Certificate No							

Consultant/Engineer's Representative
Date

Engineer
Date

Employer
Engineer

Consultant
Contractor

Contract No
Contract

Interim Payment Application No
Period Ending

CLAIMS

S.No.	Description	Claimed by Contractor		Recommended by Consultant		Recommended by Project Manager		Approved by SCADIA		Remarks
		Amount (AED)	Time	Amount (AED)	Time	Amount (AED)	Time	Amount (AED)	Time	
Total carried to Interim Payment Certificate No										

Consultant/Engineer's Representative
Date

Engineer
Date

Employer
Engineer

Contract No
Contract

Consultant
Contractor

Interim Payment Application No
Period Ending

Amount of Advance Payment
Recovery Method: Fixed Monthly Deduction or
Percentage of Monthly Value Deduction

Advance Payment Bond Details
Bank
Bond Ref No
Date
Amount

ADVANCE PAYMENT / RECOVERY AND REMAINING AMOUNT

Certificate No.	Advance Payment Made	Previously Remaining	Recovered in this Certificate		Remaining in this Certificate	Remarks
			Fixed Monthly Deduction	% of Monthly Value Deduction		
Total Advance Payment and Recovery Carried to Payment Certificate No						

Consultant/Engineer's Representative   Engineer
Date   Date

Employer
Engineer

Contract No
Contract

Consultant
Contractor

Interim Payment Application No
Period Ending

RETENTION

Description	Amount (AED)
Retention	
Release of Retention	
Retention Amount Remaining Carried to Payment Certificate No	

Consultant/Engineer's Representative   Engineer
Date   Date

Employer
Engineer

Consultant
Contractor

Contract No.
Contract

Interim Payment Application No.
Period Ending

LIQUIDATED DAMAGES / PENALTY

S.No.	Description	Amount (AED)
	Liquidated Damages	
	Penalty	
	Total Liquidated Damages/Penalty to Payment Certificate No.	

Consultant/Engineer's Representative
Date

Engineer
Date

Employer
Engineer

Consultant
Contractor

Contract No.
Contract

Interim Payment Application No.
Period Ending

OTHER DEDUCTIONS

S.No.	Description	Amount (AED)
	Total Amount of Other Deductions Carried to Payment Certificate No.	

Consultant/Engineer's Representative
Date

Engineer
Date

Employer   Contract No
Engineer   Contract

Consultant   Interim Payment Application No
Contractor   Period Ending

PREVIOUS PAYMENTS CERTIFIED

Payment Certificate No.	Certification Date	Amount (AED)
Total Previous Payment Certified Carried to Interim Payment Certificate No		

Consultant's/Engineer's Representative   Engineer
Date   Date

Employer   Contract No
Engineer   Contract

Consultant   Interim Payment Application No
Contractor   Period Ending

MILESTONE ACHIEVEMENT

Milestone No.	Milestone Dates			Remarks
	Original Completion	Revised Completion	Actual Completion	

Consultant's/Engineer's Representative   Engineer
Date   Date

FINAL STATEMENT

Contract No: Project

Contract

Contractor/Consultant

Date

			AED
1	**Contract**		
	As per the Letter of Acceptance / Agreement:		
	1.1	Value of Contract	
	1.2	Provisional Sums	
	1.3	Effective Contract Value	0.00
2	**Adjustments**		
	2.1	Variations	
	2.2	Other Deductions	
		FINAL VALUE: AED	**0.00**

Acceptance

for and on behalf of the Contractor

____

Authorized Signatory
& Official Stamp   Date

Concurrence	Approval
	for and on behalf of Employer
Date	Authorized Signatory Date

By signing this final Statement the Contractor hereby certifes that this Final Statement represents full and final settlemet of all monies and claims due or that may become due to the Contractor in connection with the aforementioned contract.

Upon approval of the Final Statement by (Employer) and its subsequent payment that Contractor / Consultant releases, indemnifies and holds harmless (Employer) from any claims, liabilities, request for additional payments, actions, liens and obligation of every nature and from whatever sourse arising out of or in connection with the aforementioned contract and all amendments thereto.

Original No. 1 :   Contractor's / Consultant's copy
Original No. 2 :   Employer's copy   Controlled Document

Chapter 7

Variations

Variation may be defined as any change to the Works, which is instructed or approved as a variation under the Clause for "Variations and Adjustments" of an existing Contract.

A potential contract variation may be initiated anytime during the Term of the Contract as a change or variation. A contract variation may be initiated by the Employer or the Contractor (the contracting parties).

A potential variation is generally identified or generated from the following occurrences:

- Revision to Original Plans and Specifications
- Unforeseen Field Conditions
- Plan Deficiency
- Specification Conflict or Ambiguity
- Industry Regulations
- Contractor Proposed Change
- Execution of Provisional Sums
- Stakeholder Changes
- Extra work or unanticipated need
- Design Criteria Changes
- Other (to be evaluated on a case by case basis)

A variation (sometimes referred to as a variation instruction or variation order) is an alteration to the scope of works in a construction contract in the form of an addition, substitution or omission from the original scope of works.

Generally all construction projects vary from the original design, scope and definition. Whether small or large, construction projects will have inevitably departs from the original tender (more specifically the contract) design, specifications and drawings prepared by the design team. This can be because of technological advancement, statutory changes or enforcement, change in conditions, geological anomalies, non-availability of specified materials, or simply because of the continued development of the design after the contract has been awarded. In large civil engineering projects variations can be very significant, whereas on small building contracts they may be relatively minor.

Variations may generally include:

- ➢ Alterations to the design
- ➢ Alterations to quantities
- ➢ Alterations to quality
- ➢ Alterations to working conditions
- ➢ Alterations to the sequence of work

Variations may also be deemed to occur if the contract documents do not properly describe the works actually required.

However, Variations may not (without both parties consent):

- ➢ Change the fundamental nature of the works
- ➢ Omit work so that it can be carried out by another contractor
- ➢ Be instructed after practical completion
- ➢ Require the contractor to carry out work that was the subject of a prime cost sum

In legal terms, a variation is an agreement supported by consideration to alter some terms of the contract. No power to order variation is implied. Hence there should be express terms in contract which give the power to instruct variations. In the absence of express terms in the contract the contractor may reject instructions for variations without giving rise to any legal consequences, and resulting in adverse effect to the employer's requirements with regards to the planned and budgeted time and cost for a project.

Standard forms of contract generally make express provisions for the contract administrator (generally the architect or the engineer) to instruct variations (for example, FIDIC 1987 Clause 51.1). Such provisions enable the continued, smooth administration of the works without the need for another contract or a contract amendment. Variation instructions must be clear as to what is and is not included, and may propose the method of valuation.

Valuation of Variations:

Valuation of variations gives rise to additions or deductions of time and money (either or both) from the contract sum The valuation of variations may include not just the work which the variation instruction describes, but other expenses that may result from the variation, such as the impact on other aspects of the works. As seen above, variations may also (but not necessarily) require adjustment of the completion date.

Variations may be valued by:

- ➢ By applying rates contained within the BOQ
- ➢ By using star rates
- ➢ Agreement between the contractor and the client
- ➢ The cost consultant
- ➢ A variation quotation prepared by the contractor and accepted by the employer
- ➢ By some other method agreed by the contractor and the employer

Valuations of variations are often based on the rates and prices provided by the contractor in their tender, provided the work is of a similar nature and carried out in similar conditions. This is true, even if it becomes apparent that the rates provided by the contractor were higher or lower than otherwise available commercial rates. They do not become reasonable or unreasonable by the execution of variations.

In some contracts, when rates are applied to the valuation of variations, the contractor is not able to claim for additional payments in relation to profits and overheads.

If similar types of works to those instructed by a variation cannot be found in the drawings, specification or bills of quantities, then fair valuation of the contractor's direct costs, overheads and profit is necessary.

One important observation is to highlight that not all contract conditions tends to value variations based on the rates contained within the tender. For example, NEC forms of contracts do not value variations based on rates contained within the contract, but tends to pay the contractor on a defined cost plus a fee. In other words the contractor can ignore their tender pricing and claim cost plus on variations. The arguments come on items such as factory overheads and management which are very hard to evaluate. In addition, given the complexity and length of chain suppliers and subcontractors in major building works, getting forecast pricing out of all the parties down the chain affected by a variation takes time, often beyond the date by which the contract administrator has to make the decision as to whether or not to instruct the variation. They may then have to decide whether or not to proceed with a variation based on estimates from the cost consultant which in due course get replaced by the actual cost. In all practical sense both have its own advantages and disadvantages.

Source of Conflict:

Conflict can arise when work is not mentioned in the bills of quantities, drawings or the specifications contained within a contract. In common law this silence does not mean the contractor has an automatic right to claim for extra payment. The employer is not bound to pay for things that a reasonable contractor must have understood were to be done but which happen to be omitted from the bills of quantities. Where there are items that, whilst they are not expressly mentioned, are nonetheless required in order to complete the works, then the contractor should have included them in their price. The bills of quantities and specification do not necessarily have to include each and every minute detail of works that is supposed to be performed by an experienced contractor for the completion of the Works. For example in fixing glass reinforced concrete (GRC) façades it is necessary to have steel supports, and a reasonable experienced contractor must make provision for this in the contract price. Unless expressly excluded, such supports are not paid for as a variation.

Conflict can also arise when a sub-contractor qualifies that, for example, Supply & Fixing of Door is included, but Supply & Fixing of Ironmongery is excluded. A reasonable sub-contractor should foresee that a door cannot be fixed without hinges:which is a part of the ironmongery. So even if ironmongery is excluded, the sub-contractor cannot expect a variation for any of the items required to fix the doors.

Also under the pretext of variation, the contract administrator cannot change the nature of works. For example, if the contract provides for secant pile shoring, they cannot ask for diaphragm wall shoring as it will entirely change the nature of the work. Further, if the contract administrator omits work from contractor's scope, such an omission must be genuine, i.e.; the work omitted must be omitted from the contract entirely, it cannot be used to take work away from the contractor to give it to another (for example, see FIDIC

1987 Clause 51.1). Similarly, the contract administrator is not empowered to order variations to help the contractor if the contracted works are proving too difficult or expensive for them.

Limits on Variations:

FIDIC forms of contract put limitations on variations that can be instructed. If the value of the contract increases or decreases by more than 15% of the net contract sum (excluding provisional sums and day works) then the contract administrator can add or deduct from the contract sum a determined value upon consultation with the contractor, having due regard to their site expenses and other general overheads. Note that this 15% increase or decrease is not for a single item of work, but the total contract sum at completion.

Limits to variation is provided as a safe-guard to both the contractor and the employer to have a cap to the rates contained within the contract that could be applied to a variation and provides a bench mark beyond which these unit rates needs to be re-worked.

Similar provision to cap the variation limit is not uncommon to other forms of contract used in various parts of the world within the construction industry.

Conclusion:

Variations are often a source of dispute (either in valuing the variation, or agreeing whether part of the works constitutes a variation at all) and can cost a lot of time and money during the course of a contract. Whilst some variations are unavoidable, it is wise to minimize potential variations and subsequent claims by ensuring that uncertainties are eliminated before awarding the contract. This can be done by:

- ➤ Undertaking thorough site investigations and condition surveys before and during the tendering process and well documented
- ➤ Ensuring that the project brief is comprehensive and is supported by stakeholders
- ➤ Ensuring that legislative requirements are properly integrated into the project
- ➤ Ensuring that risks are properly identified and documented
- ➤ Ensuring that designs are properly co-ordinated before tender
- ➤ Ensuring the contract is unambiguous and explicit

- ➢ Ensuring the contractor's rates are clear
- ➢ Preparing concise scope of work, drawings, bills of quantities and specifications, providing for all situations which are reasonably foreseeable.

Once a potential contract variation is identified and initiated, responsible party shall perform the following function:

- ➢ Whether the proposed changes are from the Contractor or Employer, it is required that the changes are to be first validated by the Contract Administrator before progressing any further.
- ➢ Once the variation is confirmed by the Contract Administrator and an entitlement established, the Contractor is required to submit a proposal highlighting the time and cost impact of the proposed variation.
- ➢ It is likely that the proposed variation tends to change the terms and conditions of the contract. If this is the case, then a Contract Amendment is the outcome and hence has to involve the Contract drafters to do a critical review of this proposed change.

Upon obtaining the Contractor's fee proposal and schedule impact, the Contract Administrator shall perform a thorough review and evaluation to ensure that:

- ➢ the variation is priced in accordance with contractual terms
- ➢ when BOQ rates are referenced for an item that form part of the variation, the BOQ rates are used
- ➢ when existing BOQ rates are not available and new rates or lump sum items are quoted by the Contractor, substantiation by the Contractor is required either by providing extrapolation rate from existing BOQ (wherever applicable), three quotations, reference to other similar contract's rates or by providing breakdown of rates that shall be in line with the prevailing market price of similar item.

The intention of the review of the cost of variation to be done in a structured manner is to safeguard the employer against an error and overpayment to the appointed contractor. This is more important for the reason that a variation process generally tends to do away with the tendering process and hence the opportunity of obtaining the best market rate is lost when getting a work or services executed through a variation.

Contract Administrator shall thereafter, capture the pertinent information by completing Variation Order (VO) Justification form and Variation Merit Assessment (VMA) form in order to provide an auditable record of the means and methods used in order to determine entitlement for variation. Both forms shall include the following, at a minimum, along with all support documentation:

- ➢ Project reference
- ➢ Variation Number
- ➢ Contract Number
- ➢ Contract Title
- ➢ Contractor name
- ➢ Description of the work to be executed
- ➢ Reason for a variation
- ➢ Justification
- ➢ Why does this work need to be done
- ➢ How this work came about
- ➢ Entitlement for a variation
- ➢ Cost & Schedule Impacts
- ➢ Contract Documents/drawings as applicable
- ➢ Applicable signatures and authorizations
- ➢ Record of negotiation
- ➢ Additional supporting documentation substantiating the price and time impacts, as required.
- ➢ Concurrence from the Contractor regarding cost and schedule
- ➢ For a re-measurable Variation, contingency needs to be included in the proposed cost, whereas no contingency shall be included for a lump sum Variation
- ➢ Schedule Impact Analysis (if applicable)
- ➢ Estimated Final Contract Value
- ➢ All other relevant correspondence, including but not limited to, Contractor's proposal, Engineer's evaluation and review comments, record of negotiation, Emails and benchmarking,

The compiled variation document shall be reviewed and amendments, if any, carried out before seeking Competent Authority's approval.

Upon the approval of the variation, an instruction needs to be issued to the Contractor (Engineer's Instruction) enclosing original Variation Order documents in original for Contractor's sign-off.

The variation is concluded when the Contractor's authorized representative signs the Variation Order and returns one set of original document to the Employer, keeping one set for its own records.

A sample form that may be used for the purpose is provided over leaf.

Variation Order (Merit Assessment Form)			
Date:			VO No.:
Contract No.:		Contract Reference:	
Employer:		Contractor:	
Contract Description:			
Description of Variation:			
Originator:			
Request Reference:			
Location of requirement:			
Drawings reference:			
Specification/others ref.			
Variation due to (tick, as applicable):			
Unforeseen Conditions			
Stakeholder request			
Revision of original specs			
Critical Works			
Others (specify)			
As a general rule, following answers needs to be answered before proceeding with the requested Variation:			
Why does this work need to be done?			
How did this work come about?			
Why this varied work was not captured in the original scope?			

Review comments & recommendation	
Cost of this Variation (AED):	
Basis of costing:	

Authorized Signatory	Signed	Date
Authorized Signatory	Signed	Date

Cover Sheet for Variation Order (VO) No.:

Contract No.   :

Contractor   :

VO Description   :

Justification of current VO:

VO No.	DESCRIPTION	VO Value
01		
02		
03		
04		
TOTAL OF VARIATIONS		

CONTRACT VALUE   =

TOTAL VALUE OF VARIATIONS   =

REVISED CONTRACT VALUE   =

Chapter 8

Contract Claims

Claim may be defined as a legitimate request for additional compensation (cost and/or time) on account of a change in the terms of the contract.

Therefore, a claim may arise under any form of construction contract. A claim is most likely to arise under a fixed price form of contract (it may also arise in a re-measured contract, however by the very nature of such contracts, since the contractor's rights are re-measured, a claim scenario is reduced in such contracts). In fact there are very few contracts in which there are no claims, negotiations and settlements before the contract may be finally closed out.

It also follows that it is essential to know exactly what is expected of the contractor under the terms of the contract, both before signing, as well as during its execution.

Fortunately, the increasing use of standard documents and specifications has gone a long way to facilitate the expression of requirements, and thereby avoid disputes through simply misinterpretation of the terms of contract.

Contractors:

Contractors and subcontractors should avoid unmerited and exaggerated claims which in extreme cases can also lead to personal prosecution on charges of criminal fraud.

Claims must be properly constituted and documented:

➢ Proper legal entitlement must be established

➢ Cause and effect must be clearly demonstrated by contemporaneous records

➢ Additional costs must be backed up by full supporting documents

Claimant is expected to avoid unnecessary optimism when reporting settlement figures and should be willing to accept a reasonable offer of settlement without recourse to expensive litigation means that otherwise occupies management resources which could be better utilized elsewhere.

It needs to be highlighted that although a Claim may be taken to court as litigation, there is no guarantee of success in court, besides this being a costly and time consuming affair.

Employers and his Agents:

It is very important that Employers are mindful of the desirability of avoiding a claim situation arising at their project.

An Employer has an obligation to resolve proper claim entitlements in an efficient and professional way, and hence he needs to invest in front end surveys, particularly ground investigation and topographical surveys. These can help reduce the likelihood of claims to a great extent.

It is estimated that over 60% of claims arose from delays due to ground problems. Hence, it cannot be over-emphasized of the importance of ensuring that all geotechnical data is made available to all parties in the bidding process.

It is important to pick the most suitable method of procurement in relation to risk allocation and appropriate contract conditions. This includes deciding which elements of a project are to be designed by the contractor or subcontractors.

It is recommended that one needs to avoid drafting changes to standard forms of contract, which while attempting to re-allocate risk, can lead to ambiguity and uncertainty. The balance of marginal judgment, while calculating negligence, will generally favour the party that had no hand in drafting the contract. The *'contra proferentum'* rule (interpretation against the draftsman) may be applied against the interpretation of ambiguities.

Generally the earlier a dispute is settled, the cheaper is the settlement. In addition, there are considerable advantages to reducing the period of antagonism between parties to the contract.

Tender Documentation:

A number of strategies can be used in the preparation of tender documentation to help avoid claims. Some of which are as discussed below:

> ➢ Avoid dealing with items post tender. Statements such as 'to be agreed' can lead to dispute without the leverage of competition

- ➤ Phrases such as 'to suit the contractor's programme' are open ended, and needs to be avoided

- ➤ Setting a conditional date such as, 'in accordance with the architect's instruction' creates uncertainty for tendering contractors. It is not possible to enforce an 'agreement to agree'

- ➤ Avoiding ambiguity in design responsibility, such as, 'the contractor shall complete any design required after the consultants have finalised the drawings provided for tender purposes'

- ➤ Ensure that programmes, resource charts and method statements supplied by contractors with their tenders are provided for tender assessment only and are not adopted as contract documents or as the basis for variations

- ➤ If possible avoid 'letters of intent' as they encourage arguments over details in the contract not covered in the letter of intent. There are many cases where disputes have gone to Court with no signed contract in place. In case it's a must that a letter of intent is required, at the very least, the letter of intent should limit activity to pre-construction activity, such as engineering design and pre-ordering of long-delivery items of manufacture. It is also beneficial to define payment terms in a letter of intent as this can be one of the most contentious matters of legal disputes. There is no exact legal definition of Quantum Merruit, and so a letter of intent should describe how overheads, profit and indirect costs are to be treated.

Design:

Many claims are based on delays resulting from design consultants issuing schedules, drawings and specifications after construction has begun. Conflict can then arise due to arguable deficiencies in that information, such as:

- ➤ Missing, or not produced at all
- ➤ Late is providing the design document
- ➤ Incorrect design
- ➤ Insufficient to order or build
- ➤ Impractical part or full design
- ➤ Unclear or conflicting
- ➤ Inconsistent with pricing information

> ➢ Inappropriate or not fit for purpose
>
> ➢ Uncoordinated with other information

Some flexibility however is allowed by standard traditional contracts for the design team to issue further drawings and details reasonably necessary either to explain or amplify the contract drawings.

There can be an onus on the contractor to raise any queries on newly received information within 28 (less or more) days of its receipt or forfeit their right to additional payment.

Contractor's Master Programme:

Many contracts require the contractor to draw up a contractor's master programme within a defined time after the execution of the contract. The contract documents should specify the level of detail required by the contractor's master programme, however, the contractor should make allowance for the following:

> ➢ Realistic time for carrying out each section of the work, with proper consultation and agreement with the major subcontractors involved
>
> ➢ Sensible periods for specialist design and manufacture, including approval periods for checking conformity and co-ordination with other specialist input
>
> ➢ Providing consultants with an even workload for the approval of specialist drawings
>
> ➢ A stated system for recording progress against programme and future updating to reflect the enforced changes

Upon receipt of the contractor's master programme, the employer's team should examine and challenge any aspects of the programme that cannot be justified. This programme is most likely to be the basis upon which all future claims for delay, extensions of time, disruption and loss and expense are based and judgments made. Challenging the contractor's master programme at a later date when claims are submitted is arguing from a position of weakness.

The employer should not 'approve' the contractor's master programme, as approval might be considered to relieve the contractor of liability for programming the works in such a way as to achieve the completion date.

It needs to be highlighted here that as it is produced after the execution of the contract, the contractor's master programme does not impose any obligation on the contractor beyond those imposed by the contract documents.

Cause and Effect:

Global claims, made by lumping or grouping or grouping together many different causes of delay to make a case for continuous disruption and cumulative effect, has not always found favour with either the Dispute Adjudication Board (DAB) or the courts. This method of 'death by a thousand cuts' can be fairly easily counter-challenged by the employer's team, citing all of the contractor's deficiencies such as labour shortages, poor management, plant breakdowns and subcontractor non-performance. This all leads to the argument of parallel, concurrent or contemporaneous delay.

It is better to be specific rather than generic. This is a more painstaking exercise requiring more intellectual rigour, as the claimant lists each alleged default, linking it against the consequential delay and its knock-on effect, backed by contemporary records. This approach is obviously a more precise way of establishing quantum and will lead to a more factually based judgment. In other words, to succeed, a claimant needs to establish a noticeable link between the breaches pleaded and the consequential delay and/or the associated costs.

Notice and Particulars:

Under all general forms of contract, any party has to give the other party a notice as soon as a breach is apparent so that it can be remedied or its consequences mitigated. Failure to do this expunges the right to additional payment for loss or expense.

It is highlighted that commercial law also generally have similar requirements and hence we may consider the requirements in parlance or look into particular contract documents that describes such requirements.

The delay or loss and expense notice should:

> Identify the specifics of the breach and legal entitlement clauses within the contract

> Disclose as full information as possible, including the effect of the delay

> Identify relevant dates and periods of delay involved

> State any criticality and effect on the completion date

The employer's team should immediately check the factual basis of such a notification and comment on any content that appears to be subjective.

Concurrent Delay:

Concurrent delay is a situation where several causes of delay are running in parallel. An example might be where consultants details were issued late, but an industrial dispute delayed progress of critical work at the same time. In more recent judgments the courts have disregarded arguments about which was the dominant delay and judgment has been made on the basis that the loss should lie where it falls.

Therefore, a contractor may be entitled to an extension of time and relief from damages but not entitled to loss and expense if the delay has been attributed to both parties.

Quantifying Claims:

Quantifying claims may involve a number of considerations as mentioned below:

Costs:

Actual cost is the proper basis for evaluating claims. It is a popular misconception that the contractor is bound by its tender rates as its full entitlement. Costs may include allowance for inflation resulting from delay.

Preliminaries:

Preliminaries include set-up costs, running costs and dismantling costs. Thus extensions of time should not include set-up or dismantling costs but merely running cost at the time of the breach and its associated period of delay.

Disruption:

Disruption describes loss due to inefficient productivity and it is extremely difficult to assess.

Often the most effective approach is to localize the claim to a specific area of breach. Then compare individuals productivity prior to and after the disruption occurred against the productivity during the period of disruption. Generic claims based on statements such as 'this was the tender price and this is the outturn cost' are unlikely to succeed.

Head office or factory overheads:

There could be many other basis of calculating head office or factory overheads, however Hudson's formula appears to be the one most readily accepted by the courts and hence recommended to be used in a contract:

(HO Profit %/100) X (contract sum/contract period (weeks)) X (delay (weeks))

In applying the above formula the following should be subtracted:

Credit for staff time included in the project costs as visiting supervision.

Any additional overhead recovered within the final account, such as the variation account.

Credit where resources were re-deployed due to the on-going delays. Therefore, salvaging from a delay event: A recommended approach expected on any modern day contract from an experienced contractor.

Loss of profit/opportunity costs:

This is only valid when the claimant can prove breaches of contract directly prevented it making a profit elsewhere. Deductions must be made for additional profit that has been paid on the project as a result of extra work instructed and priced within the final account.

Finance charges and interest:

Finance charges and interest on extra capital required to fund costs arising from breaches in the contract are recoverable providing:

Interest rates are proven and reasonable (e.g. market rates prevailing during the period of breach).

If financed within the corporate group, the rate will be that received from monies it has placed on deposit.

Claims Management:

Upon the receipt of a claim from the Contractor under the relevant clause of the Contract the Contracts Administrator is required to review the request by looking at the notifications submitted by the contractor earlier and the timing thereof.

The Contracts Administrator may request further detail and particulars if required and capture the details within a merit assessment form including time (if applicable) and cost analysis thereof.

The findings shall be based on the below mentioned criteria:

➢ Whether or not the contractual clause references (if any) used in the Contractor's claim are correct and/or appropriate for the claim in question.

➢ Whether or not there has been compliance with time periods and actions where such are required by an applicable contract clause.

➢ A review of the claim event(s) to verify cause and the responsibility thereof.

➢ If time related, ascertain whether the Contractor has used its best efforts to mitigate the consequences of any delay.

➢ Whether the records, correspondence copies, documentation, invoices, etc., used in the Contractor's submittal are correct and appropriate.

➢ Whether the party produced the required deliverables within the scheduled period.

➢ A review of the content of the party's deliverables.

If Contract Administrator's assessment establishes that the claim has merit, the full submission shall be reviewed by the Contracts Administrator, together with other relevant departments within the Employer organization (including the Engineer, if applicable).

The following tasks are a pre-requisite to the formal Claim Report:

➢ Retrieve, assemble and collection of all cost data and documentation including the Contractor's contemporary records, as required.

➢ Ensure that the cost data is signed and dated by the person who collected or produced it.

➢ Solicit signed and dated factual statements from persons involved, including review of the Contractor's contemporary records.

➢ For time-related claims, conduct a schedule impact analysis and update as-built schedule.

➢ Compile and compute the costs associated with the claim.

➢ Submit the resulting cost and/or time analysis to Competent Authority for review and approval.

➢ The above process needs to be carried out within the time periods stipulated within the Contract.

Preparation of Claim Report:

The Contracts Administrator shall liaise with other relevant departments to prepare a claim report, which typically shall include the following:

➢ An executive summary of the claim

- ➤ A contractual analysis of the claim
- ➤ A delay analysis of the claim (if applicable)
- ➤ Detailed cost analysis of the claim
- ➤ Copy of the Contractor's/Consultant's claim submittal
- ➤ Summary of pre-claim correspondence
- ➤ Summary of information from field notes, diaries, reports, meetings, in-person and telephone conversations and similar records (utilizing the Contractor's records, as required)
- ➤ Statements from persons involved in the occurrences leading to the claim
- ➤ All relevant contractual provisions, including those on which the claim is asserted
- ➤ Legal and/or other expert opinions (if applicable)
- ➤ Summary of schedule analysis, if applicable, defining schedule impact
- ➤ Summary of post-claim discussions/negotiations with the Contractor
- ➤ Summary of post-claim correspondence to and from the Contractor
- ➤ Conclusion
- ➤ Recommendation

Claim Finalization:

After the Claim report has been reviewed and approved by the Competent Authority within the organization, the Contracts Administrator notifies the Contractor in writing of the decision.

If the Contractor does not agree with the claim evaluation, it has an opportunity to object by notifying in accordance with the Contract terms. A secondary review may be required in this case. In case the Contractor does not agree to the secondary review too, dispute resolution mechanism may be kicked-off to see an amicable resolution of the claim in reference.

Chapter 9

Risk (within the Construction Industry)

Construction risks are said to be part of any and every project. However, the perceived risk can be addressed scientifically to help minimize the associated ill-effects.

The development of a project is carried out in several phases, all involving hazard, uncertainty and risk.

Hazard:

A hazard can be understood as a situation that sets some level of threat to life, health, property, environment, personal integrity, and so on. From the health and safety point of view, a hazard may be understood as a condition with the potential to cause physical impairment or health consequences in people (or any other type of life). In a project environment, a hazard is anything that may affect the success of project activities or the project as a whole. Similarly, companies, ventures, physical assets, the environment and society face hazards. Most hazards are potential or latent but when they become active or effective, they can generate emergency situations. A hazardous situation that becomes effective can cause an incident, an accident or a disaster.

Uncertainty and risk:

Uncertainty is not the same as risk. The two terms are distinct and have different meanings. Uncertainty refers to the occurrence of an event about which little is known, while a risk is the outcome of an event which is predicted on the basis of statistical probability. Uncertainty exists when there is more than one possible outcome and risk exists when a decision is expressed in terms of a range of possible outcomes.

The first step in risk assessment is to identify hazards, after which it may be possible treat risks, thereby preventing them. However, an exact definition of risk is exclusive and its measurement is still controversial:despite the ubiquity of risk in almost every human activity.

In literature, the word 'risk' is used with many different meanings. It may be suggested that a risk is a factor, event or influence that threatens the successful completion of a project in terms of time, cost or quality. However, there may be other definitions of risk.

Some of the common definitions of risk are as below:

➢ A situation where there exists little or no knowledge of its outcome

➢ The variation in possible outcomes that exist in nature in a given situation

➢ High probability of failure

➢ Lack of predictability about structure, outcome, or consequences in decision or planning situations

➢ The chance of something happening that will have an (adverse) impact on objectives

Looking at the various definitions of risk and their relationship with the previous concepts, it can be suggested that, although the risk concept has been defined in many ways, it is characterized by two main factors:

1. the likelihood/probability of a particular hazard actually taking place, and

2. the impact or consequences of that.

Actually, many risk standards state that it is important to understand these two component elements to fully define a risk. While some definitions of risk focus only on the probability of occurrence of an event that may possibly affect the achievement of a given process, more comprehensive definitions consider both the probability of the occurrence and its consequences.

Risk is the effect of uncertainty on the achievement of objectives. An effect is a deviation from the expected, and can be positive and/or negative.

Objectives can have different aspects (such as financial health and safety, and environmental goals) as can apply at different levels (such as strategic, organization-wide, project, product and process)

Uncertainty is the state, even partial, of lack of information related to knowledge of an event, its consequences or likelihood.

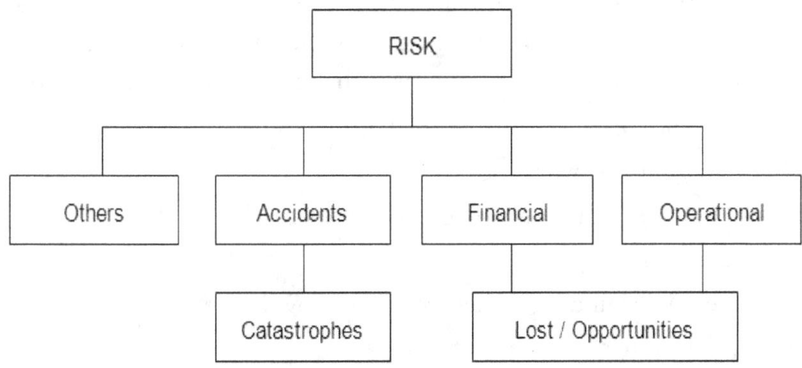

Basic Risks of Construction Projects:

The construction industry has a high rate of work accidents and a poor reputation for coping with problems, with many projects failing to meet deadlines, cost and quality targets. In extreme cases the risk of time and cost overruns can compromise the economic viability of the project, making a potentially profitable investment untenable. Compared to many other activities, construction is subject to more risks due to unique features such as long duration, complicated processes, unpredictable environment, financial intensity and dynamic organization structures.

It is argued that construction is undeniably a risky business and that risks are unavoidable in any project, risks such as tax risks, interface risks and local site risks are the most common and inevitable risks in construction projects. Other risks that may be less likely to occur are *force majeure events or changes in law. However, should these* risks occur, they will have significant impact on the project. Delay claims and claims for increased costs, injuries to workers, etc. are the most common risks in construction projects. The accumulation of all these risks or the combination of them can be termed "project risks".

Construction project risks are interrelated and interdependent. The customary origins for project risks are the following:

- Performance, scope, quality, or technology issues
- Environment, safety, and health concerns
- Scope, cost, and schedule uncertainty
- Political concerns

Risks in construction projects may be classified in a number of ways according to their source. Naturally, risk will be peculiar to each particular project and each project participant, however, it is recognized that all construction projects share common risks that can be classified as follows:

- Construction
- Changes in the work
- Subsurface geological and geotechnical conditions
- Site access
- Level of detail design delivered by the owner
- Late drawings and instructions
- Availability of resources
- Accidents (such as collision, fire and so on)
- Damage to persons or property
- Defective design
- Cost of tests and samples
- Actual quantities of work
- Equipment commissioning
- Financial and economic
- Inflation
- Funding
- Performance
- Labour productivity
- Equipment productivity
- Suitability of materials
- Defective work
- Conduct hindering performance of the work
- Labour and industrial disputes

- Security
- Vandalism
- Terrorism
- Corruption
- Assaults
- Negligence
- Intrusion
- Contractual and legal
- Delayed dispute resolution
- Delayed payment on contracts and extras
- Change order negotiation
- Insolvency of contractor or a subcontractor
- Physical conditions
- Subsurface geology geotechnical conditions
- Subsurface conditions and ground water
- Topography
- Natural catastrophes
- Political and societal
- Soil availability for construction
- Environmental pressures
- Regulations (safety or labour laws)
- Public disorder
- Commotion or strike

Construction risks may be broadly sub-divided into the following six categories:

1. Technical Risks
2. Construction Risks
3. Environmental Risks
4. External Risks
5. Organizational Risks
6. Project Management Risks

Below mentioned criteria provides the basis of the above risks:

1. **Technical Risks:**
   - Design process
   - Owner involvement in design
   - Inadequate and incomplete design
   - Change in seismic criteria
   - Errors or in completion of structural/geotechnical/foundation
   - Wrong selection of materials
   - Take off data (traffic demand, water consumption demand, etc.)
   - Need for design exceptions

2. **Construction Risks:**
   - Inaccurate contract time estimates
   - Construction procedures
   - Construction occupational safety
   - Work permissions
   - Utilities
   - Late surveys, incomplete or wrong
   - Delayed deliveries and disruptions
   - Worker and site safety
   - Innovative projects
   - Unsuitable equipment and materials

3. **Environmental Risks:**
   - Environmental factors (such as projects close to a wild river, floodplain, coastal zone, high sensitivity for paleontology area, etc.)
   - Environmental analysis incomplete or wrong
   - Offsite and onsite wetlands
   - Hazardous waste preliminary site investigation wrong
   - Lack of specialized staff (biology, anthropology archaeology, etc.)
   - Inaccurate assumptions on technical issues in the planning stage
   - Fact sheet requirements (exception to standards)

4. External Risks:

- ➢ Contractual relations
- ➢ Landowners unwilling to sell
- ➢ Priorities change on existing program
- ➢ Funding changes for fiscal year
- ➢ Stakeholders request late changes
- ➢ New stakeholders
- ➢ Additional needs requested by stakeholders
- ➢ New information required for permits
- ➢ Inconsistent costs, time, scope, and quality objectives
- ➢ Permits and licenses
- ➢ Force majeure factors
- ➢ Political factors change (political interference)
- ➢ Political climate
- ➢ Economic instability
- ➢ Market conditions
- ➢ Exchange rate fluctuation
- ➢ Public safety regulation
- ➢ Social factors
- ➢ Local communities pose objections
- ➢ Environmental factors
- ➢ Environmental regulations change (for example, effluent water quality requirements)
- ➢ Water quality issues
- ➢ New information required for permits
- ➢ Environmental impact statement required
- ➢ Historic site, endangered species, or wetlands present
- ➢ Pressure to compress the environmental schedule

5. Organizational Risks:

- ➢ Inexperienced staff assigned
- ➢ Losing critical staff at crucial point of the project
- ➢ Insufficient time to plan

> ➤ Unanticipated project manager workload
>
> ➤ Not enough time to plan
>
> ➤ Priorities change on existing program
>
> ➤ Inconsistent cost, time, scope, and quality objectives

6. **Project management Risks:**

> ➤ Project purpose definition (needs, objectives, costs, deliverables) are poorly defined or understood
>
> ➤ No control over staff priorities
>
> ➤ Too many projects
>
> ➤ Consultant or contractor delays
>
> ➤ Estimating and/or scheduling errors
>
> ➤ Communication breakdown with project team
>
> ➤ Lack of coordination/communication
>
> ➤ Inexperienced workforce/inadequate staff/resource availability

It is very important to capture all potential risks in a project and undertake all necessary actions or make provisions for eliminating or preventing them from occurring. Alternatively, the effects of risks may be reduced and allocated to the party best prepared for managing them. This requires a systematic approach to risk management.

Risk Mitigation & Control:

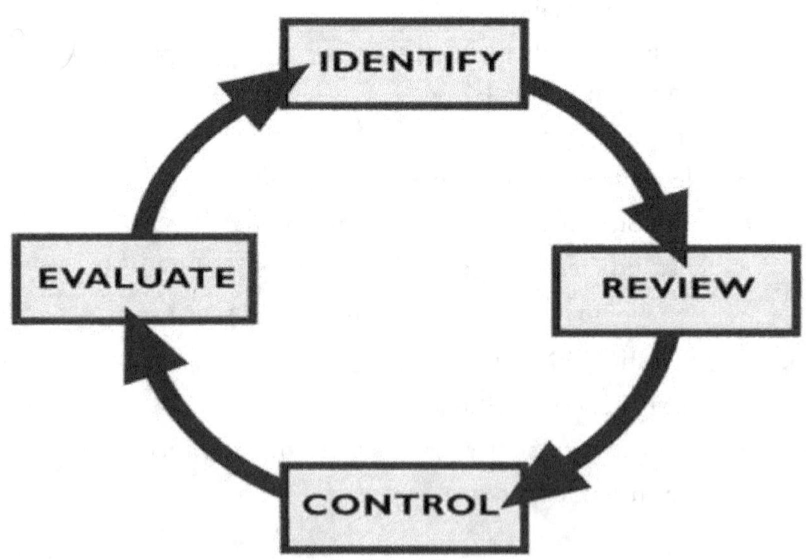

Alternative Techniques
Risk Control
Risk Financing
Exposure Avoidance
Loss Prevention
Loss Reduction
Contractual Transfer
Retention
Transfer

Chapter 10

Contract Close-out

Contract closeout begins when the contract has been physically completed, i.e., all services have been performed and products delivered. Closeout is completed when all administrative actions have been completed, all disputes settled, and final payment has been made. The process can be simple or complex depending on the contract type for cost-reimbursement contracts. This process requires close coordination between the contracting office, the finance office, the program office, and the contractor. Contract closeout is an important aspect of Contract Administration.

Contract closeout management is a collaborative effort between the various Employers departments and hence coordination and communication holds the key.

The importance of time within which the Work has to be performed cannot be reiterated enough, particularly within a construction contract, due to the large value and volume of resources that is involved from both Employer and the Contractor. Therefore, any modern day construction contract without an expressed reference to the time of completion is unheard of. The contractor is therefore, bound to do the works within the specified time and shall be liable for damages if he fails to do so, subject to the entitlement of extension of time.

Contractor also has an entitlement to carry out the Works. Hence, if the Employer prevents completion, he will be liable in damages to the contractor. A very common example is to fail to give possession of site to the contractor.

Importance of time in a Contract can be understood by the fact that, where no time period has been specified, the Contractor is obliged to complete the Works within a reasonable time.

A Contract audit process also may affect the Contract closeout. Contract audits are required to determine the reasonableness, allow ability, and allocation of all costs incurred under the Contract. Although a good Contract Administration practice would have ensured that there has been already a pre-award review of the contractor's proposal, there is a cost-incurred audit of the contractor's claim of incurred costs and a close out audit to reconcile the contractor's final claim under the contract. This shall be an easy task in case of a lump sum contracts, however in case of re-measurable contracts, the assigned Contracts Administrator shall closely work with the audit team and the other Stakeholders in arriving at the final Contract value.

The following are the recommended best practices for contract close-out procedure:

Establishment of a separate closeout function within the contracting organization emphasizes the importance of contract closeout.

The best time to concentrate on contract closeout documentation is during the progress of the contract itself, it is definitely not a good idea to leave this important task to the end. A practical time for the Contract Administrator to concentrate on the contract close out is during the time of the preparation of the Taking over Certificate (TOC) that shall signify Substantial Completion.

Using Contractor support may be an efficient way to accomplish contract closeout when in-house resources may be limited.

Such administrative functions as creating the closeout file, soliciting required closeout forms from internal organizations, obtaining the contractor's release are duties that can be performed through contractor support as long as the forms are executed and approved by the Contractor Administrator.

Although the contract specialist continues to work with the contractor through physical completion under "cradle-to-grave" contract administration, this does not prohibit a separate group from performing the closeout function.

A suggested good practice could be rewarding employees through incentive awards for the highest number of closeouts completed is a good motivation factor.

Cross-training in contract closeout is good for a Contract Administrator as it helps him to understand the importance of writing good Contracts.

In construction contracts, claims often cause closeout problems. An alternate dispute resolution (ADR) technique therefore, is recommended to be included within the Contract.

Contracting approach may also be altered to achieve a faster and stress-free contract closeout. One example could be Partnering Agreement between the Employer and the Contractor. Creating a partnership agreement with the Contractor helps avoid disputes. Having a partnership agreement signed by all parties to the Contract creates a buy-in to the overall goal "Completion on time, within budget, and without claims."

Using specific monetary thresholds for quick closeouts may be practicable so long as Employer's and Contractor's interests are protected, low risk is involved, and the indirect rates can be verified.

Having knowledge of Contractor's history of incurred costs, billings, variations, claims and performance are additional factors to be considered when establishing thresholds for using quick closeouts.

Closeout documentation recommended is to always use a checklist and include it in the contract file when closing contracts. This helps to assure that all actions have been completed.

Contract Completion:

Full and complete performance is a requirement not only to discharge contractual obligations of an Employer and a Contractor in a construction contacts, but also serves the purpose of permitting the Employer to take possession of the Works and to allows the Contractor to rightfully leave the site. Therefore, confirming that the intention of the Contract has been accomplished.

Contract close-out activity has the following attributes:

➤ Contract closeout is an often overlooked aspect of contract administration as a project manager generally views closeout as an unnecessary function and intends to move his team to a new project, leaving a lean team to complete the close out

➤ After final delivery of goods or services some offices believe that the contract is closed

➤ The closeout function is often regarded as the most distasteful activity of the contracting process

➤ The closeout specialist is frequently acting in the capacity of a problem solver

➤ Knowledge of the contracting process, use of contract terms, and excellent interpersonal skills is critical to closeout process success

Physical completion of a contract:

A contract is considered physically complete when:

> The contractor has completed the required deliveries and the employer has inspected and accepted the Works or Services

> The contractor has performed all services and the employer has accepted these services

> All option provisions (if any) has expired

> The employer has given the contractor a notice of complete contract termination

Questioned Costs:

Those amounts on which audit action has been completed and which are not considered acceptable as a contract cost will be shown by the auditor as questioned costs. This category includes amounts for:

> Those items specifically identified as unallowable under the contract terms, statute, public policy, applicable Government regulations, or legal advice.

> Those items which, although not specifically unallowable, are determined to be unreasonable in amount, contrary to generally accepted government accounting principles, or not properly allocable to the contract considering the relative benefit received or other equitable relationship.

> Those items questioned for other reasons, usually based on buyer engineering or technical advice.

Administrative Completion:

A contract is considered administratively complete when all administrative actions have been accomplished, all contractual releases obtained and the final payment made.

Contract Closeout:

The wrap-up of a physically complete contract, which involves reviewing the contract file and finalizing all administrative requirements under the contract, i.e., technical, desk review, contractual and accounting actions, closeout audit/ review, storage and timely retention and/or disposal of the contract file.

Conclusion:

A good contract administration program is essential to improving contractor performance in modern complex construction contracts. In the long term, this not only helps the direct contracting parties (employer and contractor) but is significant to help develop the construction industry by reducing avoidable (and sometimes unnecessary) dispute resolution methods that at times, are time consuming and definitely expensive.

The best practices that have been included in this book are a step at providing practical guidance that shall help improve the contract administration process.

Project contracting officials need to realize the importance of good contract administration. Convening a forum to discuss these best practices shall help organizations to focus more attention to bottlenecks and may begin using the outcomes to help resolve problem that is normally encountered.

Structuring a contract administration by the type of activity, i.e., contract and agreement monitoring, invoice reviews, variations and claims reviews, contractor performance evaluation using various Key Performance Indicators (KPIs) may also help to better allocate contract administration resources so that these best practices can be useful.

Lessons learned report:

The lessons learned report is an assessment of lessons that can be learned from a project that could be applied to other projects. This is particularly useful to employers who are regular developers and/or organizations that are regularly engaging contractors to procure projects, and may run a continuous improvement programme. It may also be a requirement of some funding organizations and banks.

A lessons learned report may be prepared as part of a post project review, undertaken during the defects liability period. The purpose of a post project review is to look at the effectiveness and efficiency of the project delivery process. The lessons learned report focuses more specifically on how things could be done differently in the future.

The lessons learned report would generally identify:

> Mistakes that could be avoided in the future

> Successful strategies that might be adopted in the future

> Procedures or resources that could be improved

It may be prepared by an in-house team, by members of the consultant team or by independent employer/client advisors. If such services were not a requirement of original appointments then new appointments or re-appointments may be necessary.

Ideally, the requirement for a lessons learned report should be included in tender documentation so that members of the project team are contractually obliged to provide the necessary information and input to the report. They may be required to provide information as the project progresses (such as key performance indicators, which might require information from sub-contractors) or to maintain up to date lessons learned logs.

It is important to agree to the following:

➢ The purpose of the report (who is it for and how they will use it)

➢ The scope of the study required

➢ The reporting procedures and timescale for the study

➢ The stakeholders that will be involved

➢ The techniques that will be used

➢ The information that is available

The report might also include an assessment of the project, or simply focus on the lessons that can be carried forward. Assessments may be both qualitative (based on research, interviews and workshops) and quantitative (such as key performance indicators or benchmarking assessments).

Qualitative assessments may include:

➢ Cost compared against similar projects

➢ Progress compared against similar and benchmark projects

➢ Complaints assessed by interviewing managers on and off site

➢ Nature of incidents and work time lost

➢ Quality and quantum of plant and material in use

➢ Nature of defects

➢ Customer satisfaction surveys

Quantitative assessments may include:

➢ Cost vs budget

➢ Project progress relative to milestones

➢ Number of complaints

➢ Number of incidents/accidents

> ➢ Number of working hours spent on different aspects of the works
> ➢ Use of materials
> ➢ Number of defects
> ➢ Number of disputes
> ➢ Amount of waste generated
> ➢ Amount of recycling
> ➢ The number of variations

However, it is important that it does not simply become a time-consuming paper exercise. Nor should it be a PR exercise: An opportunity to pat each other on the back and claim every aspect of the project was successful. Only genuinely important aspects of the project should be assessed, and only viable and worthwhile lessons needs to be proposed for adoption.

The basic content of the report may be as follows:

> ➢ Executive summary
> ➢ Background: Including the wider context of other projects that the report will feed into, and details of any abnormal characteristics or events
> ➢ Detailed assessment of different stages or aspects of the project
> ➢ Things that can be taken forward to other projects
> ➢ Things that can be changed on the project being assessed

Aspects of the project that may be assessed could include:

> ➢ The quality of briefing documents
> ➢ The effectiveness of communications
> ➢ The performance of the various members of the project team
> ➢ Quality issues
> ➢ Technical issues
> ➢ Health and safety
> ➢ Certification
> ➢ Variations
> ➢ Claims and disputes
> ➢ Collaborative practices

Furthermore, for each lesson the report needs to describe:

> ➢ What went wrong/right

- Why it went wrong/right
- Seriousness, i.e.; is it worth avoiding/replicating in the future
- If so, how can this be done

Post project review of construction projects:

A post project review may begin during the defects liability period, when the client first occupies the development (called Taking Over of the Property, signifies issuance of TOC and therefore, the commencement of Defects Liability Period).

A post project review is undertaken to evaluate the effectiveness and efficiency of the project delivery process. To undertake a post project review, it is important to seek the views of contractors, designers, suppliers and the client about how well the project was managed.

This may include assessments of how well the delivery of the project performed against key performance indicators such as:

- The quality of briefing documents
- The effectiveness of communications
- The performance of the entire project team
- Quality issues
- Health and safety issues
- Certification
- Variations
- Claims and disputes
- Collaborative practices

An evaluation can then be made of what lessons can be learned from the approach taken and a lessons learned report prepared.

A wider "post occupancy evaluation" may also comprise two distinct studies:

- A post project review to evaluate the project delivery process
- An assessment of performance in use, to assess the extent to which business and design objectives have been satisfied, which may not begin until 6 to 12 months after occupation, as operations may not be properly established before then

It is noted that when the project is first occupied by the employer, it is important to visit the site immediately to identify any issues that need to be addressed quickly. It can be beneficial to establish a help-desk and rapid response team to resolve issues as they arise.

A few relevant Templates follow this page:

Partial Taking Over Certificate (PTOC)		
Date:		
Contract No.:		
Contract Reference:		
Project Reference:		
Employer:		
Contractor:		
Contract Description:		
Contract Commencement Date:		
Contract Completion Date:		
Description of Works being taken over:	Pursuant to Sub-clause …….. of the Contract, this PTOC is being issued to the Contractor signifying the taking-over of a portion of the Works (as defined within the sub-clause ….. of the Contract). The part of work being……………………	
Value of Works being taken over:		
Effective date of PTOC:		
Punch list attached?	Yes/No	
Review comments & recommendation:		
Authorized Signatory	Signed	Date
Authorized Signatory	Signed	Date

Taking Over Certificate (TOC)	
Date:	
Contract No.:	
Contract Reference:	
Project Reference:	
Employer:	
Contractor:	
Contract Description:	
Contract Commencement Date:	
Contract Completion Date:	
Description of Works being taken over:	Pursuant to Sub-clause .... of the Contract, this TOC is being issued to the Contractor signifying the taking-over of the whole of Works (as defined within the sub-clause ..... of the Contract) and signifies the commencement of the Defects Liability Period (DLP).
Value of Works being taken over:	
Effective date of TOC:	
Punch list attached?	Yes/No
Review comments & recommendation:	
Authorized Signatory	Signed	Date

Authorized Signatory	Signed	Date

Defects Liability Certificate (DLC)	
Date:	
Contract No.:	
Contract Reference:	
Project Reference:	
Employer:	
Contractor:	
Contract Description:	
Contract Commencement Date:	
Contract Completion Date:	
Description of Works being taken over:	Pursuant to Sub-clause .... of the Contract, this DLC is being issued to the Contractor signifying the completion of Works (as defined within the sub-clause ..... of the Contract) and signifies the completion of the Defects Liability Period (DLP).
Value of Works being taken over:	
Effective date of DLC:	
Review comments & recommendation:	

Authorized Signatory	Signed	Date
Authorized Signatory	Signed	Date

FINAL STATEMENT	
Date:	
Contract No.:	
Contract Reference:	
Project Reference:	
Employer:	

Contractor:		
Work Description:		
1	Contract	AED
1.1	Value of Contract	
1.2	Provisional Sums	
1.3	Effective Contract Value	
2	Adjustments	
2.1	Variations	
2.2	Other Deductions	
Final Contract Value		
Acceptance (Contractor)		
Concurrence (Employer)		
Approval (Employer)		

By signing this Final Statement the Contractor hereby certifies that this Final Statement represents full and final settlement of all monies and claims due or that may become due to the Contractor in connection with the aforementioned Contract.

Upon approval of the Final Statement by the Employer and its subsequent payment that Contractor releases, indemnifies and holds harmless the Employer from any claims, liabilities and request for additional payments, actions, liens and obligation of every nature and from whatever source arising out of or in connection with the aforementioned contract and all amendments thereto.

Chapter 11

Construction Disputes

In an international survey carried out in the year 2013, it was found that 30% of firms had been involved in at least one dispute in the previous one year. As a consequence, there is enormous interest in construction disputes but it also tends to focus on dispute resolution techniques rather than only to try and avoid them. Of course, it may well be argued that it is best to avoid a dispute, this only becomes a wishful thinking of the contracts administrator due to numerous factors playing within the construction industry.

The above is an indication of what a contract administrator may come across in his course of work. The project needs to be managed to the minutest details to see the product without the hassle of going through a dispute.

Reasons for the occurrence of Construction Disputes:

A combination of environmental and behavioural factors may lead to construction disputes. Projects are usually long-term transactions with high uncertainty and complexity, and it is impossible to resolve every detail and foresee every contingency at the outset. As a result, situations often arise that are not clearly addressed by the contract, or not understood in the same context by the contracting parties. The basic factors that drive the development of construction disputes are uncertainty, contractual problems and/or understanding, and behaviour.

Uncertainty:

Uncertainty (in project parlance) is the difference between the amount of information required to do the task and the amount of information that is available. The amount of information required depends on the task complexity and the performance requirements, usually measured in time or to a budget. The amount of information available depends on the effectiveness of planning and requires the collection and interpretation of that information for the task.

Uncertainty also means that each and every detail of a project cannot be planned before work begins. When uncertainty is high, initial drawings and specification will almost certainly change and the project members will have to work hard to solve problems as work proceeds if disputes are to be avoided.

Form of Contract:

Standard forms of contract clearly prescribe the risks and obligations each party has agreed to take. However, such rigid agreements may not be appropriate for long-term transactions carried out under conditions of uncertainty.

It is not uncommon to find amended terms or bespoke contracts that shift the risk and obligations of the parties, often to the party least capable of carrying that risk. Where amended terms or bespoke contracts are used, they may be unclear and ambiguous. As a consequence, differences may arise in the parties' perception of the risk allocation under the contract. Where the parties have agreed to the amended or bespoke terms, those conditions take effect in addition to the applicable law of the contract, which is continually evolving and being refined to address new issues.

Since contracts cannot cater for every eventuality, wherever problems arise either party may have an interest in gaining as much as they can from the other. Equally, the parties may have a different perception of the facts. At least one of the parties may have unrealistic expectations, affecting their ability to reach agreement. Alternatively, one party may simply deny responsibility in an attempt to avoid liability.

Behaviour:

Since contracts cannot cater for every eventuality, wherever problems arise either party may have an interest in gaining as much as they can from the other. Equally, the parties may have a different perception of the facts. At least one of the parties may have unrealistic expectations, affecting their ability to reach agreement. Alternatively, one party may simply deny responsibility in an attempt to avoid liability.

Common causes of construction disputes:

Construction is a unique process which can give rise to some unusual and unique disputes. However, various researches in Australia, Canada, Kuwait, the United Kingdom, United States and other developed and developing countries suggest that a number of common themes occur quite frequently:

Acceleration:

Due to high cost of a modern-day project and the associated long gestation period, it is not uncommon for commercial property owners to insist upon acceleration of a construction project. Such examples might include the completion of a major retail scheme, and the need to meet key opening dates or tenant occupation in an office development. The construction costs associated with acceleration are likely to be less than the commercial risk the developer may face if key dates are missed.

The circumstances surrounding acceleration are often not properly analyzed at the time the decision is made, and that inevitably leads to disputes once the contractor has carried out accelerative measures and incurred additional costs only to find that the developer refuses to pay.

Co-ordination:

In complex projects involving many specialist trades, particularly special systems, mechanical and electrical installations, co-ordination is key. Yet conflict often arises because work is not properly co-ordinated. This inevitably leads to conflict during installation which is often costly and time-consuming to resolve, with each party blaming the other for the problems that have arisen.

Ineffective management control may result in a reactive defence to problems that arise, rather than a proactive approach to resolve the problems once they become apparent.

Culture:

The personnel required to visualize, initiate, plan, design, supply materials and plant, construct, administer, manage, supervise, commission and correct defects throughout the span of a large construction contract is substantial. Such personnel may come from different social classes or ethnic backgrounds. In the United Kingdom skill shortages have led to an influx of personnel from central and eastern Europe, a trend likely to continue with the growth of pre-accession states seeking access to the labour market in the European Union.

Major international construction projects may employ or engage people from different nationalities and cultures. For example, a major pipeline contract in say Kazakhstan, the owner may be a joint venture comprising Kazakh, Canadian and British companies, the owner's representatives for the project for day-to-day matters may be Canadian, French, Russian or British nationalities. The contractor may a Greek–Italian joint venture that in-turn may employ labour and supervisors from more than a dozen different countries from throughout the central and eastern Europe, the Middle East and the Indian sub-continent. Projects within the Middle East invariably employ manpower from all over the globe, it is estimated that over 100 nationalities make up the overall manpower at a large project in this region.

Forming a teamwork approach across cultures can be very difficult where each culture has its own values.

Differing goals:

Personnel engaged on a large construction contract are likely to be employed by one of many subcontracted firms, including those engaged as suppliers and manufacturers. Each of these firms may have their own commitments and goals, which may not be compatible with each other and could result in disputes.

Delays:

Disputes frequently arise in respect of delays and who should bear the responsibility for them. Most construction contracts make provision for extending the time for completion. The sole reason for this is that the owner can keep alive any rights to delay damages recoverable from the contractor. On international construction projects the question of any rights the contractor might have to extend the time for completion was a matter often addressed towards the end of the contract, when an overrun looked likely. From the owner's point of view, this made the examination of the true causes of delay problematical and inevitably led to disputes between the contractor and the owner as to the contractor's proper entitlement.

Under the FIDIC and other general forms of contracts, the contractor is required to give prompt notice of any circumstances that may cause a delay. If the contractor fails to do so, then any rights to extend the time for completion will be lost, both under the contract and at law. This may seem a harsh measure, but a better view is that this approach brings claims to the surface at a very early stage and gives the recipient an opportunity to examine the cause and effect of any delay properly as and when it arises, so that the owner has some say in what can be done to overcome the delay.

Design:

Errors in design can lead to delays and additional costs that become the subject of disputes. Often no planning or sequencing is given to the release of design information, which then impacts on construction. Equally, the design team sometimes abrogate their responsibilities for the design, leaving the contractor to be drawn into solving any design deficiencies by carrying out that part of the work itself to try to avoid delays, and, in doing so, innocently assuming the risk for any subsequent design failures.

The design stage stipulated to produce error free drawings contains a lot of steps: programming and feasibility, schematic design, design development, and contract documents. It is the responsibility of the design team to ensure that the design meets all building codes and regulations. Furthermore, it needs no over-emphasize that it is during this stage that the bidding process takes place.

Programming and feasibility:

The needs, goals, and objectives must be determined for the building. Decisions must be made on the building size, number of rooms, how the space will be used, and who will be using the space. This must all be considered to begin the actual designing of the building.

Schematic design:

Schematic designs are sketches used to identify spaces, shapes, and patterns. Materials, sizes, colors, and textures must be considered in the sketches. Schematic designs generally follow the approval of the concept designs.

Design development (DD):

This step requires research and investigation into what materials and equipment will be used as well as their cost and follows on to proceed with the preparation of detailed drawings and specifications

Tender documents (TDs):

Tender documents are the final drawings and specifications (besides the ITT, Terms and the Pricing section) issued to the Bidders for a construction project. They are used by contractors to determine their bid while builders/ employers use them for working towards the construction process..

Contract documents (CDs):

Contract documents are the final terms of contract, scope of work, drawings and specifications of a construction project. They are used by contractors to plan and work on the project and the employer uses them for the control and monitoring of the actual construction process.

Engineer and Employer's Representative:

The personality of the Engineer or the Employer's Representative and their approach to the proper and fair administration of the contract on behalf of the Employer is crucial to avoiding disputes, yet a substantial proportion of disputes have been driven by the Engineer or the Employer's Representative exercising an uneven hand in deciding differences in favour of the Employer.

In domestic and international contracts, the Engineer traditionally had an independent and impartial role. This independence or impartiality was often not properly exercised, and in some cases there was clear evidence of bias by the Engineer towards the Employer. This practice was not limited to third world countries but also existed in developed countries.

It is a complete fiction to say that the Engineer under government contracts could possibly act independently of the Employer on every issue.

Some contracts are open as to the constraints imposed on the Engineer: in Hong Kong Engineers are subject to financial constraints in respect of variations and in the extensions of time that can be given. While this may be understandable from a public policy point of view, it is unacceptable for it to be done behind a veil so that the fiction of independence is preserved.

Under the new FIDIC contracts the Engineer no longer has an impartial role but expressly acts for the Employer. This does not prevent the Engineer from taking a professional view on the merits of any difference that may be at issue, but in the event of a dispute the mechanism to resolve such matters quickly by independent means has been achieved by the introduction of a dispute adjudication board.

Project complexity:

In complex construction projects the need to carry out a proper risk assessment before a contract is entered into is paramount: yet this is often not done.

There are numerous examples of projects taking much longer than planned and contracted for because there was insufficient appreciation of the risks associated with the project's complexity. Inevitably the delay and additional costs the contractor incurs, and the owner's right to claim damages for delay, often develop into bitter disputes.

Quality and workmanship:

In traditional construction contracts, disputes often arise as to whether or not the completed work is in accordance with the specifications. The specification may be vague on the subject of the dispute in question, and each party to the contract may have a different view on whether the quality and workmanship is acceptable.

This is even more so in international contracts. Although great care may have been taken to prescribe the quality of the materials and their compliance with European standards, these standards may contradict the local laws and regulations in the country where the project is being constructed, and any dispute will be governed by the law of that country.

In design and build contracts, perhaps the greatest deficiency is in the contract documentation, particularly the Employer's requirements. This inadequacy inevitably leads to claims by the contractor for additional costs, which if are not resolved swiftly can lead in turn to costly disputes.

Site conditions:

If the contract inadequately describes which party is to take the risk for the site conditions, disputes are inevitable when adverse site or ground conditions impede the progress of work or require more expensive engineering solutions.

Even if the Employer, in good faith, provides detailed information on the site conditions to the contractor, if that information is discovered to be incorrect and the contractor has relied on it and acted upon it to their detriment, the Employer may be liable to the contractor for the consequences.

Tender:

The time allowed scrutinizing the tender documents, preparing an outline programme and methodology, carrying out a risk assessment, calculating the price, and concluding the whole process with a commercial review is often very short. Mistakes in this process may have an adverse effect on the successful commercial outcome of the project. A culture may be engendered in the contractor of pursuing every claim that has a prospect of redressing any ultimate financial shortfall. This approach is detrimental to foster a close and co-operative working relationship between the Employer and the Contractor during the progress of the work, and inevitably leads to disputes.

Variations:

Variations are a prime cause of construction disputes, particularly where they are in a substantial number, or the variations impact on partially completed work or are issued as work is nearing completion. The nature and number of variations can transform a relatively straightforward project into one of unmanageable complexity. A new airport terminal is such an example. The building was planned to accommodate 6 contact gates, but through variations the building increased in size and complexity to house 9 aircraft contact gates. It was perhaps not surprising that the total cost of construction exceeded twice the original budget.

Value engineering:

This term often lacks definition in construction contracts and can lead to disputes, particularly where the saving is to be shared between the contractor and the owner. Savings in respect of the supply and installation of the material or product in question might be relatively easy to determine and agree, but these are not the only benchmarks, and a proper value engineering approach needs to take full account of the life cycle costs of any proposed change.

Contract Claims

Contractors:

Contractors and subcontractors should avoid unmerited and exaggerated claims which in extreme cases can lead to personal prosecution on charges of criminal fraud. Claims must be properly constituted and documented:

- ➢ Proper legal entitlement must be established
- ➢ Cause and effect must be clearly demonstrated by contemporaneous records
- ➢ Additional costs must be backed up by full supporting documents

Claimants should avoid unnecessary optimism when reporting settlement figures to managers and should be willing to accept a reasonable offer of settlement without recourse to expensive legal action, which occupies management resources that would be better utilized elsewhere. It is important to note that there is no guarantee of success in court.

Clients (Employer) and their agents

The client always needs to keep in mind the following:

➢ The desirability of avoiding claims.

➢ Their obligation to resolve proper claim entitlements in an efficient and professional way.

➢ Investing in front end surveys, particularly ground investigation and topographical surveys, can help reduce the likelihood of claims.

➢ It is important to ensure that all geotechnical data is made available to all parties in the bidding process.

➢ It is important to pick the most suitable method of procurement in relation to risk allocation and appropriate contract conditions. This includes deciding which elements of a project are to be designed by the contractor or subcontractors.

➢ Avoid drafting changes to standard forms of contract, which while attempting to re-allocate risk, can lead to ambiguity and uncertainty. It is needs to bear in mind that the balance of marginal judgment will favour the party that had no hand in drafting the contract. The 'contra proferentum' rule may be applied against the interpretation of ambiguities in case of a claim scenario.

➢ Usually the earlier a dispute is settled, the cheaper the settlement. In addition, there are considerable advantages to reducing the period of antagonism between parties to the contract.

Tender documentation:

A number of strategies can be used in the preparation of tender documentation to help avoid claims:

➢ Avoid dealing with items post tender. Statements such as 'to be agreed' can lead to dispute without the leverage of competition.

➢ Phrases such as 'to suit the contractor's programme' are open ended and needs to be avoided

➢ Setting a conditional date such as, 'in accordance with the architect's instruction' creates uncertainty for tendering contractors. It is not possible to enforce an 'agreement to agree'.

➢ Avoid ambiguity in design responsibility, such as, 'the contractor shall complete any design required after the consultants have finalized the drawings provided for tender purposes'.

➢ Ensure that programmes, resource charts and method statements supplied by contractors with their tenders are provided for tender assessment only and are not adopted as contract documents or as the basis for variations.

➢ If it is possible avoid 'letters of intent' as they encourage arguments over details in the contract not covered in the letter of intent. There are many cases where disputes have gone to court with no signed contract in place. At the very least a letter of intent should limit activity to pre-construction activity, such as engineering design and pre-ordering of long-delivery items of manufacture. It is also beneficial to define payment terms in a letter of intent as this can be one of the most contentious matters of legal disputes. There is no exact legal definition of Quantum Merruit, and so a letter of intent should describe how overheads, profit and indirect costs are to be treated.

Design:

Many claims are based on delays resulting from design consultants issuing schedules, drawings and specifications after construction has begun. Conflict can then arise due to arguable deficiencies in that information:

➢ Missing, or not produced

➢ Late

➢ Incorrect

➢ Insufficient to order or build

➢ Impractical

➢ Unclear or conflicting

➢ Inconsistent with pricing information

➢ Inappropriate or not fit for purpose

➢ Uncoordinated with other information

Some flexibility is allowed by standard traditional contracts for the design team to issue further drawings and details reasonably necessary either to explain or amplify the contract drawings.

There can be an onus on the contractor to raise any queries on newly received information within 28 days (or as stated in the Agreement) of its receipt or forfeit their right to additional payment.

Contractor's Master Programme:

Many contracts require the contractor to draw up a contractor's master programme within a defined time after the execution of the contract. The contract documents should specify the level of detail required by the contractor's master programme, however, the contractor should make allowance for the following:

- ➤ Realistic time for carrying out each section of the work, with proper consultation and agreement with the major subcontractors involved.
- ➤ Sensible periods for specialist design and manufacture, including approval periods for checking conformity and co-ordination with other specialist input.
- ➤ Providing consultants with an even workload for the approval of specialist drawings.
- ➤ A stated system for recording progress against programme and future updating to reflect enforced changes.

Upon receipt of the contractor's master programme, the Employer's team needs to examine and challenge any aspects of the programme that cannot be justified. This programme is most likely to be the basis upon which all future claims for delay, extensions of time, disruption and loss and expense are based and judgments made. Challenging the contractor's master programme at a later date when claims are submitted is arguing from a position of weakness.

As the master programme is produced after the execution of the contract, the contractor's master programme does not impose any obligation on the contractor beyond those imposed by the contract documents.

Cause and effect:

Global claims, made by grouping together many different causes of delay to make a case for continuous disruption and cumulative effect, may not always find favours with the courts.

It is better to be specific rather than generic. This is a more painstaking exercise requiring more intellectual rigour, as the claimant lists each alleged default, linking it against the consequential delay and its knock-on effect, backed by contemporary records. This approach is obviously a more precise way of establishing quantum and will lead to a more factually based judgment. In other words, to succeed, a claimant needs to establish a discernible nexus between the breaches pleaded and the consequential delay and/or the associated costs.

Notice and particulars:

A form of contract requires that a party has to give the other notice as soon as a breach is apparent so that it can be remedied or its consequences mitigated. Failure to do this expunges the right to additional payment for loss or expense.

The delay or loss and expense notice needs to:

> Identify the specifics of the breach and legal entitlement clauses in the contract

> Disclose as full information as possible, including the effect of the delay

> Identify relevant dates and periods of delay involved

> State any criticality and effect on the completion date

It is highly recommended that the Employer's team shall immediately check the factual basis of such a notification and comment on any content that appears to be subjective.

Concurrent delay:

Concurrent delay is a situation where several causes of delay are running in parallel. An example might be where consultants details were issued late, but an industrial dispute delayed progress of critical work at the same time. In more recent judgments the courts have disregarded arguments about which was the dominant delay and judgment has been made on the basis that the loss should lie where it falls.

Therefore, in a very general concurrent delay event aContractor may be entitled to an extension of time and relief from damages but may not be entitled to loss and expense.

Quantifying claims:

Quantifying claims may involve a number of considerations:

Costs:

Actual cost is the proper basis for evaluating claims. It is a popular misconception that the contractor is bound by its tender rates as its full entitlement. Costs may also include allowance for inflation resulting from delay or a lesser spent than the contract rates if it can be established that the actual cost incurred by the contractor has been lesser.

Preliminaries:

Preliminaries include set-up costs, running costs and dismantling costs. Thus extensions of time should not include set-up or dismantling costs but merely running cost at the time of the breach and its associated period of delay.

Disruption:

Disruption describes loss due to inefficient productivity. It is extremely difficult to assess.

Often the most effective approach is to localize the claim to a specific area of breach. Then compare individuals productivity prior to and after the disruption occurred against the productivity during the period of disruption. Generic claims based on statements such as 'this was the tender price and this is the outturn cost' are unlikely to succeed.

Head office or factory overheads

Hudson's formula appears to be the one most readily acceptedis calculated as below:

(HO Profit %/100) X (contract sum/contract period (weeks)) X (delay (weeks))

However, in applying the above formula the following should be subtracted:

➢ Credit for staff time included in the project costs as visiting supervision.

➢ Any additional overhead recovered within the final account, such as the variation account.

➢ Credit where resources were re-deployed due to delay.

Loss of profit/opportunity costs:

This is only valid when the claimant can prove breaches of contract directly prevented it making a profit elsewhere. Deductions must be made for additional profit that has been paid on the project as a result of extra work instructed and priced within the final account.

Finance charges and interest:

Finance charges and interest on extra capital required to fund costs arising from breaches in the contract are recoverable providing:

- ➤ Interest rates are proven and reasonable (i.e.; market rates prevailing during the period of breach).

- ➤ If financed within the corporate group, the rate will be that received from monies it has placed on deposit.

Alternate Dispute Resolution (ADR):

Although Litigation is an always available means of settling a dispute, construction contracts usually provide for disputes to be dealt with by agreed dispute resolution procedures involving mediation, adjudication and arbitration. It can very often be a combination of all the three. The construction sector is also subject to statutory schemes which impose adjudication procedures in the absence of contractual agreement.

Many contracts for large and complex projects in addition to the dispute resolution procedures set out above, have provided for dispute resolution procedures with obligations to negotiate in good faith, dispute adjudication boards (DAB), steering committees and partnering meetings. Also, the Chartered Institute of Arbitrators' dispute resolution clause recommends use of alternate dispute resolution methods for faster settlement of construction dispute.

Contract disputes are a complex area of law and the choice of procedure is one which requires careful consideration.

A very wide range of alternate Dispute Resolution (ADR) techniques are available. Some of them are as illustrated below:

1. Arbitration

2. Adjudication

3. Neutral Evaluation

4. Expert Determination

5. Mediation

6. Conciliation
7. Ombudsmen

Arbitration:

Arbitration is a procedure whereby both sides to a dispute agree to let a third party, the arbitrator, decide. In some instances, there may be a panel. The arbitrator may be a lawyer, or may be an expert in the field of the dispute. They will make a decision according to the law. The arbitrator's decision, known as an award, is legally binding and can be enforced through the courts.

Court-annexed non-binding arbitration:

Court-annexed non-binding arbitration is widely used in the United States. The finding of the arbitrator becomes a binding order of the court if neither party seeks a rehearing by a judge.

Court settlement process:

This is a combination of early neutral evaluation and mediation. It has been produced for use in those situations where, following a request from the parties, a case managing judge feels that the parties should be able to achieve an amicable settlement. In those circumstances, the case managing judge would then be at liberty to offer a court settlement process to the parties and, if accepted by all relevant parties to the case, that judge or any other judge would make a court settlement order embodying the parties' agreement and fixing a date for a court settlement conference, with an estimated duration proportionate to the issues in the case. The judge would then conduct the court settlement process and if a settlement were not reached, then the case would proceed with another case management judge: the judge conducting the court settlement process (the settlement judge) would take no further part in the litigation.

Early neutral evaluation:

Early neutral evaluation is a process in which a neutral professional, commonly a lawyer, hears a summary of each party's case and gives a non-binding assessment of the merits. This can then be used as a basis for settlement or for further negotiation.

Expert determination:

Expert determination is a process in which an independent third party who is an expert in the subject matter is appointed to decide the dispute. The expert's decision is binding on the parties.

Mediation:

Mediation is a way of settling disputes in which a third party, known as a mediator, helps both sides to come to an agreement that each considers acceptable. Mediation can be "evaluative", where the mediator gives an assessment of the legal strength of a case, or "facilitative", where the mediator concentrates on assisting the parties to define the issues. Where a mediation is successful and an agreement is reached, it is written down and forms a legally binding contract, unless the parties state otherwise.

Conciliation:

Conciliation is a procedure like mediation but in which the third party, the conciliator, takes a more interventionist role in bringing the two parties together and in suggesting possible solutions to help achieve an agreed settlement. The term 'conciliation' is gradually falling into disuse and the process is regarded as a form of mediation. It remains, however, a specific process available under certain contract forms.

Med-arbitration (med-arb):

Med-arbitration (med-arb) is a combination **of** mediation and arbitration. The parties agree to a mediation initially but, if that fails to achieve a settlement, the mediator takes on the role of arbitrator, with powers to make a legally binding award. The same person may act as mediator and arbitrator in this type of arrangement.

Neutral fact finding

Neutral fact finding is a non-binding procedure used in cases involving complex technical issues. A neutral expert in the subject matter is appointed to investigate the facts of the dispute and make an evaluation of the merits of the case. This can form the basis of a settlement or a starting point for further negotiation.

Ombudsmen:

Ombudsmen are independent office holders who investigate and rule on complaints from members of the public about maladministration in Government and in particular services in both the public and private sectors. Some ombudsmen use mediation as part of their dispute resolution procedures. The powers of ombudsmen vary. Most ombudsmen are able to make recommendations; only a few can make decisions that are enforceable through the courts.

Utility regulators:

Utility regulators are watchdogs appointed to oversee the privatized utilities such as water or gas. They handle complaints from customers who are dissatisfied by the way a complaint has been dealt with by their supplier.

In addition to those listed above, the following are also some of other Alternate Dispute Resolution methods:

Mini-trial (executive tribunal):

Mini-trial, also known as executive tribunal, in which each party, often through its legal advisers, makes a presentation of its case to a 'mini-trial panel'. An abbreviated version of the discovery process may have taken place in advance of the mini-trial. The panel generally consists of three members:a management executive from each party (with sufficient authority to reach a settlement), and a third party neutral who may act as a mediator or adviser. The executive members usually have not been involved in the particular dispute. After the submissions have been made, the executives seek to negotiate a settlement. The role of the third party neutral may vary. They may act as a mediator or may act as an adviser, assessing objectively both the facts and the merits of the case and advising on the most appropriate solution.

Construction adjudication:

Construction adjudication is a statutory right introduced into UK construction contracts and is applicable to all relevant contracts entered into after 01 May, 1998. It provides a temporarily binding decision which must be complied with by the parties until overturned or varied by the courts, arbitration or agreement.

Construction adjudication as a process and in spirit is being actively sought to be implemented by other countries around the world due to the prime benefit of aiding the progress of works on a project while a dispute remains unresolved.

Dispute board (dispute review board, dispute resolution board (DRB) or dispute adjudication board (DAB))

Dispute board (also known as dispute review board or dispute resolution board (DRB) and dispute adjudication board (DAB)) is a procedure where a panel, normally of three independent and well-established individuals, is appointed at the commencement of a large construction project and considers project issues and recommends resolutions of disputes. Normally the employer and contractor each appoint one member and the third member is chosen by the first two. The recommendations are normally non-binding.

Judicial appraisal:

Judicial appraisal is a procedure where the parties appoint a judge to receive written representations from each side and make an appraisal of the likely result if the case goes to court. The parties must agree the form and extent of the submissions and whether the appraisal is to be binding or not.

Med-adjudication (med-ad):

Med-adjudication (med-ad) is a process in which the appointed neutral begins conducting the process as if they were an adjudicator, but after meeting the parties' key professionals and expert witnesses together, gives a preliminary view on the matter in dispute. If the parties settle, this is recorded in writing, but if no settlement is reached within a fixed period of time the neutral proceeds to make a decision in which they are not bound by their preliminary view.

Michigan mediation:

Michigan mediation is an interesting variation on the theme and, as the name suggests, is used in the US state of Michigan. In any civil case where the primary relief sought is monetary, the assigned judge may refer the case to process. The term 'mediation' is, however, something of a misnomer: it is more properly described as a 'case valuation' process. After disclosure has been completed, the parties meet with a panel of three neutrals who are all attorneys. They hear 15-minute presentations by each party and give a non-binding evaluation of the case.

Project neutral:

Project neutral is effectively a one-person dispute resolution board.

Summary jury:

Summary jury trial is a non-binding, abbreviated mock trial using a panel of actual jury. The normal rules of evidence and procedure are normally modified to expedite the process, and negotiations generally follow the trial. It is not a very common approach and in fact has been used so far only in the United States.

Third party opinion and fixed-fee mediation:

This scheme fairly new and was launched in the year 2014 by RIBA. This is intended for low-value disputes where both parties have a genuine wish to reach settlement.

The above processes can be divided into two broad categories, as described below:

Alternative adjudication:

Alternative adjudication comprises those processes whereby a neutral third party makes a decision, such as arbitration, construction adjudication, expert determination, ombudsmen and industry regulators;

Assisted settlement:

Assisted settlement comprises those processes whereby a neutral third party offers an opinion and/or seeks to bring the parties to an agreement, such as mediation, conciliation and early neutral evaluation.

Med-arb and med-ad are hybrids of these two categories.

A case study on Pre-litigation mediation:

The dispute in reference is concerning an artificial tennis court that was not performing as expected in the sense that it was flooding during a rain. Initially the argument was between the main contractor, subcontractor and the appointed engineer. However, the following six parties were directly or indirectly affected by the dispute:

> ➤ The local authority (Employer) that had commissioned the works
> ➤ A club that inherited the tennis court
> ➤ The main contractor
> ➤ The specialist subcontractor
> ➤ The engineer, and
> ➤ The sports consultant

Various tests and attempts at correcting the problem had been undertaken, however, none was conclusive to resolve the problem. The cost of complete relaying of the tennis court surface including the sub-base and drainage, was in the order of AED 500,000.00.

The Employer's in-house solicitor recommended mediation as a suggested means to reach an agreement as the six parties in dispute (some of whom had arbitration clauses in their contracts and some did not) were not reaching an agreement and kept blaming the other parties.

All six parties agreed to the suggestion and referred the dispute to mediation and the Employer agreed to pay all the mediator's fees. A mediator, who was an experienced civil engineer, was agreed on, asked for the required written submissions and responses. Each party was given an opportunity to respond to all the other parties' submissions. This process took around eight weeks.

A mediation meeting was held about four weeks after close of written submissions and it lasted one full day. All the referenced parties represented themselves and the only lawyer present was the Employer's in-house solicitor, who had initially recommended meditation as a dispute resolution process.

The mediation meeting followed the usual format, commencing with a joint session wherein each party made a brief oral submissions followed by the mediator shuttling between the parties. The meeting concluded successfully in the late afternoon with a draft agreement having been reached that required formal approval by the Employer's senior management before it could be finalized, but which had the support of their solicitor who attended the meeting.

The settlement included the waiving of claims and fees by some of the parties and undertakings concerning the guaranteed life of the surface together with a contribution by the contractor/subcontractor towards additional maintenance of the tennis court.

Thereafter, the formal approval was obtained and the settlement concluded.

Apart from the internal costs of the parties' own staff, the only external costs were those of the mediator, which was about AED 10,000.00.

Thus an issue was resolved in a better manner than what otherwise would have been the consequence had the parties decided to follow the litigation route.

A case study on Post-pleadings mediation:

The dispute in reference concerns a commercial building in the UAE which had developed a defect about six months after the practical completion, confirmed by the issuance of a Taking over Certificate (TOC). The main contractor for the Work was a major international contractor who had subcontracted part of the Works to a local specialist contractor. The work performed by this subcontractor was apparently the cause of the defect. Several attempts to correct the defect were made without success and eventually the Engineer issued an instruction requiring the whole of the subcontractor's work to be taken out and re-executed strictly in accordance with the specification. Both the main contractor and the subcontractor argued that the problem lay with the design and hence, refused to carry out the instruction.

Thereafter, the building owner hired an architect to advise him about the problem and in due course employed another contractor to strip out and re-execute the defective work to what was in effect, a different design.

The building owner then commenced proceedings in the Court naming the Engineer (who also had designed the Works) as the first defendant and the main contractor as second defendant. The basis of the building owner's claim was failure by the Engineer to design and supervise the works and alternatively failure by the main contractor to carry out the works in accordance with the specification.

The main contractor then issued third party proceedings against the subcontractor, but the subcontractor was successful in applying to the court for those proceedings to be stayed in favour of arbitration, as there was an arbitration clause in the subcontract.

The situation was clearly very complicated for the main contractor having the additional problem of fighting both the litigation and the arbitration on the same issue. Mediation as a means to resolution was suggested by solicitors who could preempt the delay in Court.

A mediator was appointed and each party was allowed to submit a written statement of its case the mediator not later than 14 days before the mediation meeting. These were then simultaneously circulated to all the other parties.

The mediation commenced on a set-date at 9.00 AM. The mediator and the parties with their respective solicitors and advisers first met in a joint session. After a brief introduction to the proceedings by the mediator and the mutual introduction of all those present, each party was allowed 10 minutes to make a brief, oral presentation of its case. Thereafter, each party was given an opportunity to comment on the other parties' presentations. This phase took around another one hour.

Each party then retired to separate rooms and the mediator commenced his meetings with each party in turn. The process was very protracted. There were three major matters to be resolved:

1. The building owner was clearly the 'innocent' party and had to be persuaded to accept a figure less than he had expended in remedying the defect.

2. The question as to whether the defect was due to a failure in design or workmanship and the risk to both the architect and the main contractor of the court finding against them. The mediator had the task of persuading both parties to make a contribution.

3. The split of any responsibility for defective work between main and subcontractor. In reality, this issue was resolved between the main and subcontractor without any assistance from the mediator.

The mediator had at least three private sessions with each party and a greater number with the building owner and the Engineer. At no stage did the mediator overtly express his own opinion as to the merits of the respective parties' cases. He concentrated on the costs and risks of litigating and the difficulties of proving in court the various allegations each party sought to advance in its favour.

By 7.00 PM, the parties were getting close to a settlement, but some needed to take further instructions from their respective head offices, who were closed by this time of the evening. The meeting was called-off with an understanding that discussions would continue the following day by telephone through the mediator.

The dispute was finally settled about 3 days later. The building owner accepted significantly less than the amount of his claim. The Engineer, main contractor and subcontractor each contributed amounts which were far less than they would individually have had to pay had they had been found to be 100% liable by the Court.

Selection of Technique:

Whether or not a particular form of Alternative Dispute Resolution (ADR) is suitable depends upon a number of factors including the nature and value of the dispute, the attitude and financial resources of the parties, the desired outcome and the balance of representation.

Both (or all) parties must be willing to submit their dispute to a form of alternative adjudication, or willing to try a form of assisted settlement as clearly, if both parties are not willing, there can be problems in enforcing an apparently contractual agreement to try mediation or conciliation.

Litigation is, of course, the only option where one party needs to set a legal precedent or obtain an injunction, or where one party is refusing to acknowledge the problem or engage in negotiations. Any form of ADR will be worth considering where the cost of court proceedings is likely to equal or exceed the amount of money at issue.

Where parties wish to preserve an existing relationship, mediation or conciliation may be helpful. A great advantage of mediation is that the mediator is not bound merely to consider the obvious disputes between the parties but can bring in other matters, perhaps unrelated to the particular dispute, provided they may help the parties towards settlement.

Arbitration may be suitable in cases where there is no relationship to preserve and a rapid decision is needed.

Where available, trade association arbitration schemes, utility regulators and ombudsmen can provide a cheaper alternative for an individual seeking redress against a company or large organization, but they may be limited in the redress they can provide.

Early neutral evaluation might be applicable in cases where there is a dispute over a point of law, or where one party appears to have an unrealistic view of their chances of success at trial.

Where there is a technical dispute with a great deal of factual evidence, mediation or determination by an expert in that area might be best. In addition, parties involved in a commercial dispute may prefer to use a form of ADR to keep sensitive commercial information private.

In many apparently intractable, large-scale and complex multi-party cases, mediation has achieved settlement. Where there is a significant imbalance of power, mediation might not be appropriate.

Expert determination:

Expert determination is a process in which an independent third party who is an expert in the subject matter is appointed to decide the dispute. The expert's decision is binding on the parties.

Mediation:

Mediation is a way of settling disputes in which a third party, known as a mediator, helps both sides to come to an agreement that each considers acceptable. Mediation can be "evaluative", where the mediator gives an assessment of the legal strength of a case, or "facilitative", where the mediator concentrates on assisting the parties to define the issues. When mediation is successful and an agreement is reached, it is written down and forms a legally binding contract, unless the parties state otherwise.

Conciliation:

Conciliation is a procedure like mediation but in which the third party, the conciliator, takes a more interventionist role in bringing the two parties together and in suggesting possible solutions to help achieve an agreed settlement. The term "conciliation" is gradually falling into disuse and the process is regarded as a form of mediation. It remains, however, a specific process available under various Institution of Civil Engineers' (ICE) contracts.

Med-arbitration (med-arb):

Med-arbitration (med-arb) is a combination of mediation and arbitration. The parties agree to a mediation initially but, if that fails to achieve a settlement, the mediator takes on the role of arbitrator, with powers to make a legally binding award. The same person may act as mediator and arbitrator in this type of arrangement.

Neutral fact finding:

Neutral fact finding is a non-binding procedure used in cases involving complex technical issues. A neutral expert in the subject matter is appointed to investigate the facts of the dispute and make an evaluation of the merits of the case. This can form the basis of a settlement or a starting point for further negotiation.

Ombudsmen:

Ombudsmen are independent office holders who investigate and rule on complaints from members of the public about maladministration in Government and in particular services in both the public and private sectors. Some ombudsmen use mediation as part of their dispute resolution procedures. The powers of ombudsmen vary. Most ombudsmen are able to make recommendations; only a few can make decisions that are enforceable through the courts.

Utility regulators:

Utility regulators are watchdogs appointed to oversee the privatized utilities such as water or gas. They handle complaints from customers who are dissatisfied by the way a complaint has been dealt with by their supplier.

Mini-trial (executive tribunal):

Mini-trial, also known as executive tribunal, in which each party, often through its legal advisers, makes a presentation of its case to a 'mini-trial panel'. An abbreviated version of the discovery process may have taken place in advance of the mini-trial. The panel generally consists of three members:a management executive from each party (with sufficient authority to reach a settlement), and a third party neutral who may act as a mediator or adviser. The executive members usually have not been involved in the particular dispute. After the submissions have been made, the executives seek to negotiate a settlement. The role of the third party neutral may vary. They may act as a mediator or may act as an adviser, assessing objectively both the facts and the merits of the case and advising on the most appropriate solution.

Construction adjudication:

Construction adjudication is a statutory right introduced into UK construction contracts by the Housing Grants, Construction and Regeneration Act 1996, applicable to all relevant contracts entered into after 1 May 1998. It provides a temporarily binding decision which must be complied with by the parties until overturned or varied by the courts, arbitration or agreement.

Similar provisions are being introduced in contracts all around the world due to the benefits that this has on the completion of upcoming and on-going projects.

The above dispute resolution processes can be divided into two broad categories, described as:

Alternative adjudication:

Alternative adjudication comprises those processes whereby a neutral third party makes a decision, such as arbitration, construction adjudication, expert determination, ombudsmen and industry regulators;

Assisted settlement:

Assisted settlement comprises those processes whereby a neutral third party offers an opinion and/or seeks to bring the parties to an agreement, such as mediation, conciliation and early neutral evaluation.

Med-arb and med-ad are hybrids of these two categories.

Selection of technique:

Whether or not a particular form of ADR is suitable depends upon a number of factors including the nature and value of the dispute, the attitude and financial resources of the parties, the desired outcome, and the balance of representation.

Both (or all) parties must be willing to submit their dispute to a form of alternative adjudication, or willing to try a form of assisted settlement as clearly, if both parties are not willing, there can be problems in enforcing an apparently contractual agreement to try mediation or conciliation.

Litigation is, of course, the only option where one party needs to set a legal precedent or obtain an injunction, or where one party is refusing to acknowledge the problem or engage in negotiations. Any form of ADR will be worth considering where the cost of court proceedings is likely to equal or exceed the amount of money at issue.

Where parties wish to preserve an existing relationship, mediation or conciliation may be helpful. A great advantage of mediation is that the mediator is not bound merely to consider the obvious disputes between the parties but can bring in other matters, perhaps unrelated to the particular dispute, provided they may help the parties towards settlement (an approach that seldom is allowed to be brought up in case of Arbitration of Litigation).

Arbitration may be suitable in cases where there is no relationship to preserve and a rapid decision is needed.

Where available, trade association arbitration schemes, utility regulators and ombudsmen can provide a cheaper alternative for an individual seeking redress against a company or large organization, but they may be limited in the redress they can provide.

Early neutral evaluation might be applicable in cases where there is a dispute over a point of law, or where one party appears to have an unrealistic view of their chances of success at trial.

Where there is a technical dispute with a great deal of factual evidence, mediation or determination by an expert in that area might be best. In addition, parties involved in a commercial dispute may prefer to use a form of ADR to keep sensitive commercial information private.

In many apparently intractable, large-scale and complex multi-party cases, mediation has achieved settlement. Where there is a significant imbalance of power, however, mediation might not be appropriate.

Adjudication in Construction Contracts:

Adjudication is a contractual or statutory procedure for swift interim dispute resolution. Adjudication is provided by a third party adjudicator selected by the parties to the dispute. Adjudication is often is subject to a strict timetable and may be based purely on documentary submissions.

Adjudicators can adopt an inquisitorial role which may involve taking the initiative in ascertaining facts and law.

Adjudication decisions are binding unless and until they are revised by arbitration or litigation. There is no right of appeal and limited right to resist enforcement. Award of legal costs is at the discretion of the adjudicator unless this is excluded by the terms of the contract.

If parties to a construction contract do not agree an adjudication procedure, then one is imposed by statute. The adjudicator is either named in the contract, agreed by the parties or appointed by a nominating body and is usually named in the contract.

Following are the Key adjudication provisions:

- ➢ A contract must allow for the requirements for adjudication
- ➢ If the contract does not comply with these requirements, then the statutory scheme will apply
- ➢ A party to a construction contract will thereby be able to refer any dispute arising under the contract for adjudication under either the contractual scheme or the statutory scheme

- ➢ Enable a party to give notice at any time of his intention to refer a dispute to adjudication
- ➢ Provide a timetable with the object of securing the appointment of an adjudicator and referral of the dispute to him within 7 days of such notice
- ➢ Require the adjudicator to reach a decision within 28 days of referral or such longer period as agreed by the parties, or by up to 14 days with the consent of the party by whom the dispute was referred
- ➢ Impose a duty on the adjudicator to act impartially
- ➢ Enable the adjudicator to take initiative in ascertaining the facts and law
- ➢ The adjudicator is not required to act judicially when applying the law, nor is there any obligation upon him to reach the right answer
- ➢ The decision of the adjudicator is binding unless and until the dispute is finally determined by legal proceedings, by arbitration or by agreement
- ➢ The adjudicator is not liable for anything done or omitted in the discharge of his functions unless in bad faith
- ➢ If the contract does not comply with the requirements of the Act, the adjudication provisions of the Scheme for Construction Contracts would apply

The recommendation for adopting adjudication procedure for Construction Contracts:

Notice:

- ➢ It is required that the party seeking adjudication serves written notice on every other party to the contract
- ➢ This briefly sets out the nature of the dispute and the relief sought
- ➢ A copy is sent to the adjudicator of nominating body

Appointment:

- ➢ Selection of an adjudicator by a body must be communicated to the parties within five days (or as stated within the Contract) of its referral
- ➢ The selected adjudicator has two days to decide whether he is willing to act

- ➤ This person must not be an employee of a party to the dispute
- ➤ Once appointed, the referring party must serve notice on the adjudicator, accompanied by copies of all documents on which that party intends to rely
- ➤ Copies of the notice and documents are sent to all other parties in the dispute

Related disputes:

- ➤ The adjudicator may decide more than one dispute arising out of one contract, and/or
- ➤ May decide related issues arising under different contracts

Objection to adjudicator:

- ➤ The objection of a party to the appointment of a particular person as adjudicator will not invalidate the appointment or decision of the adjudicator

Powers of adjudicator:

- ➤ To open up, revise and review certificates unless the contract provides that they are final and conclusive
- ➤ To decide and order payment of sums due under the contract
- ➤ To decide whether interest should be paid

Mediation in Construction:

Mediation is a consensual process of dispute resolution in which a third party mediator, appointed by the parties to the dispute, assists in the negotiated resolution of the dispute.

There are basically two types of mediation:

1. Facilitative mediation

2. Evaluative mediation

(although in practice, there are many in-between kind of arrangements).

Facilitative mediation:

Facilitative mediation involves the participation of a neutral third party (the mediator) whose primary role is to assist the parties to reach a negotiated solution. As a facilitator, the mediator manages the negotiation process, assisting the parties to overcome deadlock and encourages them to think creatively about a reasonable solution. The mediator will also encourage the parties to focus on their underlying interests and concerns and to move away from the fixed positions that often obscure the real issues. They will assist the parties in identifying common ground and may act as a reality tester, encouraging parties to reflect realistically upon their position and upon the consequences of failing to reach a negotiated solution.

Evaluative mediation:

Where evaluative mediation is used, the mediator learns the facts of the case and each party's position. The mediator then expresses to each party a view on the overall merits as they see them. Conciliation may also be considered as a form of evaluative mediation if a settlement is not reached with the conciliator acting in facilitative mode, may issue a 'recommendation' setting out how, in his opinion, the matter should be resolved.

Techniques/Procedures:

The following are a range of procedures that may be used under the mediation procedures, such as:

- Assisted negotiation and independent chairing
- Coaching
- Early neutral evaluation
- Expert determination
- Independent intervention
- Independent investigation and review

Although mediations do not have a rigid procedure but a typical one might proceed along the following lines:

- The first step is for a mediator to be chosen, either by agreement between the parties, or by selection by an organization such as CEDR (Centre for Effective Dispute resolution) and CIArb (Chartered Institute of Arbitrators). A proposed mediator should not accept an appointment unless all parties have agreed to the appointment.
- A date, time and venue for the mediation meeting need to be fixed. A venue may comprise of a large room capable of accommodating all the participants, which is used for the joint session and a separate room for each of the parties involved in the mediation.

➢ At a set time (usually two to three weeks) before the date fixed for the mediation meeting, the parties simultaneously produce written statements, together with any documents which they wish the mediator to see, and serve these on the other party or parties and the mediator.

➢ On the appointed day for the mediation meeting, the mediator will meet all the parties in an initial joint session at which each will present a brief oral summary of their case, possibly through their legal advisers. A time limit may be allowed for each party.

➢ Each party will then retire to their separate rooms and the mediator will talk to each party in turn, either by visiting them in their separate rooms or by calling them into the main room. Such private meetings are known as 'caucuses' in the jargon of ADR practitioners. Everything that takes place in the caucuses is private and confidential and their purpose is to enable the mediator to establish his understanding of the possibilities for reaching agreement and the approach most likely to encourage a settlement.

➢ The mediator will then shuttle between the various parties as required in an effort to find a settlement to the dispute. Nothing disclosed to the mediator in confidence in the caucuses will be disclosed to any other party without the express permission of the party disclosing the information. Private meetings between the mediator and only some of the parties may take place.

➢ Working with the parties, the mediator will examine the issues arising in the dispute. The mediator does not take sides but they may challenge a position being adopted by one or other party. The mediator may suggest looking at the dispute from a different angle. They may test out possible ways of resolving the dispute. In short, they will examine the dispute and work with the parties to find an acceptable solution.

➢ During the various joint and private sessions, the mediator may useconventional negotiating techniques such as:

1. Separating the people from the problem: Being easy on the people and hard on the problem;

2. Getting behind the position to find the interest;

3. Encouraging a constructive problem-solving approach rather than dwelling on past arguments.

> The mediator may decide at any time to bring the parties together in joint session to report progress and seek mutually agreeable ways forward.

> When and if the mediator reaches the position at which a settlement has been achieved, they will bring the parties together in joint session for a final time and will work with the parties to reduce the settlement to writing by means of a binding legal agreement and/or a consent order.

> If there is a dead-lock and no settlement are being reached at the meeting (however, some progress has been made) it is still open to the parties to adjourn to another time and place. The evidence is that even when no settlement is reached at the meeting itself, the parties may often reach an agreement shortly afterwards as a consequence of the discussions and progress made at the meeting.

The process is voluntary, confidential, non-binding and without prejudice to the parties' legal positions. The fact that legal action is underway does not prevent mediation although the cost benefits of achieving settlement through mediation are obviously greater the earlier mediation is employed to resolve the dispute.

Adoption:

Mediation is now very much a core procedure in construction contracts and, whilst it's necessity remain consensual, the courts may enforce mediation clauses into contracts. The courts cannot insist that the parties reach an agreement, however they may order parties to engage in the mediation process if there is a contractual obligation and can stay legal proceedings pending mediation. An unreasonable refusal to mediate may prejudice the right of a successful litigant to an award of legal costs.

Arbitration within the Construction Industry:

Arbitration is a private, contractual form of dispute resolution. It provides for the determination of disputes by a third party arbitrator or arbitration panel, selected by the parties to the dispute. Disputes are resolved on the basis of material facts, documents and relevant principles of law.

The arbitration process is administered by an appointed arbitrator subject to any relevant contractual rules and subject to the statutory regulatory framework applied by the domestic courts. There are only limited rights of appeal and legal costs are usually awarded to the successful party.

Common law does not insist on any formal requirements for an arbitration agreement (for example it can even be verbal), however if the agreement is not in writing it will be outside the supervisory regime of the courts established by the Arbitration Act. In addition, construction projects with complex disputes require properly constituted arbitration procedures in order for them to be effective.

Arbitration clauses are traditionally found in all standard form contracts generally used in the modern construction industry, often with related adjudication clauses. However, there may be instances where the default dispute resolution is set as litigation rather than arbitration, leaving the contracting parties to specifically agree to arbitration, in case they so desire.

Arbitration remains the favoured method of dispute resolution for international projects within the FIDIC contracts and UNCITRAL model is widely accepted in international commerce.

Arbitration commences with a notice to concur which provides for agreement on the appointment of an arbitrator, failing which an arbitrator may be appointed by a nominating body (which should be named in the contract). Arbitration is now usually combined with adjudication and mediation in tiered dispute resolution procedures.

Steps undertaken in an Arbitration process:

Arbitration process generally is undertaken in two distinct parts.

Part A: Describes the steps that an arbitrator needs to take before and during a full oral hearing, and

Part B: Deals with costs.

It is difficult to deal with all issues, through correspondence, that arise during arbitration proceeding. Therefore, when submissions have been made and witness statements have taken place, an arbitrator may consider it necessary to call the parties together for meetings which are known as Interlocutory Meetings. Unless agreed by the parties otherwise, the tribunal holds oral hearing for the presentation of evidence or for oral arguments in arbitrating the disputes at an appropriate stage. The arbitrator should consider various steps before and during such hearing which are as discussed below:

Part A: Oral Hearing

Steps before Oral Hearing:

1. *What has been done so far?*

During submissions, disclosure and exchange of witness statements, situation arises that may take different dimensions and need to be directed so that both parties have full opportunity to be heard. Therefore, before full oral hearing an arbitrator should consider the proceeding that has been done so far and focus on any matters that are still to be dealt with so that both the parties could be heard and present their case fully.

2. *Administration Facilities:*

Administrative facilities required for a hearing are rooms, recording facilities, sitting arrangements, food facilities, etc. Administrative facilities of an arbitrator institution may be used in case of institutional arbitration. In case of an Ad hoc proceeding, the parties and arbitration tribunal agree on these matters.

3. *Location of Meeting:*

The arbitration can take place virtually anywhere. Therefore, important point for the place of hearing is that it should be suitable and convenient for parties. Arbitration suites for such hearing are available in major Arbitration Centres. The parties may select to use hotels or other conference facilities for such meetings. Therefore, the arbitrator is to choose the location meeting carefully that suits everyone.

4. *Rooms:*

Once the place of hearing is decided, the arbitrator should consider the number of rooms to be allocated for hearing. There should be one room large enough for the hearing. Sitting positions may be arranged in U shape, the arbitrator at one end with the parties to each side and witness may be seated in the middle facing the arbitrator.

There should be one room allocated to each party for their private discussion and one room for the arbitrator. This will allow them privacy and may serve as retiring room during hearing intervals.

5. *Sittings Timings:*

The arbitrator is required to consider the days when hearing will take place. The hearing start and finish timings should also be determined. The arbitrator should not forget that during long hearing, concentration often loose therefore sitting duration should be such which could enable arbitrator to listen, absorb and ask questions and make note constructively.

6. Overall length of Hearing:

It may be very easy for the length of hearing to expand until it is unreasonable in both time and cost. Therefore, arbitrator, in agreement with the parties, does set limits to the time a hearing will last. The arbitrator generally agree overall hearing period which should be divided in two parts giving each side an amount of time that the have to do with as they want.

7. Recording the Proceeding:

Since arbitration is a private process, the arbitrator decides with the parties that how much detailed record they wish to keep for the proceeding. This can be done using tape recorders, video recorders or other electronic systems. Therefore the extent of record keeping must be decided at the outset by arbitrator (with agreement of the parties) so that hearing arrangement could be made accordingly.

8. Interpretation and Translation:

Where the language of the arbitral proceeding is foreign to one party or arbitrator, and the services of translators or interpreters is required, it should be decided by the arbitrator for timely employment of such interpreters.

9. Presentation of Witness of facts and Expert Witness:

The arbitrator should discuss with the parties regarding presentation of witness of facts and expert witness in oral hearing. The expert witness assist the tribunal in hearing and the tribunal may appoint its expert witness. Therefore, the arbitrator should discuss the matter before start of the hearing and appoint expert witness accordingly.

Steps During Oral Hearing:

1. Order of Proceeding:

During hearing, the arbitrator should follow the order of proceedings. The tribunal and parties will agree on the order of proceeding. Generally, the claimant opens his case first stating summary of dispute. The claimant then presents his evidence (witness of fact and of opinion). Each witness will undergo examination by the party who called them and is cross-examined by the other party. The respondent then presents his case in exactly the same way.

The respondent will make his closing statements followed by the claimant. The hearing procedure will therefore, take the following sequence:

- ➤ Commencement of hearing,
- ➤ Claimant case opening,
- ➤ Claimant evidence,
- ➤ Respondent case opening,
- ➤ Respondent rebuttal evidence,
- ➤ Respondent case closing,
- ➤ Claimant case closing.

2. Arbitrator Impartiality:

During course of arbitration hearing, there are intervals of dinners and coffee breaks. The arbitrator must not allow himself to be alone with one of the parties which may raise questions regarding his impartiality. Therefore, during hearing an arbitrator must take all steps that demonstrate his impartiality.

3. Admissibility of Evidence:

The purpose of the evidence is to establish facts before a tribunal in support of the case. Therefore, different types of evidence are produced by parties to prove their case for example; facts documents, hearsay evidence (hearsay is something which a witness has heard others say), expert witness, parol evidence etc. What kind of documents/evidence should be acceptable by arbitrator and what not?

The arbitrator should take steps in determining admissibility of evidence. In determining this, he is required to consider that the evidence must be relevant to the fact under discussion and consider law of seat of arbitration in this regard.

One very important step an arbitrator is to distinguish the fine line between "authenticity" and "admissibility" of documents. Whether the document is signed, whether it is signed by the authorized person, whether it was written when it was dated, whether it is a genuine extract of the relevant record, etc. These are the points that deal with authenticity of documents. Whereas, in determining admissibility of documents, the question is not whether the document is authentic but whether a statement of fact or opinion in the document is admissible evidence of the fact or matter of opinion, which the party seeks to establish.

4. Production of New Evidence:

In case where any party present new evidence (during hearing but) at a late stage of reference, which had never been brought before the tribunal, and which may materially affect their case, or if the evidence is produced after the close of the hearing but before the award is made ,what steps an arbitrator should take in such matters?

Depending upon the nature, relevance, weight and critically of new evidence with reference to the dispute, the arbitrator is required to judge the admissibility (or inadmissibility) of new evidence and should (or should not) adjourn the hearing and grant a further hearing period.

If new evidence is not submitted until after the award is published, the arbitrator has no power to take any action and the remedy of the party seeking to reply on the new evidence.

While dealing with the new evidence, arbitrator should ensure that the parties are heard and treated fairly.

6. Intervention by the Parties and Arbitrator:

Generally, each party does not intervene to other's party evidence/ presentation, during hearing, until his opponent has closed his case. However, such interventions by party may or may not be justified depending upon nature of intervention. Therefore, the arbitrator is required to step in and either rule-in or rule-out considering the nature of the intervention.

Similarly, an arbitrator need to intervene when he is proposing to make a finding based on his own personal knowledge, so that other party against whom the finding is made can comment upon the finding of the arbitrator. An arbitrator should also question a witness the purpose of explaining an answer to the question.

7. Failure to appear in Hearing:

At the start of hearing, there may be an occasion where the respondent fails to appear at the hearing notwithstanding having been given reasonable notice of the time and place fixed by the arbitrator. The step that an arbitrator is required to take is not to stop the hearing and proceed without him and hear the case of claimant by giving all evidence/submissions/correspondence to respondent. The arbitrator must ensure that the absent party has been duly notified of the proceedings and all relevant communications have been brought in the knowledge where they could comment. An arbitrator must also consider that part absence does not mean that award will be automatically against the absent party.

In case no party appears, and if the arbitrator already has before him written submissions and evidence, the step that an arbitrator is required to take is to decide the case on the material before him.

8. Arbitrator's Notes:

An arbitrator is not obliged to make note of the evidence and submission. However, where full oral hearing is held, the arbitrator should take a note for the purpose of the comparison and checking. Sometime what is said (or not said) at an earlier stage may subsequently prove to be more important than had been realized. The arbitrator should also take a note of any applications or objections by the parties and of his own ruling during the course of hearing.

9. Natural Justice:

The arbitration tribunal is to manage the proceeding effectively ensuring that all the parties are treated equally and given a fair opportunity to present their cases and defend the cases against them. All procedural matters are subject to the mandatory provisions of the applicable procedural law. Therefore, during the course of hearing, an arbitrator must include and expand on the rule of Natural justice.

Part B: Costs

The arbitrator not only decides the disputes itself but also he has the power to decide on who pays cost of dealing with the dispute.

Arbitration Act 1996 states that "Unless the parties otherwise agree, the tribunal shall award costs on the general principle that costs should follow the event except where it appears to the tribunal that in the circumstances this is not appropriate in relation to the whole or part of the costs". *It means that the winner has his costs paid by the loser.*

Major Cost heads (as per UNCITRAL) are as follows:

➢ Fee and reimbursable expenses of the arbitral tribunal.

➢ Administrative costs of the arbitral proceedings.

➢ Fees paid to an arbitration institution or appointing authority.

➢ Cost of expert advise or assistance required by the arbitral tribunal.

➢ The legal costs of the parties if claimed during the arbitration.

The parties in arbitration claim the costs of the arbitration in addition to other monetary claim amounts. Therefore, arbitration costs should be apportioned between parties as follows;

Taxation of Costs/Recoverable Costs:

Either the tribunal or arbitration institute fixes the cost of arbitration, which at the commencement of arbitration proceeding or before the tribunal is constituted, parties are required to deposit for the cost of arbitration. Hen proceeding is over, the tribunal produces a statement of account and refund any excess money paid.

In determining the costs, parties are not entitled to recover all of his actual expenses but only a reasonable amount in respect of all costs reasonably incurred.

Equal Costs allocated to both parties:

Considering the arbitration costs heads in mind, an arbitrator should determine the cost, which should be equally distributed to both the parties. The arbitration cost incurred by the tribunal, which is attributable to both parties, is to be borne by the parties.

Costs allocated to Specific Party:

There are certain costs that are caused because of the one party like following:

> Costs of interpretations/interpreter/translation
> Party calling the expert witness
> Party seeking tribunal visit to site to support his evidence

In determining costs elements, the tribunal allocates the costs where it lies.

Interest on Money Claims Disputes:

In deciding monetary disputes, the arbitrator has the power to award the interest. An arbitrator can determine the rate of interest, kind of interest (whether simple or compound), starting date of interest (when the cause of action arose or date of dispute, etc.) and period of interest.

However, it may be noted that interest discussed above is for the monetary claim (or counter claim) and has no relevance to the cost of arbitration s discussed herein above.

Important point to be noted by the Arbitrator:

Arbitration is a dispute resolution procedure the has its origin and owes its success to the advantages that it has over other procedures of dispute resolution, and therefore, the arbitrator must endeavor to make justice to the parties in dispute without compromising on the following inherent advantages that this procedure possess :

1. Choice of arbitrator

2. Speed

3. Cost

4. Finality of Decision

5. Flexibility & Control

6. Autonomy of parties

7. Informality

8. Privacy

It is noted that International Commercial Arbitration is based on UNCITRAL model subject to any agreement in force between this State and any other State or States.

Essential Features of International Arbitration:

International arbitration is one of the many private dispute resolution mechanisms parties involved in international transactions may adopt in resolving their disputes. The United Nations Commission for International Trade Law (UNCITRAL) regulates two primary mechanisms, conciliation/ mediation and arbitration, and particular rules govern each mechanism. This chapter examines the differences between conciliation/mediation, arbitration and litigation and the factors which require consideration when opting for arbitration as the preferred method of dispute resolution.

Conciliation/mediation and arbitration:

The terms 'conciliation' and 'mediation' are used interchangeably in this chapter. It is however, acknowledged that they are two different, though very similar mechanisms. However, UNCITRAL and the International Centre for the Settlement of Investment Disputes (ICSID) refer to conciliation, whereas most private and national dispute resolution organizations and rules refer to mediation.

Conciliation/mediation refers to a private dispute resolution mechanism where a neutral third party assists the opposing parties to reach a solution in settlement of their dispute. Conciliation/mediation, when successful, results in a decision that is usually only binding as a contract. Arbitration refers to a private dispute resolution mechanism whose outcome is a legally-binding and enforceable decision with *res judicata* effect (i.e.; once a dispute has been decided upon, the same parties cannot attempt to raise the issue again by or during further proceedings). Apart from litigation no other resolution process has such universal enforceability.

In 1980 the General Assembly of the United Nations recommended the UNCITRAL Conciliation Rules to its member states. Parties have to agree on the rules by concluding a reference clause or agreement post- or pre-dispute. The UNCITRAL Conciliation Rules then govern the conciliation procedure. The conciliator may make settlement proposals to the parties which do not need to be in writing or accompanied with reasons. In 2002 UNCITRAL published a Model Law on International Commercial Conciliation which, like the UNCITRAL Model Law on International Commercial Arbitration 1985 with regard to arbitration, is intended to guide states in drafting conciliation legislation.

Arbitration and litigation:

Before examining in detail the decisions to be made when opting for arbitration as the preferred method of dispute resolution, we first need to look at the advantages and disadvantages of arbitration compared with its main comparator, litigation.

Arbitration is most often compared to litigation, logically, since they are the only two methods capable of producing binding resolution. It should, however, be appreciated that any possible advantage can, if not exploited properly, become a disadvantage (and *vice versa)* and this consideration should be applied to the advantages and disadvantages of arbitration listed below.

Advantages:

a) The parties can choose their arbitrator who, with very few exceptions, can be anyone. This means they can choose a person with particular, relevant expertise.

b) The arbitral process is private and confidential between the parties and the arbitrator. This confidence may only be breached with the consent of the parties and the arbitrator. Unless agreed by all parties, no outsider may be involved. This principle extends to sitting in by pupils (although most parties do not object to this, often welcoming it in a very positive way).

c) In choosing their arbitrator, parties will usually ensure that he can start the arbitration quickly and proceed without unnecessary delay.

d) An arbitration hearing may be held anywhere that is convenient, at any suitable time.

e) Arbitration is flexible and can be tailored to a particular dispute, making the best use of time while still ensuring a proper consideration of the matters in hand.

f) By starting and proceeding without delay, and eliminating unnecessary procedures, significant corresponding cost savings can be made, even though arbitration requires the arbitral tribunal and any hearing room and services to be paid for (while a judge and court and its facilities are usually free to the parties).

g) Parties in an arbitration are usually free to choose whomever they wish to make their case for them (advocate):the party itself or a friend or a professional accountant, architect, etc. (lay advocate) or a lawyer without restriction as to type or grade.

h) An arbitrator's award may "be enforced in the same manner as a judgment", provided it is made in accordance with the relevant statute, that is, it was made with regard to a written arbitration agreement.

Disadvantages:

a) Arbitration results in a stand-alone decision:it generally has no effect on any other decisions either in arbitration or in the courts. It has no 'precedential' value (in certain circumstances this can be an advantage to the parties, ensuring confidentiality extends to there being no report of the arbitration).

b) If a dispute relates to an important point of law, it may be that the 'loser' in arbitration will appeal the arbitrator's decision. In such a situation, it would probably be faster and cheaper to litigate the dispute in the courts rather than go through an arbitration and delay the apparently inevitable court proceedings.

c) Unless the parties in an arbitration agree, joining another party (a 'third party', who must also agree) into an arbitration may not be done.

d) Legal aid is generally not available for arbitration.

Confidentiality:

Litigation is almost always open to the public. Documents filed at court and the judgments delivered are all public documents. In contrast, arbitration proceedings, documents and awards are private as between the parties and the arbitral tribunal (and arbitration institution). However this privacy is not the same as confidentiality. Thus, an arbitral award enters into the public domain when, for example, enforcement proceedings are commenced. Various courts have ruled that in certain circumstances arbitral documents and awards are not protected by confidentiality.

Enforceability:

Judgments of national courts are enforced through the coercive powers of the state. However, arbitration awards do not have any automatic coercive powers of enforcement, which means that an arbitral award is not self-enforcing. Unless it is voluntarily complied with by the losing party, a winning party in receipt of an arbitral award will have to seek enforcement by the national court system.

National court judgments have territorial limitation and there are no multilateral conventions for the enforcement of court judgments except within the European Union. However, under the Convention for the Recognition and Enforcement of Foreign Arbitral Awards made in New York (also known as the New York Convention) an award made in one Convention state can be enforced in any other Convention state upon the production of minimal documents (arbitration agreement and arbitral award and translations, if necessary).

Speed and finality:

A court judgment is generally subject to appeal on the merits and usually only becomes final when it is no longer able to be appealed. An arbitral award is final and subject to appeal on very limited grounds (but not on the facts decided in it) and within very limited time. An example of this stringency is to be found the UNCITRAL Model Law on International Commercial Arbitration which states that an arbitral award must be challenged within three months.

Neutral forum:

Litigation takes place before national courts connected geographically to either the dispute or one or both of the parties. A party litigating before a national court must have standing to sue before the court. However, parties in arbitral proceedings can arbitrate before any forum of their choice without the necessity of such a connection. The neutrality of forum is said to be one of the major advantages of arbitration, since parties involved in international arbitration are usually from different countries and prefer to have their arbitration in a neutral country. This neutrality removes the anxiety of one party getting a home advantage and therefore the problems of perceived or actual bias.

Settlement of Dispute in Abu Dhabi (UAE):

Within UAE and in particular within its capital city Abu Dhabi, any dispute which is to be referred to arbitration is to be conclusively and finally settled by arbitration in accordance with the Procedural Regulations of the Abu Dhabi Commercial Conciliation and Arbitration Centre (ADCCAC).

Similar clause and approach to arbitration is recommended to be drafted within a contract by organizations that are keen on using arbitration as an approach to dispute resolution.

A case on payment for omissions during tendering:

A dispute concerning payments for concrete surrounds for pipe works that was not included as an item on a re-measured contract.

An experienced contractor who had been awarded laying of pipelines over several kilometers on a re-measured contract had priced for all items as requested within the BOQ including the road crossings and shallow depth pipe works. The method of measurement was based on CESMM3 and the contract was based on FIDIC Red Book form of contract.

The works however, involved substantial amount of concrete encasing to be done to the pipe works due to road crossings and due to the fact the substantial portion of the works was at very low depths from the ground level. The drawings clearly identified provision of concrete encasings in all such cases.

The contractor completed the works, as required and as contracted, however it came back to the Employer through the Engineer requesting additional monies to be paid on account of the substantial concrete encasing works that he had to do.

This was contested by the Engineer and the Employer on the basis that the tender had provision of different rates to the road crossings and to the pipes laid at shallow depths. It was also highlighted that the BOQ had provisions for the addition of rates that an experienced contractor could have used to provide new rates.

Since the contractor chose not to request for additional items and had in fact provided for different rates to pipes at road crossings and pipes to be laid at different depths, it is deemed to be understood that the rates for concrete encasing were in fact included within the rates contained in the awarded BOQ. Method of measurement identified within the Preamble also provided for an all-inclusive rate and hence it was reasoned that the request for additional monies on account of the deemed omissions are not justified and hence this claim was rejected.

Several attempts were made by the main contractor to convince the Employer, who could not accept to the request citing the Contract and the language contained within the method of measurement and to the fact that this acceptance (of a star rate for concrete surrounds) would set a wrong precedence to future contracts that would initially be let out at low cost by an experienced contractor, only to claim such a cost at a later point of time.

Different Standards of measurement (NRM, POMI, etc. may have impacted the above decisions and hence, the choice of measurement standard cannot be over-emphasized. As a general rule, a proper selection of the measurement standard is to be based on the type of anticipated Works).

What does a Client/Employer want from a Contractor?

A very obvious question and probably easier said than what is practically observed within the construction industry.

Of course, a reasonable response could be right product at the right time and within budget.

The answer however, becomes ambiguous on the understanding of the term "reasonable". With the volatility of pricing of all possible commodities that directly or indirectly is needed in construction. The rapidly rising prices of reinforcement, steel and concrete a few years ago created an extremely challenging environment in the industry. While recently the prices have been more under control, in fact fluctuating to suit some while challenge others. It appears that the construction industry may be getting ready for another wave of unstable material prices.

These problems need to be addressed by an experienced contractor. A contractor, who is supposed to be an expert in this field, needs to explore the site and anticipate the challenges that the construction process presents at a particular location. In other words, he needs to understand the surroundings and topography of the site and understand how these may impact the construction process.

In fact, not doing this important task before taking up a construction job is one of the fastest ways for a contractor to become liable to liquidity problems in future.

A general contractor/main contractor needs to consider himself on the side of his Employer and hence must not be passing-on his subcontractor's change order requests without reviewing them critically. It's the responsibility of the general contractor to review the change order and first determine if the work in question is even the responsibility of the subcontractor or the general contractor. If it is determined it is the owner's responsibility, the general contractor needs to ensure that the pricing is fair and reasonable before it is sent on to the employer.

Price has always been important and will ever be so. Like any other industry, construction industry too is a very competitive market, and the contractor therefore, needs to provide his client's their value for money. A client may want more than that from a contractor. They may want to know what the end price of the intended project will be, so they don't want the contractor to price just what's on the drawings. In fact they would like to see the overall price by suggested addition of what has been missing. Obviously in a competitive situation, the contractor can't include items in its bid that are not included on the documents. However, what the contractor can do is tell the client what it will take to complete the project. This would demonstrate that the contractor is looking out for the client and is indeed experienced.

Definitions and Interpretation

For the purposes of this book, the words and expressions listed hereunder shall have the following meanings:

Bankruptcy is a legal proceeding involving a person or business that is unable to repay outstanding debts. The bankruptcy process begins with a petition filed by the debtor (most common) or on behalf of creditors (less common). All of the debtor's assets are measured and evaluated, whereupon the assets are used to repay a portion of outstanding debt. Upon the successful completion of bankruptcy proceedings, the debtor is relieved of the debt obligations incurred prior to filing for bankruptcy.

Best Practice means those practices and methods of working which are generally exercised and adhered to when working in the environment meant for the intended Contract by an experienced contractor having expertise and experience in constructing works of similar scope, complexity, purpose and size to the Works.

Bill of Quantities (BOQ) means the priced and complete bill of quantities set out within the tender document.

Building information modeling (BIM) is a process that involves the generation and management of digital representations of physical and functional characteristics of a place/site.

CESMM means Civil Engineering Standard Method of Measurement

Commercial Bid is that portion of a Bidder's Offer which comprises pricing information only.

Commencement Date (CD) is the actual date of commencement of the referenced Contract.

Competitive Tendering Process is a tendering process wherein more than one bidder is invited to participate in a Tender or Request for Proposal (RFP).

Competent Authority means an authority competent within the law of the land to take decisions.

Contract Agreement means the agreement between the Parties identified as such.

Contract Document means the Contract Agreement, the conditions of contract, Schedules and Appendices thereto, Scope of Work, Specifications and the Bill of Quantities.

Contract Price means the sum stated within the Payment Schedule as payable to the Contractor for the design, execution and completion of the Works and the remedying of any defects therein in accordance with the provisions of the Contract set out within the Contract Document.

Contractor's Personnel means all personnel whom the Contractor utilizes on or off Site, which shall include the staff, labor and other employees of the Contractor and of each Sub-contractor; and any other personnel assisting the Contractor in the execution of the Works.

Construction management (CM) refers to form of delivery and the management of a project site.

Consultant is an entity contracted by Employer to provide professional consultancy services under a Contract.

Contract is a written agreement between Employer and the other contracting party for the provisions of works, services or goods. A Contract may also be referred to as an Agreement.

Contractor is an entity contracted by Employer to provide works or goods or services under a Contract.

Contract administrator (CA) Contract administrator assists the project manager as well as the superintendent with the details of the construction contract.

Cost means all expenditure properly incurred or to be incurred, whether on or off the Site, including overhead and other charges properly allocable thereto but does not include any allowance for profit.

Defects Liability Certificate (DLC) means a certificate issued pursuant to a defined Clause within the Contract document.

Defects Liability Period (DLP) is a time period defined within the Contract document (usually 365 Days, but may differ from Contract to Contract) calculated from the date of Substantial Completion stated in the Taking-Over Certificate.

Effective Date means the date on which the Contract Agreement is signed by both Parties.

Employer means the person (or a company) who requests for the Works to be done and as such, is ready to pay a consideration to the second party (the contractor/consultant). Employer is also referred to as "Owner" or "Client" or the first party to a contract.

Engineer means the person (or a company) appointed from time to time by the Employer under the Contract. Generally, any reference to the Employer shall be deemed to apply equally to the Engineer where powers have been so delegated by the Employer.

FEED means Front end engineering design

Force Majeure Event means any of the following that occurs within the country:

War, rebellion, terrorism or revolution.

Civil commotion (by persons other than the Contractor's personnel, agents and employees or any party for which the Contractor is responsible (including Subcontractors));

Ionising radiation or contamination by radioactivity, except as may be attributable to the Contractor's use of such radiation or radioactivity;

Catastrophic storms or floods, lightning, tornadoes, cyclones, earthquakes, epidemics, fires and explosion.

Following do not come into the category of Force Majeure Event:

Any shortage or late delivery of Plant and/or materials or consumables which the Contractor or any Subcontractor is obliged to supply under the Contract or any subcontract and/or in connection with the Works;

Any shortage of staff and labour;

Any act of a Governmental Authority in relation to visas, work permits and immigration approvals for the Contractor's or Subcontractor staff and labour;

Changes in market conditions; and

An inability to secure financing (and the effects thereof) for whatever reason occurring in relation to the Contractor, any Subcontractor, or supplier of the Contractor or any subcontractor or supplier of any tier or a guarantor or financial institution providing any Performance Security;

Governmental Authority means any national, federal, state, regional or local government (of or within any country) and any legislative, executive or judicial organs of the foregoing including any ministry, department, agency, official, court or other emanation and any reference to specific Governmental Authorities shall be construed so as to include any and all successors to such Governmental Authority which take over the function or responsibilities of such Governmental Authority.

Guaranteed maximum price (GMP) is a contract that has a specified upper limit to the project's final price.

Insolvency is a term used to describe a financial ill-health of an individual or a company. It is used to state a condition wherein an individual or organization can no longer meet its financial obligations with its lender or lenders as debts become due. Insolvency can lead to insolvency proceedings, in which legal action may be taken against the insolvent entity, and assets may be liquidated to pay off outstanding debts.

Joint Venture (JV) is collaboration between two or more companies from the same or different backgrounds and/or fields to complete a common project. Joint Ventures typically have a lead contractor that deals with most of the business aspects. The lead will usually have a bigger stake in the partnership (i.e. the lead may have a 65% stake while the second contractor might have 30% and a third might have 5%).

Law means any and all written and unwritten laws, treaties, regulations, regulatory approvals, standards, decrees, rules, decisions, judgments, orders, injunctions, authorizations, directives and/or other legal requirements of any Governmental Authority which are or may become during the currency of the Contract applicable to the execution and completion and operation and maintenance of the Works, and any and all applicable laws, by-laws, rules, regulations, directives, approved schemes and guidance of any public or private utility or other undertaking which has any jurisdiction with regard to the Works, or with whose systems or property the Works and/or the Project is or will be connected and Law shall be construed as including any and all laws which subsequently amend, extend, consolidate and/or replace the specific Laws referred to.

Liquidated Damages means the penalties for delay in completion of the Works or any Milestone Works payable in accordance with the Contract.

Malum in se is a Latin phrase meaning wrong or evil in itself. The phrase is used to refer to conduct assessed as sinful or inherently wrong by nature, independent of regulations governing the conduct.

Malum prohibitum is a Latin meaning "wrong due to being prohibited.

Milestone means any milestone set out within the Contract.

Milestone Works means, in relation to a Milestone, those parts of the Works included within the Milestone.

Multiple prime contracts (MPC) is in parlance to prime contracts. In UK, One contractor takes responsibility for the overall development (package deal), whereas in US, an employer may have five or six prime contractors.

New Rules of Measurement (NRM) has been published by the Royal Institution of Chartered Surveyors (RICS) in 2009 that is extensively used for Order of cost estimating and elemental cost planning. Non Confirmation Report (NCR) a document or a certificate that is used within construction industry to highlight the non-conformance issues during a construction stage of a project. This is generally signed by the quality inspector.

Owner representative (OR) is the representative of the owner; may be internal or external to the company.

Parol Evidence Rule prevents a party (to a written Contract) from presenting extrinsic evidence that discloses an ambiguity and clarifies it or adds to the written terms of the Contract that appears to be whole.

Payment Certificate means a certificate issued in accordance with the Contract (in particular the Payment Terms identified therein).

Performance Bond means an unconditional bank guarantee issued by an approved bank in a sum identified within the Contract for the due performance by the Contractor of this Contract which shall be in the form set out therein.

POMI means Principles of Measurement International, which is aan ingternational measurement standard.

Prohibited Act means:

Offering, giving or agreeing to offer or give to, or accepting or agreeing to accept from, any person employed by or on behalf of the Employer or any related person or Governmental Authority, any bribe, gift, gratuity, commission or consideration of any kind, including whether by action or inaction or showing favour or disfavour as an inducement or reward;

Entering into the Contract or any other agreement or arrangement with the Employer or related person, or Governmental Authority relating to the Works in connection with which commission has been paid or has been agreed to be paid by the Contractor or on its behalf;

Committing any dishonesty offence under applicable Laws;

Failure by the Contractor to disclose any actual or potential conflict of interest that may arise due to entering into the Contract;

Failure by the Contractor in advising the Employer in writing in the event that any actual or potential conflict of interest arises during the term of this Contract; and

The Contractor engaging in any activity which may give rise to a conflict of interest, and failure to establish precautions to prevent its employees, agents and Subcontractors from engaging in any activity which might be contrary to the Employer's best interest.

Project control (PC) is the tracking and reporting of the progress, time, cost and quality of a project. This function can be characterized as passive, whereas construction project management (CPM) is active.

Project director (PD) is the leader of a large project that can be broken down into sub-projects (e.g. the Channel tunnel) or the head of a PM organization

Project leader (PL) is the person responsible for achieving the project's objectives; acts as the "in-line" manager.

Project manager (PM) Person appointed as project manager is in charge of the project team.

Field Engineer: A field engineer is considered an entry-level position and is responsible for paperwork.

Purchase orders: A purchase order is used in various types of businesses. In this case, a purchase order is an agreement between a buyer and seller that the products purchased meet the required specifications for the agreed price.

Real estate management (REM) is professional property advice (it is a continuous process, as opposed to a process).

Royal Institute of British Architects (RIBA) is professional body for architects primarily in the United Kingdom.

Royal Institution of Chartered Surveyors (RICS) is the world's leading professional body for qualifications and standards in land, property and construction.

Scope of Work has the meaning given to and included within the Contract.

Site means the places provided by the Employer where the Works are to be executed and any other places as may be specifically designated in the Contract as forming part of the Site with the exception of lay-down areas and storage areas which are not contiguous to the site.

Specialized Agency means an agency that is specialized to carry out a portion of Work that is special/peculiar in nature (generally requiring a specialist).

Specification means the performance specification and other specifications and drawings, including design criteria and the scope of work, provided by the Employer and set out in the Contract. Any modification thereof shall be carried in accordance with the specific clause mentioned within the contract and approved by the Employer.

Subcontractor means any person named in the Contract as a sub-contractor or any person appointed as a sub-contractor to the Contractor, for a part of the Works, and the legal successors in title to each of these persons.

Substantial Completion means the stage when the Works are completed as evidenced by:

> - there not being any legal impediment (for which the Contractor is responsible) to the Employer's use or occupation of the Works and there are no defects or outstanding work or any matter which could prevent the Works from being used for their intended purpose;
> - all Tests on Completion required to be obtained from the Contractor in accordance with the Contract have been carried out and passed and certificates, permits and reports in respect thereof have been obtained from the Governmental Authorities;
> - all documents and information required from the Contractor for the use, occupation and maintenance of the Works and as stated in the Contract, including but not limited to as-built drawings and operation and maintenance manuals, having been supplied to the Engineer;
> - all warranties, guarantees, and service agreements required by the Contract having been complied with, supplied and assigned to the Employer by the Contractor;
> - all services or facilities having been certified by all appropriate consultants as having been correctly installed and/or having performed to Specification;
> - all spare parts required by the Specification have been provided (unless the Specification permits these to be provided after the issue of a Taking-Over Certificate) and
> - The Works and Site are clean, free from refuse and rubbish.

Superintendent It is the superintendent's job to make sure everything is on schedule including flow of materials, deliveries, and equipment. They are also in charge of coordinating on-site construction activities.

Taking-Over Certificate (TOC) means a certificate issued pursuant to a defined Clause within the Contract.

Technical Bid is that portion of a Bidder's Offer which comprises all technical and un-priced submission.

Tender Document is asset of documents issued to the Bidders to solicit Bids or Offers. It typically comprises an Invitation to Tender, the Instructions to Bidders, the Form of Tender, Scope of Work, Specifications, Drawings and the Form of Contract.

Tendering Process refers to the entire process of tendering, from the issue of tender document to the bidders till the award of the Contract and its execution by both parties.

Tests on Completion means the tests specified in the Specification or otherwise agreed by the Employer and the Contractor which are to be made by the Contractor before the Works or any part thereof are taken over by the Employer.

Time for Completion means the time for completing the execution of the Works as stated within the Contract (this is generally subject to extension under specific clauses dealing with time extensions within the Contract.

UNCITRAL means the United Nations Commission for International Trade Law (UNCITRAL)

Works means the Permanent Works and the Temporary Works or either of them as appropriate, and relates to the actual deliverables from a Contract in return for a consideration.

Information Source:

1. Chartered Institute of Arbitrations, UAE Branch: Introduction to International Commercial Arbitration by Dr. Emilia Onyema.

2. UNCITRAL Model Law on International Commercial Arbitration

3. College of Estate Management Notes on: Construction Law.

4. Book on "Construction Law" by John Uff.

5. Commercial Management in Construction by Ian Walker and Robert